PORTFOLIO PORTRAITS

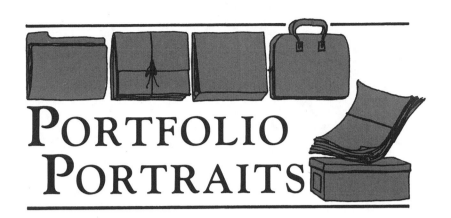

PORTFOLIO
PORTRAITS

edited by
Donald H. Graves
and
Bonnie S. Sunstein

HEINEMANN
Portsmouth, New Hampshire

IRWIN PUBLISHING
Toronto, Canada

Heinemann
A division of Reed Elsevier Inc.
361 Hanover Street, Portsmouth, NH 03801-3912
Offices and agents throughout the world

Chapter 3 originally appeared under the title "Portfolios across the Curriculum" in *Workshop 3: The Politics of Process,* ed. Nancie Atwell (Portsmouth, NH: Heinemann, 1991) and is reprinted by permission.

Chapter 4 originally appeared as portions of chapter 8 in *Seeking Diversity: Language Arts with Adolescents,* Linda Rief (Portsmouth, NH: Heinemann, 1992) and is reprinted by permission.

Every effort has been made to contact the copyright holders for permission to reprint borrowed material. We regret any oversights that may have occurred and would be happy to rectify them in future printings of this work.

Library of Congress-in-Publication Data
Portfolio portraits / edited by Donald H. Graves and Bonnie S. Sunstein.
    p. cm.
    Includes bibliographical references (p.).
    ISBN 0–435–08727–4
    1. Portfolios in education.   2. Students–Rating of.   3. Language arts.   I. Graves, Donald H.   II. Sunstein, Bonnie S.
LB1029.P67P67   1992
428–dc20   92–915
                                                    CIP

Canadian Cataloguing in Publication Data
Main entry under title:
Portfolio portraits
    Includes bibliographical references.
    ISBN 0–7725–1938–2
    1. Portfolios in education.   2. Students–Rating of.   3. Language arts.   I. Graves, Donald H.   II. Sunstein, Bonnie S.
LB1029.P67G73   1992   428   C92–094364–0

Design and cover illustration by Mary C. Cronin
Printed in the United States of America
95 96   9 8 7 6 5

Keeping track is a matter of reflective review and summarizing, in which there is both discrimination and record of the significant features of a developing experience. . . . It is the heart of intellectual organization and of the disciplined mind.

John Dewey
Experience and Education

CONTENTS

ACKNOWLEDGMENTS

The authors wish to thank the many teachers and students who generously opened their portfolios to us. They welcomed us into their classrooms and shared insights about their collections. It is this sustained reassessment of the meaning of the portfolio that continues to teach us.

The University of New Hampshire supported the work of the Writing Laboratory and the authors of this book, most of whom are now former doctoral students of the PhD program in Reading and Writing. We especially thank Donald Sundberg, executive director of Sponsored Research for help with arrangements, and Sue Ducharme, secretary at the Laboratory, who handled numerous details attendent to the production of the book.

We are most pleased that Heinemann Educational Books has added this book to their long collection of publications that focus on the rich contributions of teachers and students. Philippa Stratton, editor in chief at Heinemann, supported us from the outset of the project. Joanne Tranchemontagne, production editor, has displayed immense patience in following through on all the necessary details that make a book more than just another copy on someone's shelf. The many "thank yous" written in the margins of the copyedited manuscript by the contributors acknowledge Donna Bouvier's expert copyediting. And finally, Mary Cronin's very special artwork was a delightful surprise, making a portrait of the book itself.

INTRODUCTION

In schools these days, the word *portfolio* can mean anything from cumulative student writing folders to elaborate personal scrapbooks. On classroom shelves, portfolios can look like student-made cardboard boxes or publisher-made textbooks complete with reproducible worksheets between hardcover bindings and velcro tabs. At professional conferences, we hear experts recommend portfolios as alternatives to grading. In our professional journals, we read about portfolios as new systems for evaluating teacher performance. Several states are mandating portfolio assessments for entire school populations. The popular press is joining the conversation. *Time Magazine* called it "the portfolio approach to testing" and described it this way: "In addition to taking formal exams, a portfolio student selects his or her best work during an entire year of study, and at term's end explains the choices." *Time* cites students in English classes as they "assemble poems, plays and essays," and "submit to a forty-five minute creative writing session to determine how well they perform under pressure" (July 15, 1991, 63).

As teachers, we wish the activity would slow down. It is too early to close our portfolios with words like "approach to testing," "best work," "assemble," "submit," or "perform." We are still asking questions about portfolios and experimenting with our answers. How do we use them for assessment? Is assessment the same as evaluation when we use portfolios? Who's doing the assessing? Who's doing the evaluating—our students? us? the administration? the state? And with what criteria? How can students learn to evaluate their own literacies? Are students able to define their literacies well enough to document them in a portfolio? Are we? Can we achieve standards for grading if everyone's portfolio looks different? Should we grade portfolios at all? Can portfolios be used to assess reading or writing on a large scale? on a small scale? How do portfolios differ from folders? or scrapbooks? or journals? The portfolio as strictly an evaluative device might limit its contribution to a student's education. Students and teachers need to participate; we need to be both disciplined and exploratory.

Portfolio Portraits does not attempt to offer definitive answers to any of these questions. Instead, we offer glimpses into portfolios through the eyes and words of real portfolio keepers in schools. All we can say for certain is that our definition of portfolios ought to move, grow, and change as we see what portfolios can do and as we continue to apply them in practice for ourselves and for our students.

Portfolios mean more than evaluation or assessment. They are tied to our definition of literacy. When we read and write constantly, when we reflect on who we are and who we want to be, we cannot help but grow. Over time, portfolios help us identify and organize the specifics of our reading and writing. They catalogue our accomplishments and goals, from successes to instructive failures. Portfolios ought to be personal documents of our personal literacy histories. Keeping a portfolio is a long and disciplined process. We need to allow portfolios some growing and breathing space before we freeze them into a definition or a standardized mandate.

This book was born in Don Graves' seminar for teachers and doctoral students during the 1989–90 school year. We were teaching and researching in schools where teachers and students kept portfolios, from first grade through college and graduate school. We all kept portfolios, and we all still do. We thought and wrote and read about portfolios for a year. We talked to all kinds of portfolio keepers, from two "at risk" second graders to a school superintendent. We kept our definitions open and they shifted. As fifth-grade teacher Mark Milliken said, "If there *is* a should, it ought to be *to have*" a portfolio. So we continue to keep our own portfolios, and we watch and learn from others who keep them.

This book contains three sections: descriptions of portfolios in classrooms, the politics of portfolios, and portraits of portfolio keepers. Don Graves' introductory chapter, "Portfolios: Keep a Good Idea Growing," looks at shifting definitions of portfolios and offers seven principles to insure growth. He describes his own personal growth as a portfolio keeper and the shifts he has made in his teaching over three years as he assigns portfolios in his classes.

CLASSROOM PRACTICE

Jane Hansen likes to say that a portfolio ought to show who we are and who we want to be. The first section of *Portfolio Portraits* illustrates classes where portfolios are kept—first grade, fifth grade, eighth grade, sophomore year of college, and a graduate master's course for teachers. In the teachers' voices, the chapters describe how portfolios can link theory to practice for students and teachers. As they collect and select the evidence of their literacy, they begin to define literacy for themselves and develop their own goals.

Margaret Voss was a researcher in a first-grade classroom. She describes Laurie Mansfield, a third-year teacher, who set out to organize a record-keeping system with portfolios and discovered that, through portfolios, she began to learn about each of her students as individual decision makers and learners. As she worked with portfolios, Laurie made subtle shifts in her role as a teacher to allow for strengths she hadn't noticed before in the children.

Mark Milliken, a teacher in Stratham, New Hampshire, writes about how he and his fifth graders guided each other as they defined what their portfolios should be. They designed various ways to construct their portfolios, planned what to include, and decided how they would share the contents. Mark describes the conferences with his students about their accomplishments and goals. He writes about his record-keeping system, his contact with parents, and his current goals for change.

Linda Rief profiles some of her eighth graders as they learn to evaluate their own reading and writing through their portfolio selections. Although her class is an English class, many of her students choose to include pieces they have written for other classes. Her chapter highlights the range and breadth of the reading and writing she encourages in her class. As Linda's students choose what to put into their portfolios and as they write about their choices, they come to identify precisely what they value, and Linda comes to trust their ability to set goals and evaluate themselves.

Elizabeth Chiseri-Strater admits that her years of experience using writing folders for assessment prevented her from seeing broader possibilities for portfolios. She began using portfolios in a college sophomore writing class as "dressy writing folders," ways for her students to show off the "Sunday best" of their writing. The sophomores taught her a broader definition as they constructed profiles of their literacy and assessed themselves with disciplined reflection. Elizabeth offers samples from her students' portfolios, her letter to them at the end of the term, and the form they used for self-evaluation.

In the final chapter of this section, Jane Hansen shares her experiments with portfolios in classes of teachers as they viewed themselves as readers and writers. The "Dear Jane" letters they wrote periodically in her class were the way they documented their own growth. As they wrote, these teachers were able to establish new goals for themselves. By keeping portfolios as tools for self-evaluation and exchanging reflective letters about what they saw, they developed ideas for their own teaching. Jane highlights two teachers' portfolios and quotes from their letters and hers.

POLITICS: EXAMINE POSSIBILITIES, RETHINK DIRECTIONS

Section Two moves away from classroom specifics and takes a look at the larger issues related to portfolios. As the chapters in the first section illustrate, no matter what their age, students can't learn to be self-evaluators without discipline and help. Teachers using portfolios in their classrooms need to create a climate safe for risk taking, but they also must demand that students understand the specifics of reading and writing. In chapter 7, Don Graves offers suggestions for helping students learn to evaluate their own work: inviting experiments, naming the conventions they see in their reading and use in their writing, developing lists of the practices they've learned to recognize as they write and read both fiction and nonfiction. He offers ways for teachers to intervene with students so that students can keep track of their own values and develop their own goals. Don shows that the more we help students learn what to look for in reading and writing, the better they become at evaluating themselves.

Jay Simmons steps back to look at the current situation in large-scale testing and performance assessment. He asks that teachers be central contributors to new evaluation models and demonstrates the kind of information that can derive from a carefully designed portfolio system. He argues that measurement doesn't have to focus on just the product of students' writing. It can reflect students' views of their own abilities and intellectual processes as they articulate their own choices and purposes. Jay describes his own large-scale portfolio research study, shows the model itself, and shares his findings: that product-based tests hurt the weakest writers and the poorest schools. He calls for more portfolio assessment on a large scale so that we can begin to measure more than just the products of student literacy.

Dan Seger reviews the term *portfolio* as it is used in fine arts and financial investment. He surveys the multiple notions of portfolios that have found their way into schools and suggests that each informs a different purpose for keeping a portfolio. He offers examples of three kinds of reading and writing portfolios currently used in schools. In each case, the purpose reflects what's in the portfolio and where the student stands in relationship to it. A student's stance in a portfolio, Dan concludes, is as crucial to its contents as the purpose and type of assessment for which it is used.

PORTFOLIO KEEPERS: FOUR PORTRAITS

As Don Graves, Jay Simmons, and Dan Seger point out, portfolios in schools ought to be most important to those who assemble them. Our final section offers portraits of four very different people who keep portfolios: a school superintendent, a college senior, and two second graders. My chapter is about Ken Greenbaum, superintendent of schools in rural Moultonborough, New Hampshire, who was involved in a project that entailed a three-year collaboration between administrators, staff, and students at all grade levels and a team of teacher-researchers from the University of New Hampshire. As a member of the collaborating team I worked with Ken designing and implementing the Long Distance project. Ken attended classes, kept a journal, wrote papers, and worked in classrooms alongside his staff. Before his teachers and students got involved with portfolios, Ken wanted to try keeping one himself. My chapter describes Ken, his collection, and his reflections about it in a two-hour interview that was conducted two months after Ken began keeping his portfolio. Ken's professional work mirrors his personal convictions through collecting and documenting his own reading and writing and through our long, reflective conference, Ken organizes his own literacy knowledge.

Tom Romano writes about Meg, a college senior doing a semester-long research project. She studies nineteenth-century writer Mary Shelley and writes as she reads. Tom encouraged Meg to keep a personal portfolio to organize her research and document what she learned as she studied Mary Shelley and wrote in many genres. In this portfolio, the focus of Meg's paper governed her selection process. She saw both successes and failures, and through keeping a portfolio she had time and a place to explain them. In her weekly interviews with Tom, Meg found self-confidence and learned the joy of intense involvement with one topic. Meg's story shows how a specific portfolio, kept for one purpose during a long-term independent project, can help a student understand her own capacity for creative flow. A high school teacher for many years, Tom admits that this project is not typical. But he shows that encouraging more long-term independent work and providing opportunities for detailed self-assessment in high school and college classrooms can lead to the kinds of self-discoveries that Meg made.

The final two chapters are portraits of two second graders—both the same age, both boys, but poles apart in their literacies. Each is astoundingly articulate in unconventional ways, but might be headed for difficult careers under traditional school structures. Joey is a non-reader who might be considered learning disabled in most schools. Cindy Matthews studied and worked with Joey for a year in a process-oriented classroom. She studied a side of his literacy that does not get examined in most standardized assessments. She assembled a portfolio with him that demonstrated his growth.

Xiao-di Zhou, the subject of our final chapter, moved to this country from China, knowing no English, in June of the year before he entered second grade. In China, he had been an above average first grader. Both his classroom teacher and his ESL teacher worked with him and saw enormous growth during the course of the year. However, when his mother, Dan-Ling Fu, a doctoral researcher, asked him to put together a portfolio at home, she discovered that he had a much deeper understanding of what made him a literate person than did both his teachers and herself. Without help, Xiao-di described the differences in both culture and language that he had come to understand over time. His standards for his own literacy were higher and broader than others' for him because he assembled his own portfolio by drawing from his entire experience, not just the pieces his teachers or his mother had observed.

AN INVITATION

Like Xiao-di, Joey, Meg, and Ken, the more we know about our own literacy, the more we understand about ourselves and what our portfolios can show. The longer we keep our own portfolios, the more fiercely we need to defend their right to exist as we define them. By studying our own organizational patterns we gain a view of the details that inform our choices and hence an edge on understanding what we value in literacy. Our own portfolios can show the links between ourselves and our learning, between learning and teaching, between teaching and assessing. Our students' portfolios similarly provide an invitation for self-evaluation. As we reflect on growth, we grow still more.

In the 1991 New Hampshire Writing Program, teachers from across the United States kept portfolios and experimented with them together over the summer. Everyone's portfolio looked different during the summer program, and as the three weeks went by, each differed from itself the week before. Some looked like folders; some were two-sided pocket files with clusters of papers and explanatory post-it notes; some looked like scrapbooks. So what did they all have in common? What were the differences between them? These teachers share their thoughts at the beginning of each section.

Susan Stires, a teacher from Edgecomb, Maine, gathered a complex answer into a simple description: "With a scrapbook, everything gets pasted down." But with a portfolio, we can open ourselves and our students to possibilities. We can help them recognize that nothing in learning is pasted down. Over a long period of studying literacy, we have learned that writing is usually better with one more revision, that reading is more interesting with one more interpretation. Portfolios need to stay open as we track the details of our growing literacies.

In 1916, John Dewey described education as "the cumulative movement of action toward a later result." (*Experience and Education*, 87). More than seventy-five years later, we invite you to open definitions, explore possibilities, and document disciplines with us. Opening our own portfolios can help us and our students understand Dewey's concept of cumulative movement over time, our own literate actions toward literacy.

Bonnie S. Sunstein

1

PORTFOLIOS: KEEP A GOOD IDEA GROWING

DONALD H. GRAVES

As educators we are mere infants in the use of portfolios. Artists have used them for years as a means of representing the range and depth of their best and most current work. Only in the last five years have educators latched on to the portfolio as an alternative to evaluating the literate work of students, principally in the area of writing.

But as young as this notion is, there are already signs that using portfolios in education is becoming a rigid process. In a few short years, states and school systems have moved from reading about portfolios to mandating them as evaluation instruments for large school populations. Some small pilot studies were conducted to get some "minor" bugs removed, but sustained, long-term learning about the possibilities of portfolios as an learning/evaluating medium may be lost to us in the rush to mandate their use.

Portfolios are simply too good an idea to be limited to an evaluation instrument. Early data that show their use as a medium for instruction is more than promising. We need to explore the many uses of portfolios for at least another five years, and perhaps indefinitely. Without careful exploration, portfolio use is doomed to failure. They will be too quickly tried, found wanting, and just as quickly abandoned.

The rapid expansion and use of portfolios is understandable. Writing tests have exploded in volume in the last ten years; but the type of tests used is often problematic. For example, twenty-seven of the fifty states use the one-prompt test. Students are asked to write from forty minutes to an hour and a half on such prompts as "Write about something

1

significant in your life" or "Write about a trip you will take to the moon." Countless other commercial tests use writing prompts as well. Yet writers and teachers of writing have instinctively known that such artificial prompts, and test conditions generally, bear little resemblance to the everyday practice of good writers. Many educators believe that portfolios provide a quick and good antidote to the use of prompts on an annual test.

Unfortunately, when portfolios are used for large-scale assessment, the temptation is to try to standardize their use in order to make comparisons among participating individuals and groups easier. Students therefore are usually told what genres they need to have in their portfolio. In addition, some feel that portfolios containing highly variable content make the task of team evaluation too difficult. Evaluators therefore prescribe both the genres and the number of pieces of writing to include. In some cases, they bypass student judgment altogether and make the portfolio selections themselves, reasoning that students won't always select their best work for outside evaluation.

As educators we feel great pressure to show "results." We want to show we are willing to be accountable for our teaching. For years we have sold the public on the reliability of our evaluation approaches, particularly if they involved numbers. It is only reasonable to expect that the public is still hungry for the numbers that will assure them that sound evaluation is taking place. Further, our culture craves certainty in a very uncertain time.

Despite these pressures, we have to be careful not to overpromise portfolios as evaluation instruments in order not to lose their obvious long-term potential. In addition to endangering the potential of the instrument, our race to use portfolios with large populations runs the risk of bypassing the participation of the people most vital to its success: teachers and students. Further, in a too-speedy effort to employ the medium, teacher time is wasted, time that is in short supply in intensified teaching days. For all these reasons, it is essential that we slow down and learn.

I contend that there is plenty of time to learn about the possibilities of portfolios. If we are committed to a learn-as-you-go process, with research continuing to inform practice and research continuing to reshape research, we can effectively link the process of teaching and evaluation. Above all, we will continue to monitor the effect of evaluation on the student's own learning.

Students are used to being told what is good and not good in their work. If students are to improve their own judgment about their work, and if their work is to show improvement because of their own struggle with quality, a different use of class and teacher time is required. From the outset, students must be helped to make judgments about their work. Rather than quickly assembling work in May for the annual portfolio review, students must constantly shuffle their work and write letters and other statements in which they evaluate their work throughout the year. This is slow work for both teacher and student.

Research has a history geared more to prove the soundness of a notion. I contend that research—especially portfolio research—ought to be geared more to learning than proving. This requires a different use of time for both researchers and teachers. Rather than the quick-hit intervention, studies must be geared for the long term, with a whole series of learnings during the course of the investigation.

In addition to time, we need to build in a number of principles to help us keep portfolios in a state of growth and to insure that we stay on the learning road. Many of these principles require us to situate ourselves where learning can take place. This requires us to keep portfolios ourselves as well as help students to learn how to read their own work. The pace is slow, but thorough. It requires strategic planning, involvement, and reflection, repeated again and again.

Seven principles to insure growth are examined in this chapter:

1. Involve the students.
2. Help the staff keep portfolios of their own.
3. Broaden the purpose of portfolios.
4. Keep instructional opportunities open.
5. Reexamine issues in comparability.
6. Study the effect of school policy on portfolio practice.
7. Enlist the ingenuity of teachers.

Research questions and recommendations accompany each of the seven sections that follow. The effective use of research as an informing medium will help to keep the portfolio movement from stagnating or from being used erroneously as a quick solution to complex issues.

INVOLVE THE STUDENTS

If we focus on the student as one of the essential evaluators in the portfolio process, then we place ourselves in a teaching/learning role. Students cannot handle this step without sound teaching and demonstration by the teacher. Along with teaching we must gather data on some of the essential questions regarding students' changes in their ability to work with portfolios, learning, and literacy.

The history of student involvement in evaluation is a bleak one. Traditionally, students work, they pass in their papers, and teachers make the qualitative judgments while students wait anxiously for their grades from the teacher. With each successive year, from kindergarten through high school, students participate less and less in evaluating their own work. We seem to believe that if students receive grades at the top of their papers, view the number of errors circled at the top, or read short comments ("awkward," "irrelevant," "thin," "good," "excellent," "top of the line," "sloppy"), they will have learned how to evaluate their own work.

The portfolio movement promises one of the best opportunities for students to learn how to examine their own work and participate in the entire literacy/learning process. What we don't know is the best way to involve students in the process of maintaining effective portfolios. More research is required to secure better understanding of this essential step. A number of questions point to ways we might examine this step and remind ourselves of which data are needed to continue our learning with portfolios:

- How do students change what they value in making selections for their portfolios?
- How do students adopt strategies from the teacher or from other students for reading their own work?
- How can the variance in the contents of student portfolios over the course of a year be described? (Standardization of portfolios can lead to orthodoxies that exclude both teachers and students from participation; therefore, this question is an important one.)
- How do various teacher statements for portfolio use affect students' participation in the process of maintaining portfolios? (I suspect that the more teachers allow students' own literate/learning life beyond the school to enter the portfolio process, the more the students will be involved.)
- What is the effect of different teacher approaches to helping students make more effective judgments regarding their portfolios? (We need to gather data on the various ways teachers both delegate student evaluative responsibility—and take back that responsibility.)
- What is the students' perception of how teachers maintain their own literacy/learning portfolios? What hypotheses can be drawn between students' understanding of teacher portfolios and how they maintain their own portfolios?
- How do students with different culture and language backgrounds work with the portfolio? How do they change their understanding of the purpose of the portfolio?

Although data on these questions can be gathered by outside researchers, most can be acquired by teachers themselves. If teachers enlist the students' help in conducting the research, not only will valuable data be gathered, but the research questions themselves will lead to more effective evaluation by the students. In short, good research questions are instructive to both students and teachers. They can be made a natural part of teaching and therefore would not require as much extra time as might be supposed.

The teacher-researcher's view in embarking on portfolio work should be one of partnership with the students: "Here is a new way to keep our work and to choose what is important. I am going to need help in finding the best way to help you and me make it work. I'll want your comments on what works and doesn't work."

HELP THE STAFF KEEP PORTFOLIOS OF THEIR OWN

As I travel across the country and speak with various professionals engaged in portfolio study, I am surprised to find that many have not kept portfolios themselves. They are not unlike professionals who teach writing without writing themselves. They are unacquainted with the actual process of making decisions about what to include in a portfolio from their own work, and they are unfamiliar with the heady moment of sharing one's work with students or another professional.

From the outside, the process of maintaining a portfolio appears to be a simple task, uncomplicated by strong emotions or tough thinking. We need more policy makers, administrators, and teachers who know portfolios *from the inside.* Their decisions about portfolio use must include the reality of living and growing with the process of keeping one.

All of the authors in this book maintain their own portfolios and have kept them for several years. Further, they know what it feels like to share the contents of their work, as well as to read the written comments of colleagues or students who respond to their work. We began keeping portfolios three years ago. Maintaining our own portfolios has contributed more to our understanding of their possibilities and use than virtually any other aspect of our work with them.

Our portfolios are very different today than they were when we first began. And they are remarkably different from each other in their presentations. They all include profiles of ourselves as readers, writers, and thinkers in written work. Further inspection reveals a wide range of contents: fabrics, photos, tape recordings, published work, recipes, short stories, poems, lists of books, photocopies of book jackets. Portfolio containers vary from large pocketed folders and loose leaf notebooks to boxes. Some writers divide their work into sections for special projects, writing, and reading. Others sort their work by themes or chronology. All, however, write a letter or carry written commentaries that reflect on the contents of the portfolio and their judgments on the relative importance and quality of the work.

We have come to value the variance in our portfolios and the highly individual way we present ourselves to ourselves and others. We borrow ideas and approaches from each other and at the same time discover new approaches to share with our students at the university and in the public schools.

In sum, if the portfolio movement is to remain fresh, we must maintain portfolios ourselves. Our colleagues and students will continue to teach us, and we will continue to learn how to help them if we have to interpret our latest discoveries in keeping our own portfolios.

The following research questions may help to maintain growth in our own use of portfolios (*staff* refers to colleagues in a school building— teachers, administrators, etc.):

- How does the staff change their view of the function of a portfolio during the process of keeping one?
- How does the staff change their view of how portfolios might be implemented in the classroom based on their own experience with maintaining a portfolio?
- How does the content of staff portfolios change? What is the relationship between content and how the staff views both port- folio function and classroom implementation?

BROADEN THE PURPOSE OF PORTFOLIOS

The portfolio movement began as a means to evaluate student work, principally in the area of writing. That was where I began. I gave this directive to my students: "I'd like you to maintain a portfolio in which you show the range and depth of your written work. I'll keep one with you. The portfolio will contain your experiments to show range and some area of literacy in which you choose to focus to show some depth of knowledge."

I was surprised to find that, as a result of this directive, my students experimented with a broader range of genre than I had seen before. Depth, however, was not shown. People didn't choose to tunnel in and mine something of importance to them. I suspect that simultaneously handling both range and depth in reading and writing was a little too demanding, especially for students just starting out with portfolios.

The next time I tried portfolios I left range and depth out of my statement. I had found that portfolios caused people to experiment, though I was not sure why; my own sharing of experiments may have contributed, or students may have picked up notions from each other.

I suspect that both factors contributed. In any case, this time I directed them more simply: "Put together a portfolio that shows you as a literate person. I will do the same."

Students asked, "How should I do this?" Their questions implied that they assumed there was a certain way to do portfolios. I replied that I expected diversity, since I kept changing how I presented my own work and thinking. I told them I couldn't recommend a standard approach. (Chapter 6 presents a much more detailed picture of how this approach works.)

Although my new directive worked quite well and the students' reflections on why they chose certain elements for their portfolios were well thought out, I sensed that there was still a lack of connection between their lives and their literacy. I changed my directive again to accommodate a broader range of what students might include. A teacher in Winnetka, Illinois, had said something two years before that had made me wrinkle my brow in thought for some time. She said, "You know, all through school I played the oboe. The oboe was the center of my life, but no one in school ever knew it. In fact, much of my life was disconnected from school things. Suppose if I had kept a portfolio then. I could have put in a tape recording of me playing the oboe." I decided to put her idea to work and said to my students, "I'd like you to have two sides to your portfolio. On the right side put what is important to you as a literate/thinking, reading/writing person. On the left side put anything that is important to you in your life not included in the right side. How you represent these things is up to you. Be sure to comment on the quality of your contents as well as the patterns you see in your values and work. I'll do the same with my own portfolio."

Although I suggested that students separate their contents (left and right side), I allowed for any variations they thought might be effective. I expected an explosion of material, and got one. Music, sports, family, cooking, relationships, politics, issues in environment, history, hobbies, lists, schedules, and photos crowded the left side. Initially, the right side (as in my asking for depth in my first portfolio direction) suffered. The new left side took precedence over the right. People (myself included) were surprised to see important elements in their lives that had not entered their literate side. Gradually, however, the left side came to relate more with the right and vice versa. In fact, after our initial categorizing, most of us saw little point in maintaining any kind of separation. Life and literacy became more closely connected.

We've since transferred this approach from a university classroom to our work in the public schools. Students put all kinds of work into their portfolios that they see as important to them as learners. Teachers do the same. As a result, students are drawing a much better profile of themselves as learners. They now connect literacy with their everyday living—in school and out.

Jane Hansen and Dan-Ling Fu interviewed an eighth-grade student on two different occasions. The student, Dan, from a youth offenders' school, had done little literate work during the school year. At the time of the first interview, Jane Hansen found that the boy had but one piece in his portfolio, a piece of writing about a self-chosen book, *Elephant Tree*, about a boy who was constantly in trouble.

A week later, on his own, Dan had added more elements to his portfolio:

- A sign that says, "Between four and seventeen is your best time." "At four you know all the questions, and at seventeen you know all the answers," Dan explained.
- A Valentine card from his mother. Dan lives with his father but wishes to live with his mother.
- A letter from his ex-girlfriend's parents that expresses their support and love for him while he was in the placement school. They urged him to think positively about himself. Dan said, "They asked me to visit them when I get out of school and also to visit their daughter, though we broke up. They are like parents to me and mean a lot to me in my life."

This use of a portfolio provides a place for literate artifacts in Dan's life. It becomes a staging ground of significant literate events. In this instance it is immaterial to Dan and his teacher whether his collection is reviewed by outsiders.

As in Dan's case, and with countless other students, we are finding that portfolios are extremely powerful instructional instruments. The "So what?" of literacy, a major question for so many of our students, is answered in a concrete way through the use of such portfolios. Even if none of these portfolios ever receives an external evaluation beyond the classroom, their value for instruction would be assured. (However, opening portfolios to more individual uses by teachers and students raises issues of individuality versus comparability if portfolios are to be used effectively on a broad scale for assessment.)

Research questions that encourage more thinking on the idea of broadening the purposes of portfolios are the following:

- What are several classrooms' experiences in broadening the use of the portfolio from simple beginnings to more complex involvements?
- What problems do teachers have to solve in order to have more effective portfolios?

- What is the relationship between teacher statements about the purpose of the portfolio and what students actually do with them?
- How much do students bring literacy beyond the school into the portfolio? What process does the teacher use to help students expand their portfolios?

KEEP INSTRUCTIONAL OPPORTUNITIES OPEN

More work needs to be done with portfolios that more broadly represent important curriculum areas in the student's life. If we are to open the portfolio to elements in the student's life beyond the school, then we need to encourage students to look at various elements in their school day. A statement like the following could encourage students: "Include items that you think demonstrate that you have learned important things. Make your portfolio a collection of all different kinds of things you've learned. For each item write a short note about why you think it belongs in your portfolio."

In this way the portfolio provides a history of learning. What constitutes significant learning requires much help and demonstration on the part of the teacher. For most children, learning as a concept may remain a lifelong abstraction, or it may be trivialized by the notion that it consists of simple right or wrong answers (if I answered the math problem correctly, then I learned; if I didn't, I haven't learned).

A learning portfolio opens up the possibility of children viewing learning as taking place across the curriculum. Something learned in math may also constitute learning in science; learning how to take notes on a social studies project may become important in recording observations during science.

Teachers may wish to maintain a classroom portfolio of significant projects and events from September through June. This approach will help a class to acquire a concept of their history as a learning group. Classroom portfolios may also remind students of what they learned individually.

How significant artifacts from individuals or classes are represented in a portfolio is limited only by the ingenuity of the teachers and students who work together. Photos, video and audio tapes, drawings, snapshots of projects, anthologies, published student and class work, and lists are but a few ways to represent class histories.

Collections and histories, however, are only as good as they are put to use. Although writing folders have done much to help students gain a sense of personal history as writers, folders are seldom used as a medium for reflection. Teachers have not asked students to take out their folders for more critical examination, or as a medium for planning future work. Portfolios will only be as strong an opportunity for growth in learning and literacy as we put them to use. How to help students use their portfolios as a medium for reflection is one of the important challenges in future work with the medium.

The following research questions are offered as a means to determine how to keep instructional opportunities open:

- What are the diverse ways in which a large number of teachers use portfolios?
- How much is the portfolio integrated into the everyday, ongoing, evaluative life of the classroom? How can this integration be described?
- How do students' sense of personal learning histories change through the use of the portfolio? How is that awareness of a change of history connected with a change in the quality of portfolio contents?
- How can the relationship between a classroom portfolio be described in relation to individual portfolios? What are the strengths and weaknesses of such an approach?

REEXAMINE ISSUES IN COMPARABILITY

Jay Simmons's work (see chapter 8) shows that making relative judgments about student work through portfolios need not sacrifice individual expression. Although the number of pieces students could choose had to be limited, student judgments were not bypassed. Further, teachers and students were consulted as part of the evaluation process.

The reasoning behind providing single prompts on large group tests has been that evaluators are not able to achieve interrater reliability with divergent topics. Simmons's high interrater reliability figures where there was high correlation in teacher judgments on dozens of pieces demonstrate that well-prepared professionals can effectively handle a range of genre, topic, and assignment. Far more research on interrater reliability needs to be done with highly divergent contents in student portfolios. We tend to underestimate well-prepared teachers' abilities to review student work.

Further, as Simmons's work shows, we need to examine the traits in student work that tend to contribute to highly regarded portfolios. For example, Simmons shows that when students are able to keep a piece of writing "open" or work on a piece over a longer period of time, they do well with their portfolios. Most evaluation structures do not inform teaching. Rather than set benchmarks, research ought to reveal potential for more effective teaching and learning.

The following questions are posed as a means to gathering more information on these issues:

- How can professionals handle more diverse portfolios while maintaining acceptable interrater reliability?
- How can new variables contributing to higher portfolio ratings be discovered?
- What are the case examples (by school and community) in which portfolios have been effectively used to interpret progress to parents, administrators, and other school personnel?
- How does a longitudinal portfolio (kept over the school life of the students) deal with the politics of comparability?

STUDY THE EFFECT OF SCHOOL POLICY ON PORTFOLIO PRACTICE

If portfolios are to continue to grow, we have to examine the effects of policy on their use. When cities, states, or school systems mandate their implementation, the undertaking is often so massive that the careful monitoring of how the policy affects the classroom is bypassed.

Rex Brown's book *Schools of Thought* (1991) carefully examines the effects of test and instructional policy in literacy. Brown follows a state law through the various levels of interpretation from state government to local administration to the actual instruction in the classroom. Through careful interview and observation he documents the quality (or lack of quality) of thought in teacher-student interaction. Our policy on using portfolios for evaluation, or even instruction, may be a lofty one, but if the actual effect on student thinking in the classroom is negative, then the instrument has been misused.

Perhaps we ought to consider policy as a reflection of what works. For those teachers and students who demonstrate effective work in the classroom with portfolios, a process of gradual expansion might be considered until policy becomes a reflection of what is already working.

A research question is posed here in order to study the effect of school policy on portfolio practice: What are the effects of policy from legislative law or board or administrative action concerning the implementation of portfolios? Each level of personnel now writes an interpretation of the policy statement with regard to why the policy is required, what action is required of that level based on the policy, what personal or professional skill or knowledge is needed at that level to carry out the policy, and what the classroom would look like if this policy is implemented.

ENLIST THE INGENUITY OF TEACHERS

Teachers, like students, are often the last persons to be consulted in the process of moving to effective practice. Teachers, more than professors, administrators, or policy makers, will determine the success of portfolio practice. As teachers tinker and share their tinkerings with other teachers, good practice will advance.

Accordingly, we need to sponsor a host of promising proposals for different approaches to the use of portfolios. Such practices can fall in the realm of action research, with some investigations conducted with outside researchers at the request of teachers who invite the researchers to their rooms.

In order to capitalize on the ingenuity of teachers, a range of portfolio projects ought to be sponsored in which teachers are asked to find the best ways to handle portfolios with regard to:

- How to involve students more effectively.
- How to use time more effectively.
- How to use resources.
- How to raise the quality of the portfolio.
- How to acquire resources from administrators.
- How to collaborate with other professionals.
- How to interpret data to parents.

FINAL REFLECTION

The use of portfolios is in its infancy and, like most infants, the possibilities of portfolios are limitless. The challenge to educators is to learn how to keep the portfolio movement fresh with information; sound participation by all persons, particularly teachers and students; and informed research.

The health of the portfolio movement will be measured in the diversity of its practice and the breadth of its use, whether for evaluation or instruction. Because portfolios are in their infancy we stress diversity in our explorations in order to begin to learn how to use them more effectively. We invite you to explore with us.

A teacher thinks . . .

My portfolio will guide the quality of my work. Could this work for kids? I don't want anyone but myself to assess my personal portfolio, but there are many people who have every right to assess my professional work. Could kids create a personal portfolio and a professional portfolio (school stuff)? Would it help to separate the two?

Suzanne Harrington
Teacher, grades K–1
Quakertown, Pennsylvania

As skeptical as I have been about the portfolio, I realize it gave me a further nudge to focus on myself even more, and most important, it has convinced me of the value of reflecting and evaluating what goes on in it and why. . . . I like the concept of this being a "living" portfolio. It is not cast in stone. It breathes and changes as I do. I have been encouraged to look into myself—what makes me who I feel I am—since beginning this portfolio. I have seen a value in myself that I wasn't always sure existed. And, for today's kids, who seem to have so little sense of worth, of identity, or of hope of ever discovering any, I feel the portfolio could serve to open up a whole new understanding and appreciation of themselves and those around them.

Donna Galella
Teacher, grade 8
New York, New York

I

CLASSROOM
PRACTICE

When student teaching, I immersed myself in preparing to field questions from the six groups I was responsible for, created lessons to match needs of the students, read volumes of fiction and criticism, sweated blood, and loved it all. The one thing I balked at was evaluation: taking aim and leveling a grade at a living, breathing human being. Sixteen years later I don't feel any more comfortable. . . . Using a system that values process over product has made it only a little easier. . . . [but] student involvement in evaluation has all the ingredients of success . . . for both student and teacher. . . .

This fall, they will keep notebooks with responses to reading. . . . They will enter the time and date they read at least five times a week. . . . Three times a week they will write a response in their spiral-bound reading journals. . . . Each student should write a reading letter to another classmate. . . . One day a week will be a mini-lesson on a short story all have read. . . . Another day will be to share a book, one per student per grading period. . . . Once a week they will share drafts of writing. . . . They will keep three-ring writing books, write in a variety of genres. . . . At the end of four weeks, we will have a mini-lesson to determine what made the better pieces better. . . . They will choose the criteria and, after eight weeks, evaluate two self-chosen best pieces. These two pieces will be a part of the portfolio. . . . Each student will write a cover letter explaining how the idea came and what processes [were] used through the final version. . . .

I will share my portfolio with them, explaining why I have one, what it represents, how it changed from the first time I put it together, how I have changed it, where I'd like to be by the end of the first term. At intervals when I make changes, I will share with them. I'll let them ask me the questions I'll be asking them in later conferences. . . . At the end of the term I will conference again about the portfolio. The change should reflect the student's progress in . . . literacy, not just a lateral shift to . . . a change in appearance. And evaluation will be based on the growth of the portfolio.

Jamie Cure
Teacher, grades 9–12
Lakewood, Ohio

2

PORTFOLIOS IN FIRST GRADE: A TEACHER'S DISCOVERIES

MARGARET M. VOSS

Laurie Mansfield had only vague impressions of portfolios when she decided they were worth exploring with her first graders. A third-year teacher committed to process writing, Laurie knew her writing workshops were running well. She could see growth in spelling, skills, story concepts, writing forms, and illustration; but even better, the children loved to write. They worked well alone or together, and the fifty-minute writing workshop was the favorite part of their day. Still, Laurie felt she needed more of a handle on her students' growth. Maybe portfolios could help with her record keeping, could show her the specific kinds of skills and strategies her children were applying.

Laurie was eager to begin. She read a few background articles (Rief 1990; Vermont Department of Education 1989), thought about her writing philosophy and goals, and planned the way she would introduce portfolios to the class. She planned to start with only five students, for she expected that children so young would need her help in making their selections, and she wanted to have sufficient time with each of them. Though her primary goal was to help her record keeping and assessment, she also hoped to learn what the children thought of themselves as writers.

Within a few weeks, Laurie's view of portfolios deepened and changed. She came to see portfolios as much more than record keeping, for they empowered her young writers and taught her about more than their writing skills. Portfolios were vehicles through which she learned about individuals—their thinking, their decision making, their learning.

17

And as her goals for the portfolios changed, her teaching role underwent subtle changes, too.

As a researcher, I was privileged to observe those changes. I had previously worked with Laurie in my role as writing specialist in the district, and now that I'd returned to my home school to find a teacher interested in exploring writing portfolios, she welcomed me into her classroom. As soon as I made the suggestion, Laurie's enthusiasm was obvious. She immediately said, "Oh, I have an art portfolio. Why didn't I ever think of that for writing? That's just what I need to help my record keeping and to spice up the year." I was excited by her excitement and by the chance to find out how very young children would react to portfolios. But, like Laurie, I had no prior experience using portfolios in the classroom, so my main interest was to see what Laurie, the teacher, would learn about portfolios. We agreed to begin right after February vacation.

I visited Laurie's first grade about twice a week from late February through early May. After most visits we talked briefly during her lunch break or later by phone. I tried to be more an observer than a participant, though I provided Laurie with a few materials to read, and when she asked me what I thought, I discussed things with her. I solicited her ideas rather than offering my own, or I suggested alternatives she might consider, for I wanted to see how her experiences in the classroom influenced her decisions. I encouraged her to create her own writing portfolio and to show the children her art portfolio, and we talked briefly about some ideas for mini-lessons. I asked Laurie to keep a journal and to share it with me. But mostly I remained in the background.

FIRST GOALS

Laurie defined a portfolio as a collection of "best" work, which the children would select with her approval. In her class, before she instituted portfolios, students kept two folders. One, the working folder, included things the writer was still working on. The other, a cumulative folder, included all finished work (some published, some not) or pieces that had been abandoned or temporarily set aside. Looking through the folders at midyear, Laurie was pleased with the quality of her students' writing. They wrote a variety of fiction, nonfiction, and poetry, and their story concepts and skills had improved tremendously since September. But Laurie said much of her awareness of students' growth was "up in my head." She tried to record lists of skills on the students' working folders, but it was hard to keep them up. She had more success with a weekly chart she carried on a clipboard, an idea she got from consultant Mary Ellen Giacobbe. There she would note when she conferred with a child and "jot a few key words" about new skills or things the student was working on. But, Laurie said, "I'm not all that happy with my record keeping. I have a hard time assessing where a child should be. . . . I have a hard time making a formal assessment of writing, and I don't know if they'll be ready for the basic skills test in third grade. That's two years away, but they need a good start now." She thought that portfolios might show her more about her young writers to help her in assessment.

Even as she thought about what portfolios could do for her, however, Laurie was aware of the importance of students' self-evaluation. Sometimes the working folders would overflow, and the children would sort through them, moving items into the cumulative folders. Laurie spoke animatedly of the realizations children made as they looked at their old work: "Look how I used to write my letters," "I fill a page with my picture now," "Look how much more I'm writing." She hoped children would similarly note their progress as they chose pieces for their portfolios. She thought the portfolios would show "how they see themselves as writers" and "give me a sense of their development, differences between the best of October and the best of March."

GETTING STARTED

How should portfolios be introduced to the children? Laurie decided to start with just five students. She figured that such young children would need her help in making selections and that five would be all she could handle at first. She planned to take the five aside in a small group to get them started. But at the last minute, she decided to introduce the idea to everyone, explaining, "They know what's happening with each other and would have seen what was going on with the five. I didn't want the others to feel I was keeping things from them." She still worked first with the identified five, but only after she discussed the idea with everyone in a mini-lesson. The others, she said, would have portfolios as something to look forward to. Furthermore, she felt this phasing-in would help with classroom management; she wouldn't have to be too many places at once.

Her original requirement for the portfolios was simple: choose your best. Pieces could be any type of writing or pictures—published or not, short or long, done at school or at home. Laurie intended to help children select, and she expected to approve the choices. In the introductory mini-lesson she said to the children, "You'll be the number one chooser. I may give you a suggestion every now and then, and I'd like to take a peek before you put it in. Usually I'll say yes. You're good at choosing. You know what you're capable of."

The children discussed the ways the portfolio would differ from their working folders and cumulative folders. Portfolios were to be their "very best." "Who knows one piece you'd put in?" Laurie asked. Many hands went up. Katherine said, "My poem book." Laurie replied, "Yes, you could put in the whole book or just one best poem." Another child called out, "I'll put my sledding story." Someone else spoke of a story he had begun at home. Then the children went off to write, as Laurie called together the five children with whom she planned to start.

Laurie thought carefully about which five children to work with first. She chose Katherine and Annie, hoping to boost their self-confidence. Both were self-critical, and she hoped they would become more positive and happier about what they created if asked to choose their best. Cindy, on the other hand, needed to branch out more. Known as the class poet, she did "beautiful writing," but needed to be more judgmental and evaluative of her own work. Patrick and Steve appeared to need structure; the former had trouble following through and the latter frequently lost control when given choices. Portfolios might provide some structure to help them focus.

FIRST REALIZATIONS

After the introductory mini-lesson with the class, Laurie met with the five children. When she asked Steve to choose something for his portfolio, he identified a published book, My Award in Soccer, but when Laurie asked why he chose it, Steve shrugged and said, "I don't know." That didn't surprise her; Steve seldom showed much of himself. As the small group dispersed to join the others and write, Laurie headed straight to Steve. She gave him a folder to make into a portfolio. He slipped a book right in.

Laurie: Why did you choose that one?
Steve: It's exciting.
Laurie: Will everything in your portfolio be exciting?
Steve: No, but so is My Award in Soccer.
Laurie: You plan to put that in?
Steve: Yes.
Laurie [as they leaf through his folder]: Is there anything besides My Award in Soccer that would say, "Look at Steve, he's a great writer?" [Steve picks up a story he had written about Thanksgiving and tries to read it, but he has difficulty with the invented spelling and inaccurate punctuation.]

Laurie: What do you think of that one?

Steve: It's messy. I put too many periods.

Laurie: That's the piece where you first tried periods, remember? And you used uppercase *I.*

Steve: Ummm. [*He puts that story down and picks up another one.*] I'm gonna put this in here, too. The illustrations are better.

Laurie: So one is in here because it's exciting—

Steve: Yes, exciting and good.

Laurie: Good in what way?

Steve: I writed better and drew pictures better.

Laurie: When you say you wrote better, do you mean spelled better or used words better?

Steve: Both.

At that point, Annah Dupuis, a specialist who works with Steve, came into the room, and Steve tried to tell her what he was doing. When he couldn't quite articulate it, he lapsed into silence. Trying to help him, Laurie gestured toward the work on his desk and touched one sheaf of papers.

Laurie: This is your best as a writer, right?"

Steve [*emphatically*]: No! [*He points to the other story.*] *This* is my best. *That* is my *second* best.

Then he picked up the "second best," mumbled something to himself about its pictures, and grabbed a marker. Laurie's and Annah's eyes met in surprise and delight. No one said anything else to Steve; they didn't want to interrupt him. He was busy illustrating the "second best," improving it.

That first conference surprised and stunned Laurie. She confessed later, "Steve doesn't say a lot of what he's feeling, but eventually he told me. I would never have known how he feels about himself as a writer. He really thinks! For him to say, 'This one's good because the illustrations are better' introduced me to a new Steve—or a new Steve for me. Also, when he said, 'My best, my second best,' and he could prove it, that's coming from him. The assessment isn't coming from me."

The revelation about Steve's thinking caused a subtle shift in Laurie's goals for the portfolios. Immediately she sensed the importance of the student's decision making, and her second goal—that children evaluate themselves—became her primary goal. Her next conference led her to further awareness.

When Laurie approached Cindy, Cindy had already chosen one thing for her portfolio. Laurie asked, "Why is that one your best?"

Cindy replied, "It's the one I put the most work on and the most words. Every page has a little circle with a picture on it." Laurie affirmed, "That's very creative," and Cindy explained further, "There's a girl down my street—she's a fifth grader. She gave me the idea. She draws lots of things and puts little circles around them." Laurie made a mental note of Cindy's awareness of the source of her idea, her valuing of experimentation, and her multiple reasons for choosing that piece. Then Laurie talked to Cindy a bit about the content of the piece and of the portfolio. "This story is all about Annie's report?" she asked. Cindy nodded. Laurie asked, "Would you put a poem in there?" Cindy replied, "It depends. Depends on the way it's published, the way it's illustrated, and if I like the way the words are." Then she picked up the story again and turned to the first page, showing her teacher each page and summarizing as she went: "See, this starts at circle time, then it goes through Annie's report. . . ."

Laurie commented later how pleased she was that Cindy chose her story about Annie's report. "That interested me. She hasn't been motivated to write expository stuff, and I haven't wanted to insist. I've just let her go with her poetry. But the other day she started to write about Annie's report. Annie had made rabbits out of cotton—things you could touch—as part of her report, and Cindy was impressed by it, so she wrote about it. . . . She knew that story was progress for her. And I loved her answer about how she'd choose a poem to include." This was the child whom Laurie had thought was not judgmental enough!

The first session on portfolios had shown Laurie that her students could do more than she realized. She found that Steve could make and justify his own choices and assess his work. She saw that Cindy appreciated her own risk taking and growth in trying a new genre and that she used several criteria to judge her writing. Laurie realized that, through portfolios, she and the children would learn much about themselves and their learning. Laurie also felt less overwhelmed than she had at first, though she still wanted to be involved in all portfolio conferences. She said, "From the discussion during the mini-lesson, I learned that most have an idea of what they like. Now that I see they all have a clue of what they like, I think I can get all the children involved very quickly. I don't think I'll feel overwhelmed with five. I can add one or two a day."

As she jotted a few notes on her chart, Laurie observed, "I was worried about what *I* should do. But now I'm learning from them." Already the focus had shifted. Within a few days, Laurie's role was to change still further.

FURTHER DISCOVERIES

Dennie Palmer Wolf has written about the portfolios kept by secondary school students in Pittsburgh's Arts PROPEL project (Wolf 1988, 1989). One of the major purposes of that project is "to make visible the individual's ability to formulate novel problems, engage in a number of thinking processes, and reflect on the quality of his or her own work" (1988, 87). One way to do that is through "reflective interviews" in which students review the progress of their own work and reflect on their growth and goals for the future. Such interviews "provide an occasion when teachers can assess just how self-aware students are: do they have an eye for their personal styles? Have they spotted their own weaknesses? Do they realize where they are particularly strong? But, at the same time, students can enter the assessment process through the interviews" (28). While the Arts PROPEL portfolios are more sophisticated than those in Laurie's classroom, Laurie's first graders are taking initial steps toward that kind of self-assessment. Laurie saw this in conference after conference, as in this interchange with Cheryl.

Laurie: Why keep a portfolio?
Cheryl: They're nice to have special stories that I like.
Laurie: Why keep something special like that?
Cheryl: I thought of them. They're my own idea.
Laurie: If I were new to you and asked you to show me what kind of writer you are, what would you show me?
Cheryl: Right here.
Laurie: Oh, it's fiction! You can write fiction?
Cheryl: I can write real stories, too.
Laurie: You can put nonfiction in here, too?
Cheryl: Yes, and some with just a few words.

They spent a few minutes discussing the differences between non-fiction and fiction and pieces with few words and pieces with many words; then Laurie pointed out some of the specifics of Cheryl's drawings and the beginning, middle, and end of her story.

Laurie: So what goes in [the portfolio]?
Cheryl: Definitely this one [*indicating a story about space*].
Laurie: This will be your first chapter book. It's interesting that you put a separate set of pages for each new chapter. Why did you do that?

Cheryl: I didn't want to get carried away. If I put too many pages, I would get confused. Sometimes I get a headache if I have too many pages.

Laurie: You are starting to think in a very organized way. [*She notes the chapter idea on her chart.*]

Cheryl had the young child's typical appreciation for *all* her work ("They're my own idea"), but she also appreciated the range of her writing (fiction, nonfiction, short pieces) and, with her teacher's help, she appreciated her new organizational strategy of chapter divisions.

Filled as they were with evaluative talk, conferences such as the one with Cheryl showed Laurie how much she could learn from the children—and how much she could trust them to discover and do on their own. This realization affected her role in a number of subtle ways. It also led to a readjustment of what constituted a portfolio.

THE TEACHER'S CHANGING ROLE

As the emphasis shifted from assessment and record keeping to the children's self-evaluation and awareness of their learning, Laurie no longer saw herself as the controlling agent. She gave attention to individuals, reflected on their commentary, let them teach her about themselves. She no longer expected to assist in portfolio selection, and she ignored her original intent to approve all inclusions. As she handed over control, the students astounded her with their awareness. "I'm getting such insight into the kids and their thinking!" she said.

When she first introduced portfolios, Laurie started a journal in which she jotted her reactions once or twice a week. Her journal entries reflected her concern about taking too much control. For example, shortly after she introduced portfolios, she wrote about a conference with Jeremy.

Jeremy is finally getting motivated about writing. He finally finished his beautifully illustrated story about whales. . . . He was very proud of his accomplishment and hurried over to show me. After a few minutes of discussion about his words (expository) and his illustrations (incredibly accurate for a seven-year-old), I asked him if he was going to put it in his portfolio. He immediately grinned and said yes. Problem—when I ask them if they are going to put pieces into the portfolio, am I suggesting they should? Are they interpreting my words as such? Should I keep quiet and not mention the "P" word except in a mini-lesson about the "P" word? I am not going to lose this thought of the day—I am going to keep track of what I say—and how—and kids' responses.

Over the next couple of weeks, as she continued to ask "Are you going to put that in your portfolio?" she noted that children sometimes said yes, sometimes said no. After talking it over with me and watching the children's reactions, she decided that they were reading her question the way she meant it—as interest, rather than as the implication that they *should* make that choice. But Laurie remained aware of her questioning style and worked hard at turning decisions back to the kids. This new sensitivity influenced all her conferences, not just those dealing with portfolios. She became a more reflective listener and responder.

THE TEACHER'S USE OF TIME

Before portfolios, Laurie talked to the children about their work, but the conferences always seemed rushed; she felt she should ask a couple of brief questions, make a few marks on her chart, then move on to the next youngster. Two years ago, when she started teaching writing in a workshop setting, she worked hard at keeping conferences brief so she wouldn't take control away from the writer—and so she could reach more children.

Having already established a writing community, Laurie now saw her role in a new light. "I don't need to be with each one as they make portfolio choices. That's not my work. My work is at the end of the semester when I look at the portfolio and have conferences with them to ask what's in there and why. I can see that really helping me understand their development and how they see themselves." She felt less frantic and more attuned to individuals as she held conferences; some remained very brief, even less than a minute, but others—particularly those in which children discussed their decisions about portfolios—sometimes took up to ten minutes. "It's wonderful to realize that I don't have to feel guilty about spending time learning about one child; now I see that the others go on learning even when I'm not hovering over them. They do fine, and I learn more about each one when I can take more time."

FINE-TUNING THE DEFINITION OF *PORTFOLIO*

At the beginning, Laurie's only requirement was that the children choose their best work. She did not pressure students to rush into their choices; rather, she gave them as much "think time" as they needed. She wanted them to make decisions, using what Linda Rief calls "internal criteria," in contrast to the "external criteria" imposed by the teacher (Rief 1990). But after four or five weeks, when some children had chosen nothing and others had put only their single favorite book into the portfolio, Laurie decided to impose some simple external requirements. She set a deadline three weeks ahead, asking children to choose at least three pieces that represented a variety of the kinds of things they could write and the different things they could do as writers. This meant a slight change from Laurie's earlier definition that the portfolio was to represent "your best." Showing variety might sometimes mean including experiments and risks.

Although Laurie originally stated that she must approve work selected for the portfolio, in practice she did not do so. The portfolios were more for the children than for her, and she found that students made good, well-justified decisions on their own. However, she sometimes wished kids would include certain pieces that they had overlooked—pieces that Laurie judged to be representative of their growth. She talked of Melissa, who "had written a cute story and worked hard at it. . . . It was a nice achievement for her. Words and illustrations complemented each other; she worked hard to get them just right. [When she didn't choose it], I almost wanted to say, 'Melissa, that needs to go in your portfolio.' " But she refrained.

Now Laurie found a way to solve that dilemma without usurping the students' ownership. Of the three pieces each student was to select, both Laurie and the student had to agree on one. When Laurie announced the new directions in a mini-lesson, several children sighed audibly in relief. One of them was Patrick, one of the original five students. In an earlier conference, he had indicated that he chose his pieces by "going eeny-meeny." He and a few others found the decision making overwhelming. They were glad to know that their teacher would now help them choose.

Laurie decided to require a range of work in students' portfolios after she brought her art portfolio to school. She wrote about it in her journal.

> Today I brought in my own artistic portfolio I had compiled during my college and high school years. I brushed off the dust and was amazed at the variety of media I used. As I showed this to the children, I expressed my amazement at how many different types of drawings, paintings, etc. I also showed the children how I had done a pencil drawing and liked it so I had decided to do a silk screen print of it. Richard piped up, "You published it, Mrs. Mansfield!"

The children saw parallels between the art and their writing—even more than Laurie did. She wrote:

> I also showed them three large drawings of the same subject, a woman's summer sandal—but done in three different ways—in a progression of

stages—the kids saw how it was similar to the writing/content revision/ editing/publishing processes. It amazed them that what I had done in art is what they are doing in writing. It also amazed me to actually see a correlation I didn't know was there.

After that lesson, Laurie noted, "The motivation factor was at an all-time high."

That day Annie and Katherine tried something entirely new. Laurie noticed Katherine's portrait of Annie with Annie's name written underneath. She asked, "Are you going to write any more about Annie?" (Later in her journal, she asked herself, "Was I leading her? Good? Bad?" The results subsequently showed that if she *had* led Katherine, it had been effective intervention, for the girls spent several days deeply involved in the project her question inspired.) Katherine said she didn't know enough about Annie to write about her, so Annie said, "Well, why don't you ask me some questions?" Laurie took the opportunity to tell them that that was called an interview, and the girls were excited to begin.

The next day Annie interviewed Laurie. When Annie had trouble getting started, Laurie joked, "What do you want to know, my shoe size?" and Annie took her at her word. She found out her shoe size, eye color, favorite animal, and so on, listing the information down the page. "She was taking notes!" Laurie exclaimed later. "I was getting goosebumps." Annie went on to interview many of the children and considered writing a book about the whole class. Yes, it would go into her portfolio. Laurie remembered her concern that both Annie and Katherine were overly self-critical about their writing. Watching them as they experimented, Laurie no longer worried about developing their self-confidence as writers; they were demonstrating positive feelings and acting on them.

Different children had already tried particular kinds of writing— fiction (an imaginary trip in a submarine, a fantasy about baby-sitting a younger sister), personal narrative (trips, soccer games, birthday parties), informational books (dinosaurs, whales). In addition, everyone had done a report on a mammal; some included their reports in their portfolios. Martha had made a greeting card for her mother; a couple of children had written letters. But now, attempts at new genres really flourished. With the new emphasis on variety, several children followed the lead of Annie and Katherine and began writing interviews, and more children decided to try poetry. Paul, who had earlier written a thirty-seven-page story about a car race, wrote a two-sentence "poem." Jeremy intended to write a book about birds, but his first page was modeled on a poem Cindy wrote about a starfish. Laurie noted not only his poetic writing, but the expression and perspective in his illustration: a large bird with outstretched wings soared above a tiny house.

Besides helping youngsters branch out into new genres, the art port-folio inspired them to new realizations about writing. At sharing time, when Annie showed portraits of her friends, she commented, "Heather had on a white shirt, but I drew gray because it looked better." Laurie said, "Speaking as an artist, I would do that—make little changes or leave things out that I wasn't that interested in." This led the group to a discussion of stories based in truth but fictionalized, such as Andrea's tale about baby-sitting her sister: some of the details in it were true, but she had not really been left alone and in charge of cooking dinner for her younger sibling. The class also talked about Nick's problem when writing about a trip to Italy. Wanting the story to be accurate, he consulted a globe to see if he could say the characters had driven there from the United States and realized they had to take an airplane. These young children were beginning to weigh questions of accuracy versus poetic license and to consider which approach was appropriate for a particular type of writing.

PORTFOLIOS AND REPORT CARDS

Though the emphasis shifted, Laurie did not give up her intent to use portfolios to help her assess her students' growth. In her district, the report card for primary grades consisted of a list of skills and accomplish-ments graded "Excellent," "Satisfactory," or "Needs Improvement." Laurie always wrote a narrative to accompany the report card. In her anecdotal account, she tried to include information "not just on periods and spacing, but the creative, imaginative side and the development of organization—that's important." She sometimes referred to the chil-dren's working folders to help her. She said, "Folders tell me what's going on all year. I can see where the child has come from, where he's gone, and what he's already achieved in form and mechanics, writing forms, and illustrations, too." But, helpful as they were, folders did not provide the full story. Besides, they sometimes overflowed with drafts, making it hard for Laurie to sort through everything. For much of her narrative, Laurie relied on her general knowledge of the students rather than documentation.

It was to help with the narrative accounts that Laurie hoped to get information from the portfolios. She believed the portfolios would give her a quick view of children's growth in mechanics, story elements, writing forms, and so on. She was disappointed when report card time came around just three weeks after she had introduced portfolios. "There wasn't enough to go on," she said. "Some kids had chosen only one thing, and a few had none at all." But then she remembered the conferences in which she discussed portfolio choices with individuals.

Those discussions gave her rich information about the thought processes of the children and their views of themselves as writers. They helped to show how students were writing with "expression, emotion, concern, thought." The portfolios themselves, representing simply the "best" products, showed her some things, while the working folders and interviews showed her others. Now that Laurie was urging students to include a variety of writing in the portfolios, she felt portfolios would help still more in assessment.

Laurie found additional information about the children from another source—the daily charts she kept. Before she used portfolios, Laurie used to simply record the title of the piece the writer was developing, indicating where the writer was in the process (revising, editing, and so forth) or the new skills she and the writer had discussed (see Figure 2–1). Now

---

FIGURE 2–1   Weekly Chart from December (Pre-Portfolios).
Laurie used the chart primarily to indicate what children were working on, noting titles and recording when a child was ready to edit.

	MONDAY 12/11	TUESDAY 12/13	WEDNESDAY 12/14
Cindy	✓ Edit Lost Tooth		
Brett			✓ My Friend Claudio and Me
Sue	✓ I Wish the World was different	→ Edit	
Keith			✓ Book bound + Published – Author's Chair
Daniel	✓ Illustrating – Author's Chair		
Philip		✓ The Pond Writing so it can be edited	
Bonnie		✓ Added pages to I'm Excited Xmas is coming.	
Paul		✓ Adding pages to I went to Florida. Almost ready to edit.	
Matt			✓ Edit The Beach – very short story.

LM.

she found herself recording "quotes from the kids and notes about kids, their insights—for example, I wrote down what Colleen said about writing a pop-up book at home and I didn't even have a conference with her." Laurie said, "I need to revise my chart. I need more room to write!" Her goal of better record keeping had been accomplished, but in a different way than she had anticipated. The daily chart, still a quick and simple way to keep track, was evolving into a fuller anecdotal account, an ongoing descriptive assessment of the events and discoveries in the classroom (see Figure 2–2). Combined with the portfolio, Laurie indeed had more specific information about learners that would help her write more meaningful narratives at report card time—and

---

FIGURE 2–2   Weekly Chart from April (Post-Portfolios).
Laurie recorded more information about things children were trying or saying. For example, see her notes about Daniel and Sue (S = share; TTT = time to think).

	MONDAY 4/22	TUESDAY 4/23	WEDNESDAY 4/24
Cindy		✓ Fishing - Just Beginning	conferencing w/ Bonnie
Brett			✓ TTT "Paul, can I have a conference?"
Sue		✓ Tiniest Puppy - creative, good thoughts. fiction. The Baby Whale - very organized for Sue ⓢ	
Keith	✓ Finished illustrations Working on Cover - Chose Stone Soup for portfolio.		ⓢ
Daniel			✓ Deep sea water TTT
Philip			✓ Drawing a boat sinking person yelling help! Copy over My House for Port.
Bonnie	＊Today said, "I have a poem I wrote at home for my Portfolio,"(why) "I feel good about it."		
Paul	✓ The Car Race - Chapters - Very well organized. ✓ Editing - great deal of dialogue. ⓢ ＊ "This is a very long book and I feel it's worth the effort"		
Matt	See Matt about Port. →	✓ Doesn't want to Publish whale story. "I did better pictures at home." ＊check folder Wednesday	

LM.
∧ ∧

would help her know her students better every day, not just at formal evaluation time.

REFLECTIVE WRITING

Laurie was impressed by an idea from a fellow second-grade teacher, Phyllis Smith. Whenever children in Phyllis' class read a classmate's published book, they could write to the author on a special page inserted in the book. That gave Laurie an idea. She thought, "Others tell the author what they liked; authors themselves need to have a chance to write what they like about [their own] book—what they liked about writing it, their favorite part. . . . " She realized that the portfolio would be a perfect place to include such reflection. When portfolios were new, Laurie felt that it was enough to ask the children to select their favorite work; reflection came as they made the choices and as she interviewed them about their decisions. Now she decided that at the end of the year she would ask students for a written reflection about their portfolios. Like others who use portfolios (see Brandt, Rief, Wolf), Laurie was discovering the power of the reflective nature of portfolios.

Such reflective writing by students led to a clearer enunciation of their goals. Laurie at first wasn't sure how to arrange for student goal setting. She brainstormed aloud. "I could have a goal conference with each kid, write on the portfolio or regular folder things they want to accomplish. . . . " Finally she blurted out an obvious solution: "I could just go ask them." She also started noticing students' spontaneous goal-setting comments. When Jeremy announced, "I'm going to write a bird book," she jotted down his goal. Whether students were setting more goals or whether she was simply more attuned to them, Laurie wasn't sure, but since introducing portfolios she felt a greater sense of purpose among the young writers in her room. Students and teacher alike came to have a rich sense of the writer's history; goals for the future evolved naturally from that awareness of past and present growth.

Some teachers recommend including drafts in portfolios to show the writer's process as well as growth over time (see Rief: D. P. Wolf: Krest). In Laurie's first grade, most rewriting was done on the original draft, so a given piece automatically showed different drafts (except for published pieces). Laurie said, "Putting developing drafts with published pieces would help me, but I don't see it helping them." But then she reconsidered. "The more they see it, the more they recognize the process themselves." In the future, she planned to ask kids to include all drafts of pieces chosen for the portfolios.

LAURIE'S WRITING PORTFOLIO

From the beginning, Laurie realized it would be a good idea for her to keep a writing portfolio of her own, but she felt she wasn't much of a writer. Sure, she had written a poem for the class, but that was about it. Then one day, about three weeks after portfolios were introduced, Laurie alluded to her own writing portfolio. "I'll bring it in," she promised.

"What's in it?" Rich demanded. She replied, "A letter to an old friend of mine, a drawing I really like, a poem." "We see your writing all the time," Jim noted, referring to the daily agenda, the directions, the notices, the notes to parents that he saw his teacher write. Laurie suddenly became aware of her role as a model. While she still didn't "sit down to write" during class (due to the demands of the many children who needed her attention), she resolved to do quick, functional writing "while the kids are there. I no longer see it as wasted time, but as modeling." And she would keep her own portfolio. "Next year," she said, "right from the start, I'll bring in a portfolio of mine—the art one and a writing one—and I'll keep up my own writing portfolio over the year. I'll use that to introduce the idea—something visual and real to touch and to figure out." She said, "It doesn't have to have lots of stories in it, just the kinds of writing I do—letters and cards and maybe occasionally something more elaborate. That's me as a writer!"

As a result of the portfolio project, Laurie discovered another side of herself as a writer: a journal writer. At first, she kept journal notes simply to help me, the researcher who was observing her and the children. Later she laughed as she noted, "My first entry was a very short paragraph. The second day I wrote a page, and before I knew it, the entries were becoming longer and longer. I started the journal as records to share with someone else, but it became something for me. Next year, I will definitely keep a teaching journal. Even if I don't write in it every day, I learn so much from putting down my thoughts and rereading them later. It helps me figure out what's important in my teaching."

BEYOND THE WRITING WORKSHOP

Laurie intended to keep urging her kids to branch out, to include different kinds of writing. In the past, she hadn't allowed youngsters to write in their science journals during writing workshop, but now she did. She hoped someone might choose a special entry to put into his or her portfolio. She exclaimed over an elaborate illustration Ben included ("That picture was really important to him") and suggested that others might have pictures to include.

"Next year," she said, "I think I'll start the portfolio selections right after Christmas and give students four to six weeks to choose two things for it. The next month I'll ask for two more things plus at least one from outside school—from their nonschool lives, whether it be stories, letters to friends, or a grocery list they helped Mom write." Already one child had brought in a tiny scrap of cardboard with a few sentences on it. Laurie wanted to emphasize that writing was not just for school.

SURPRISES AND CHANGES

Laurie found it surprising "how little work portfolios were!" Since children already wrote regularly and saved their work, they were able to select and reflect quite easily. The biggest surprise for the youngsters was taking a close look at the things they had written. They were, as Laurie said, "amazed at their own development—formation of letters, content, spelling, everything!" As Steve put it, "I used to write like *that*?"

But the best thing about using portfolios was the new way in which Laurie related to her students. As she said, "I had more insight into the children because the portfolio system led to a large part of my assessment. It required me to have real conversations with them, writer to writer, friend to friend." Yes, her record keeping improved, and the children learned. The surprise was that Laurie herself learned so much more than she expected.

3

A FIFTH-GRADE CLASS
USES PORTFOLIOS

MARK MILLIKEN

> *Gramma said when you come on something good, first thing to*
> *do is share it with whoever you can find; that way, the good*
> *spreads out where no telling it will go. Which is right.*
>
> Forrest Carter, The Education of Little Tree

My fifth-grade class and I came upon something good this year when we started using portfolios across the curriculum in an attempt to involve students and parents in the assessment process. We started with what we knew.

I asked the kids to recall the work they had collected from last year and handed on to me: a writing sample and a list of their five favorite books. We talked about what this sample and list showed about them as learners. Then I wrote "portfolio assessment" on the board and asked what they thought it meant. Very little. Then I asked them to talk with their parents about their thoughts on portfolios, and my students came back the next day with the following information.

Portfolios

- contain something you feel good about
- are very neat
- show some type of an inventory
- depend on what you are working on

Krystal's mother, an interior decorator, volunteered to let us look at one of her portfolios. Ms. Chase kept her portfolio in an impressive black case that zipped closed. It was large and contained pictures, letters, and magazine covers. The kids gathered around our horseshoe table to get as close to it as they could. After plenty of study and discussion we generated a list of what the portfolio showed about Ms. Chase:

- What she works on
- What work she likes best
- Her best examples (samples)
- Newspaper articles about her work
- What kind of designs she does
- How good she is
- Before and after examples
- Magazine covers showing her work
- Very professional case

We now had a much better idea of what a portfolio was. Ms. Chase's portfolio became the real-life foundation that the class continually referred to when they had questions about how to proceed with their own portfolios. The kids were also excited by the physical appearance of the model. This was the point at which the portfolio concept became theirs. I asked how we could apply this idea to school, and they looked at the list, still on the board, and substituted school-related items: they could show what they were good at, include before and after examples of their writing, and provide information about themselves as readers, mathematicians, and social studies and science students. And so we jumped in, none of us able to predict what the outcome would be. We had two weeks before grades closed for term two.

I drifted around the room that first day, observing the progress, and became worried by the amount of time the class was spending on constructing their portfolios: out came construction paper, scissors, glue, rulers, and tape. The room bustled with excited work, and I had a sinking feeling in my belly. After a good part of the morning had passed in this fashion, I stopped the class and asked how they felt things were going. They had a few questions:

- Are we just evaluated on our best work?
- How do we put math in?
- Can we work on them at home?
- Do we only put in work from term two?
- If it's messy do we have to do it over?
- Can we have before and after examples from term one?
- Can we put our whole social studies log in?
- Do we have to finish today?

Their questions reassured me that they understood portfolios and helped me to guide their course. I like to operate in this manner: to let the class jump in after a little introduction, then to stop and ask what's going well and what they want to work on next. From their questions

I knew that although they were still constructing the physical port-folios, their minds were already at work on the contents.

The first question, about evaluation of best work, sparked a discussion of assessment and how people show progress. We also talked about whether Ms. Chase had included only her best work, and they remembered that she did show pictures of work in progress so that we could see her growth.

The question about math referred to the fact that they had done a lot of work with manipulatives. How could they show these in a portfolio? Many students decided to draw pictures and diagrams representing manipulative work, which pleased me because, as my experience shows, going from concrete manipulatives to representational pictures is the natural development of concept attainment. The portfolio concept was already blending with my curriculum.

I wanted the portfolios to stay at school at this time. I had visions of partially assembled portfolios going home and staying home, and students with half their work at home and half at school. I explained this to my students, and they understood.

We addressed the questions that students raised about work from terms one and two by referring to Ms. Chase's example. In order to show a progression of work, an artist compares earlier and current efforts. In my classroom the kids save all of their work: a file cabinet contains two drawers devoted to student files, which are managed by the students themselves. These include math folders, which hold any loose papers and tests, spelling folders, folders for drafts of writing they are no longer working on, and, as the year progressed and we worked with portfolios more, folders for any material they no longer wished to include in their current portfolios.

My students also do a lot of thinking, writing, and experimenting in academic journals or learning logs. Each student has a log for each subject, and these are another great resource for demonstrating progress. They wondered how to represent this work in their portfolios; some asked if they could include the whole log. Once again we talked about Ms. Chase's portfolio and discussed whether or not she showed all of her work. We concluded that she decided which work would best represent her abilities, and this was what my students did with their logs: they rewrote or photocopied their best log entries for inclusion in the portfolios.

My favorite question was "Do we have to finish today?" because it showed how new the concept was. Portfolios take so much time and thought, contain so much information, and yield so many insights, that putting one together would take much longer than a day.

KINDS OF PORTFOLIOS

The physical portfolios—the cases—fell into five categories: handmade nonfunctional, handmade functional, loose-leaf notebook, trapper keeper, and photo album. The first time we used portfolios there were many handmade varieties; by the end of the year most students were using one of the three other options.

The first category of portfolios looked almost exactly like Ms. Chase's portfolio. Made of construction paper with black covers, they even had little black handles. I termed them nonfunctional because every piece of work represented in them had to be pasted onto construction paper pages and could only be used once. Our goal was to have ongoing portfolios that changed as the learner changed. The process the kids went through in thinking about and developing the portfolio case was much like the thinking that goes on in the first drafts of writing. Next year I will stipulate that whatever format they use must be functional, that is, able to grow and change.

Some handmade portfolios were functional. They had pages with construction paper pockets for each subject, which allowed papers to be taken out or added. There were a few drawbacks here: the pockets turned out to be narrower than regular-sized paper, so students had to trim their papers with scissors. These portfolios also deteriorated with each use—something I did not have to point out as some students started using other, sturdier types of cases. An unexpected offshoot of using portfolios was an improvement in students' organizational habits. Parents also noticed this and commented positively about it.

Trapper keepers became a popular alternative. We even noticed that the pocketed folders came with the word *portfolio* printed on them. This kind of notebook helped a number of my students organize themselves because each subject could have a separate folder.

Amber's reading folder exemplifies how the trapper keeper worked. On one side she included a reading log entry she had chosen to represent herself as a reader for the term. In the other pocket of the folder she inserted each term's reading list—a record of all the books she had read, including the author, number of pages, date begun, date finished, a rating of easy, average, or hard, and a scale of 1 (worst) to 5 (best). With portfolios, the reading record has taken on new meaning since students can see the lists from each term together in front of them. By term three Amber had three reading lists in her folder pocket, and the assessment process had become much more concrete in terms of what these records showed about her, in addition to her feelings about herself as a reader.

Loose-leaf notebooks turned out to be my favorite portfolio method. It is easy to flip forward and backward through a student's work, nothing has to be pulled out and shuffled through, and many of the students become better organized by using this format. The only pitfall was the need to be careful and accurate when punching holes in papers. Many students made their own dividers between subjects using construction paper, which they had custom-fitted and decorated with the subject title and sometimes a table of contents within the subject.

Photo albums were also very effective. I found it interesting that Katie, who had spent a lot of time constructing a nonfunctional portfolio the first time around, was the one who came up with the idea of using photo albums during a discussion about what was going well with our portfolios and what we wanted to change. The photo albums were great for demonstrating growth in a student's work. Students just peeled back a plastic sheet, placed a page of work where the photographs usually go, and smoothed the plastic cover back. This worked well for reading lists, spelling tests, learning log entries, and other items that were one page long. For work that was longer, students used the photo album like a loose-leaf notebook and included papers punched with three holes.

These are the five kinds of portfolio cases my students developed as they worked with and reflected on portfolios this year. I think it was essential for them to have a choice about how they developed their portfolios. I did comment on strong points I noticed as students revised their approaches and reminded them of the purpose of the portfolios: to represent their work.

PORTFOLIO LETTERS

Because I wanted my students to reflect on their portfolios as a whole, I asked them to write a letter to me about them with the understanding that the audience for the letter would ultimately include their parents. We decided that the letters should tell what was in the portfolio, why it was there, and what it showed about them as learners. The drafts of these letters were treated just like other pieces of writing composed during writing/reading workshop: students drafted, shared, and received feedback about what others liked, learned about, and wanted to hear more about. We also asked questions we thought parents might ask. Sharing provided great models. As with other genres, the portfolio letters improved the more experience students had writing them and the more they responded to other writers and were responded to in turn.

PORTFOLIO PLANNING

I realized that I needed a way to know what students were planning to put in their portfolios and what they had already put in. The first time they created portfolios I had each student write down a specific plan for the contents. The second time around, at the end of term three, I asked if anyone had really looked at their plans once they had written them; the response was no. So we scrapped that idea and came up with a portfolio checklist. As a class we brainstormed subject by subject all the things they had done during the term. The resulting list went on the board and was later transferred to paper and put into a folder so students could look through it to help them reflect on the term's content. Students then made their own rough checklists, which afforded me a quick point of reference as I walked around the room to see where students were in their portfolio work. This is Ryan's writing checklist for term three:

Writing

- Nonfiction example
- Fiction example
- Skills test
- Spelling
- Poetry (3–5 poems)
- Memorized poem

I asked that checklists be kept updated—that areas be checked off as they were completed—and out on desks during workshop time as I circulated and talked with students about their efforts. Once, when a student had checked off fiction on his list, I asked to see what he had included for his sample. It was a short paragraph from a long story that didn't show very much about him as a writer, and he had the opportunity to find a more representative sample before submitting the portfolio at the end of the term.

The checklists help me focus on work in progress, and, based on what I see happening, I can talk to the whole class about the direction their work is taking and guide the direction of the portfolios as they are being made rather than waiting until they are completed. As a colleague described it, I try to lead from behind by asking questions.

PORTFOLIO CONFERENCES

I expect students to complete their portfolios about one week before the term ends. "Complete" means that the contents represent the student as a learner at this point in the school year. Then I have a conference with each student. Beforehand I go through the portfolio and take notes on a record-keeping sheet that has three columns. The left column is where I take my notes. Here I record strengths, changes, improvements, questions, and concerns—any areas I want to address with the student in conference. I take this information to our conference, but I keep my mouth closed and listen to the student first.

I have found it crucial to let students take me through their portfolios at our conferences. I try not to touch the contents. They show me their work. And I try to look at the work as if I have never seen it before and know nothing about it. My most frequent question to students is "What does this show about you?" In the far right column of my record-keeping sheet I record their observations about their work and their responses to my questions. The conversation is focused on the work in front of us. If a student tells me that he or she has improved in an area, I ask if the portfolio shows this.

For example, in our conference, Jim told me that his writing had improved a lot because he was using more details and "showing more then telling." I asked him if the piece he had chosen to represent his writing showed this improvement. He said it did and started reading part of it out loud. After a moment he stopped and said, "You know, this doesn't have much detail. I think that should still be a goal of mine for next term." I asked if it was just because he hadn't chosen his best sample, but he said no, he really needed to improve in this area. In this way, evaluation becomes concrete because we constantly refer to the specific work in front of us. On those occasions when a student felt he or she had improved in an area but the portfolio sample didn't show that growth, we brainstormed ways to revise the sample.

RECORD KEEPING

As I mentioned, my record-keeping sheet has three columns: one for my responses, one for students' responses, and a middle column for goals for next term. This organization represents a coming together of my perceptions and those of my students. If I see an area that needs strengthening yet the student hasn't mentioned it, we discuss it, and it becomes a new goal. Students often set more appropriate and challenging goals than the ones I come up with, as my experience with Ryan illustrates.

As I studied Ryan's portfolio at the end of term three, I noted my concerns about his reading. He had finished only two books during terms one and two and was on his third book for term three. I wrote in the teacher comment column that I was concerned about his effort and reading pace. I wanted him to set a goal for himself of reading more.

During our conference, I asked Ryan what his three reading lists showed about him as a reader. Ryan became very animated as he told me, "I've found tons of good books this year. Like *Hatchet*—it's a great adventure. I'm not a very fast reader, but I understand what I read. They read a lot faster, but I bet they can't tell as much about what they read as I can."

"They," in Ryan's quote, referred to Hal, who sat in the same response group as Ryan and literally read a book a day. Ryan also mentioned that he liked to reread pages and that he is a morning person. Sometimes he reads in bed lying down, but he gets really tired doing that, so one goal of his is going to be to sit up in bed to read. He mentioned that he had already read more books this year than all of last year. He said that sometimes he forgets his books at school and has nothing to read at home. We talked about this and agreed that his main goal for reading would be to remember to take his books home.

Thank goodness I had kept my mouth shut. In focusing on quantity with Ryan, I had missed the point. Until recently, Ryan had a history of difficulty with reading. Then he discovered the novels of Matt Christopher. I had forgotten about where he was as a reader, as my concern over quantity indicated. Listening to Ryan talk about his work gave me the complete picture. I don't know how I attempted an accurate assessment of students' work before we started using portfolios.

I also learned about how students felt about themselves in relation to the subjects under study. Ryan wrote about math in his portfolio letter:

> Two of my favorite things to do this term were % (percentages) and problem solving because I had fun doing them and I feel that I learned a lot, for example 0000000000 = 70%. I feel good about it. What I've learned about myself is that I thought that I couldn't do fractions as good as I can. Now I feel better about myself. I want to do better at word problems because I feel I can do better at word problems.

Another student, Jeff, wrote about essay tests in social studies. After immersing themselves in the Revolutionary War, the kids had taken a test that included five essay questions the class had generated on themes or concepts about the war that they felt they should know. Jeff had really bombed on the essay section. In his evaluation I learned why. Jeff wrote, "I had a hard time writing the essay questions because I knew more about the Boston Tea Party but I didn't put it in the answer. I thought you just put in what was really, really important."

In our conference, when we talked about Jeff's misconception of essay tests, I learned that he thought of them as outlines. He is now aware that an essay test is a place to demonstrate all of what he knows about a subject. Jeff's goal for social studies became "to show what I know when it comes to essay questions." Again, I was impressed with what I learned about students when I asked them to tell me what their portfolio showed about them. I had assumed that Jeff hadn't applied himself during the test. Out of a poor test score came a valuable, lasting lesson for Jeff and for me, because of the portfolio conference.

PARENTAL RESPONSE

When reporting student progress to parents, I write a narrative based on the outcome of the portfolio conference, the students' strengths, and the goals the student plans to work on. Parents' response to the port-folios and the concrete evidence of their children's growth was very positive. Before the portfolios went home I wrote a letter explaining our work. Then, because I wanted to be sure that students had a chance to take their parents through their portfolios as they had me, the class and I talked about asking their parents when would be a good time to sit down and talk. I could imagine my students going home and trying to set up appointments with their parents. (At parent conferences I did hear some funny stories about this.)

In a questionnaire that I included with the letter to parents, I asked what impressed them about their child's portfolio, whether it helped them, what they wanted to know more about, and what questions or suggestions they had for me. Parents were generally impressed with the pride their children showed in themselves and their work as they shared the portfolios. A number of parents felt that it was helpful to see a comprehensive, concrete picture of the specific work we were doing in school. One parent said that the portfolio helped her visualize the report card. Parents' concerns included spelling errors and the kind of specific skills the students were acquiring. They also wanted to see more math.

I shared this parent feedback with my students, and they decided they needed to work harder on editing the portfolio letters. Since in our spelling program students learn to find and correct the words they misspell in their writing, the portfolios provided a lot of practice in finding, circling, and correcting misspellings. I jotted "sp" on a line that contained a misspelled word, and these misspellings were to be entered into the student's own "misspeller's dictionary," on which each writer was tested weekly. This was hard work, and it helped us develop a better peer-editing system. Labeling portfolio work also became very impor-tant because there were pieces of writing, such as log entries, that were not meant to be polished pieces.

In April students came up with a great solution to their parents' wish to see more evidence of skill growth: they decided to pick a piece of writing from September and edit it. Afterwards I asked them to jot down their reactions on the back of the edited pieces. Students and parents saw very clearly which skills had improved and which still needed work. As Kylie commented in her portfolio letter, "And I thought I learned all I needed to know about skills in the fourth grade!"

Parents' desire to see more math also told me what they valued. During the next term, I asked the class to increase the amount of work they chose to represent themselves as math students. This was especially important because we were using a lot of manipulatives, a new concept for many of the parents. Because the portfolios helped enhance communication with parents by offering a clear picture of school, they became a vital link between children's home and school lives.

FINAL PORTFOLIOS

At the end of the year the portfolio took on a broader perspective. I asked students to look back through their earlier work and see what they noticed. Because of the time span involved, this last portfolio of the year grew to be the most valuable one. The students saw striking growth when they looked at what they had done in September and October.

Many students included a science experiment from the fall and another from the late spring in the final portfolios. The write-ups of the fall experiment tended toward superficial observations; in contrast, the spring experiments included materials needed, observations; hypotheses, and conclusions. For example, in summarizing her October plant experiment, Katie wrote: "[My plant] is a lot lighter at the top of the plant and the leaves are practically yellow," while her account of her May steam and bottle experiment, in which a balloon placed over the mouth of an empty bottle expanded when heated and was pulled into the bottle when cooled, included a different kind of thinking: "I think this happened because the steam made the molecules spread farther apart so there wasn't room for something else such as the balloon to come into the bottle because it took up so much space. But when the molecules got cold there was room for the balloon, so it got sucked in and started to blow up [inside the bottle]." These two conclusions set side by side clearly demonstrated an increased involvement with increasingly sophisticated concepts. The fall/spring comparison of pieces of writing and other content subjects was also effective and dramatic.

GOALS FOR NEXT YEAR

First and foremost, I am interested in inviting students next year to view portfolios as an ongoing process, something they keep in mind every day as they work and become more aware of examples of exceptional thinking. If their portfolios are in their thoughts throughout the term, they may have less collating to do at the end, which will save class time.

I also plan to invite parents *and* students to come to parent conferences. I think this would further strengthen the link between school and home. I envision students taking us through their portfolios. This year parents loved hearing what their children had told me about the portfolios and comparing it to what they said at home, so why not put it all together?

Recently, during a summer course I taught, I developed portfolios with adult students. They wanted to see how others in the class had used portfolios, so they paired up, swapped, and wrote response letters to their partners. The letters were so valuable that they included them in the portfolios. I also noticed a spreading of ideas and techniques. Using partners worked so well with adults I would like to try this kind of sharing with next year's fifth graders.

I am also considering including photographs of student projects and performances, and I'm looking for ways to incorporate different kinds of portfolios by involving the local business community—graphic artists, photographers, jewelers, and architects—and engaging students in a discussion of the similarities and differences that we see in their portfolios. But the real key, next year and always, is to keep portfolios fluid, changing, and responsive—and to keep the students at the center.

4

EIGHTH GRADE:
FINDING THE VALUE
IN EVALUATION

LINDA RIEF

*"We must constantly remind ourselves that the ultimate purpose
of evaluation is to enable students to evaluate themselves."*

Arthur L. Costa

S arah was adamant. "They don't know me as a person and a writer.
They don't know how I've improved." I watched as Sarah read the one
mark on her writing sample—a 7. On a test mandated by our school
district, Sarah had received a 7 out of 8, certainly a good score. It didn't
matter. "What does this tell me?" she continued. "I'm one less than an
eight and one more than a six. So what?"

Sarah was right. The writing sample didn't show who Sarah was as a
person or a writer, and the response she received didn't help her. No
one who had read her piece knew where she'd been, so how could
anyone tell how she had grown? How sad, I thought, especially when all
the evidence was right here in the classroom.

PORTFOLIOS: A WEALTH OF INFORMATION

The evidence was in Sarah's portfolio. In my classroom, the portfolios
have become the students' stories of who they are as readers and writers—
rich with the evidence of what they are able to do and how they are able
to do it. Each portfolio is a collection of each student's best work.

I impose the *external* criteria for the portfolios—each student's two
best pieces chosen during a six-week period with all the rough drafts that
went into each piece, trimester self-evaluations of process and product,
each student's reading list, and, at year's end, a reading-writing project.

The students determine the *internal* criteria—which pieces, for their
own reasons. I invite them to work on reading and writing from other

disciplines and to include them in their portfolios, if they think their efforts are some of their best. Joel's portfolio has a piece entitled "The King and His Achievements," a paper written for social studies but worked on in a remedial reading class and English. Sara and Jennifer each included a children's book about a little boy investigating tidal pools along the coast of Maine. It was written for science, based on their field trips while studying marine biology. In English class Jen wrote while Sarah, studying the work of Trina Schart Hyman and Jan Brett, drew the illustrations.

A CHANGING VIEW: TEACHER AS LEARNER

My classroom has evolved slowly. When I first started teaching I used to make all the decisions about what the students read and wrote and what they learned from that reading and writing. I tested them on all the information.

But times have changed. I've turned much of the responsibility for learning over to them. They choose what they write, what they read, and what they need to work on to get better at both. I invite them to try different genres of writing and I share a variety of literature that I love with them. They used to keep writing folders and were judged on all their writing. Now *they* select the best pieces to revise and rework. The portfolio of best pieces is separate from the working folder of works in progress.

I keep a portfolio also. If I don't value what I ask the students to do, they seldom value it either. We have to trust ourselves as learners first, before we can understand the trust we put in students. My portfolio this year has an educational article entitled "Seeking Diversity," a poem, a personal narrative about my mother's sewing, and a letter written to the governor nominating our parent group for a state award for support of our Arts in Education program. I keep a writer's/reader's notebook, which includes my list of books read. I begin my writing and reading with my students. I share drafts in progress and reflections on or reactions to books read. I have to trust my own possibilities as a learner if I'm going to trust and value my students as learners.

EVALUATION: THE LAST HOLDOUT

For years, however, I was the final decision maker about how well each student did. But then I began to wonder what would happen if I considered my students the best evaluators of their own reading and writing, both in progress and as a final product. I not only have them choose their own topics, but I have them choose the pieces that are going best.

So that they will have a selection, I ask them to write at least five rough draft pages a week. Further, I not only have them choose their own books, but I have them select the ones they want to respond to.

Over time, the quality of the students' work has changed. I see more diversity and depth to their writing, their reading, and their responses to literature. I have discovered that the students know themselves as learners better than anyone else. They set goals for themselves and judge how well they reach those goals. They thoughtfully and honestly evaluate their own learning with far more detail and introspection than I thought possible. Ultimately, they show me who they are as readers, writers, thinkers, and human beings.

As teachers/learners we have to believe in the possibilities of our students, by trusting them to show us what they know and valuing what they are able to do with that knowledge. The process of turning the learning back to the students, from choice of topic or book all the way through to the evaluation of their own processes and products, produces students like Nahanni. I chose Nahanni not because she had the best portfolio, not because she was the most articulate, but because she was a little better able to reflect on what she did. Through Nahanni's portfolio I want to show the possibilities in diversity, depth, growth, and self-evaluation. This kind of evidence shows the value in evaluation. This kind of assessment *matters.*

ONE STUDENT'S STORY

Nahanni's portfolio is typical of the diversity and depth of writing and reading I am now seeing in my students. I think several things have contributed to that change: the students have been immersed in reading and writing in more and more elementary classrooms, they are more sophisticated and articulate as language users, and I am actively seeking and expecting good writing and reading.

For the year she has ten final drafts: three poems, a personal narrative, a character sketch, a letter, a pen-and-ink drawing, a play, an essay, and a picture of her final project for the year—an acrylic collage representing her interpretation of the book *Night* by Elie Wiesel. Everything that contributed to the final draft—lists, rough drafts, sketches of ideas—is attached to the final draft of each piece. Nahanni's reading list and her evaluations of herself as a writer and reader are also in the portfolio, just as they are for all my students.

As a final project for the last six weeks of the year, I want the students to synthesize what they know about themselves as readers and writers. I ask them to review all their reading and writing with two questions in mind: What surprises you? What do you want to know more about? Next, I ask them to investigate that one theme, one topic, one genre, one author—whatever it is—by reading and writing in three different genres. Nahanni's project, an in-depth study of the book *Night,* is also in her portfolio.

Nahanni ranked "Looking Across Rows of Music Stands" as her best piece for the year.

Looking across rows of music stands
   I see an ordinary face—
      a quarter note on a sheet of paper.
I know the face has laughed and cheered,
   and laughed some more,
      and cried.
Violins raise, bows sway, and the ordinary
   quarter note frowns and comes alive.
The lone quarter note is gently carried off
   the page and lightly danced onto the air.
Hidden behind Beethoven's Fourth, one little
   second plays along.
A royal theme, issued from the staff,
   fades, then crescendos to a wail.
My loving ear fills up with sounds
   of staccato arpeggios, an Allegro,
      and a triste.
And so, to my dear little—quote—
   unimportant second,
   I give my ballad of soft support.
Bring your laughter and your cheers,
   your sorrows, and your fears,
We'll laugh together, heal the pains,
   use up some tears.

      We'll share in both.

Nahanni reflected on her poem in her trimester self-evaluation and why she chose it:

My best piece is my best . . . because it meant the most to me. I used music to portray a friendship. I think there are layers of understanding, and to enjoy the poem you don't need to understand all the layers.

   The piece that is the least effective means nothing to me. It was an assignment. [An assignment from me: an essay entitled "MacBeth and Lady MacBeth, the Perfect Marriage." Why? Because every few years my past history as a learner haunts me and all the essays assigned to me hover like ghosts wailing "There must have been a good reason. . . ." But after reading two of the hundred plus essays, I'm bored to tears and the ghosts are put to rest for a few more years.] That's why the pieces that are my best are so important. I chose topics that were important to me.

Now I know that in order to write something well, you have to care about it. The first important thing is that you like a piece of writing, then you worry if anyone else likes it. . . . I've learned to add detail to get something across. I've learned to care about my writing and write it in order to resolve things, because even when I read a piece over, I always learn something.

I think writing is like visiting places; you see different things each time. You read a piece of writing and you think you read it and saw it, but then you go back and read it again and see new things. . . .

Writing isn't just a school subject. It's part of how we think. I write because I need to figure out what I'm thinking.

Nahanni's final version of the poem, however, is a far cry from her first draft, which looked like this:

Letter to my best friend—You are my very best friend and I think you know I don't mean that in what you'd call a "superficial" way. . . . It feels like we are always one person. I want you to know how much I care about you. Never forget me, I will NEVER forget you. The times with you will never leave me.

How did she get from this early draft to such a different final version? Nahanni's second draft looked like this:

Two worlds collided and they could never ever tear us apart.
Two hearts that can beat as one, there aren't a single thing we cant overcome. We're indestructable.
The light of a billion stars pales
As we comfort each other . . .
. . . the universe and a billion stars—and you and me.
Crowded there with others or alone.
At times it seems—we will always be together
So bring your laughter and your cheers
your sorrows, and your fears.
We'll heal the pains, use up some tears,
we'll share in both.

poem or letter (She asks herself.)

Nahanni's first breakthrough on this piece came when she answered my question, "Where did you first think of writing this to your friend?" She said she looked up in music class across rows of music stands and saw her friend—just an ordinary face. "What does an ordinary face look like?" I continued.

"Like . . . like . . . a quarter note on a sheet of paper . . . just an ordinary note." And Nahanni was off. She made lists of musical terms. Played with them in phrases. Literally cut the phrases apart and made two piles—the ones that related best to what she was trying to say about friendship and the ones that didn't feel right to her. She read drafts in progress to her peers and to me for responses to what was working, to hear the questions we had, and to get suggestions.

Although questions are at the heart of conferences, I always point out first what I liked or heard or what stuck with me. The questions then help the writer decide what to add, what to delete, what direction the piece might take in terms of focus and format, and even how to organize the ideas. Timing is key. When I know my students well, I begin to know when I can ask questions that push their thinking—push them to make evaluative judgments as they write.

In a conference I asked Nahanni to elaborate on the poem's development ("Tell me more about how you did this"):

In my first draft I didn't tie in much about music to my theme of a person— or face. I made a quarter note be the face. I use a piece of music to interpret what the face fears and what I feel about that face. I did away with a rhythm and pattern I had in each stanza of some of my earlier drafts. I feel now that what I have to say is more important than trying to shape and twist the words into specific phrases and lines. This is one of my best pieces because I've worked so hard, making all the words say exactly what I mean.

At the beginning of the year, Nahanni set three goals for herself: to try writing poems, to write longer pieces, and to send a piece off for consideration for publication. To meet her second goal she wrote two prose pieces, one entitled "Melted Wax" and the second, "Unable to Forward".

At the time, all I was worried about was what to say to Emily. At the time I was too nervous to know. Now I know . . . this is for Emily.

Our knobby knees and skinny, six-year-old legs stuck out from underneath the little baby table that Emily and I sat at. Dinner was over and her father, Steve, brought us the cake and lit the six colored candles.

Emily had made her wish and was just about to blow out the candles, when Steve came in and told us her mother would have to be taken to the hospital. Linda had been suffering from cancer for some time. She didn't feel especially well tonight, and thought it best to be in the hospital.

I remember watching the scene, trying to look unafraid. Unafraid for Emily, her mother, and myself. How would I comfort my friend? As I sat in the little chair, I watched with fascination as the six candles sank into the cake, spluttered and went out, leaving melted wax and small burnt holes in the frosting. I wanted to tell Emily to hurry and blow them out before it was too late, but I didn't.

"My mother made this for me when she was in the hospital." We were in Emily's room. She was showing me a needlepoint design.

Linda died that night on her daughter's birthday. Those six candles had been too short. They hadn't even given Emily the chance to make her wish come true. Whatever the wish had been, it just spluttered and burned out until nothing was left except for small burnt holes in her cake.

He leaned against a tree in his "garden" of driftwood branches. My father stepped out of our shiny, white Buick and walked hesitantly up the highway with outstretched hand. The old man shook his hand heartily and, patting him on the back like an old acquaintance, said, "I'm glad you stopped in, friend, for one reason."

He instructed my dad on how to "plant" a dried up tree stump in the orchard. He had the stump roped to a live tree and had been struggling to lift it into the ground. Lucky for him that my dad came by, because that stump was HEAVY.

My brother wasn't so keen on joining my father in meeting the old hermit, but he followed as I quietly climbed out of the car. We arrived just in time to see my father and the old man heave a dead tree stump into an upside-down, mushroom-like position.

We picked our way down his rocky pathway into a low-ceilinged room that was more like a cave. I stepped carefully in and then quickly withdrew. My brother and I cringed and waited at the door in the sunlight. My father, no hesitation in his voice now, turned to us and said, with a gleam of amusement in his eye, "Come on in, kids, this is great."

The gnomelike man showed us his house. It didn't take long. It consisted of two rooms, bedroom and kitchen. My eyes slid quickly over the old photographs, the sink overflowing with green wine bottles, and the cat food strewn across the floor.

My father crouched, hands on knees, squinting to see a picture on the cover of *National Geographic*. "Hey, that's you!"

"Yeah, that's me!"

"This is great!" My dad was looking at a black and white photograph of the hermit sitting in the corner of his house. In the picture he held a plaster figure of the Virgin Mary, which I noticed above a chair in the same corner.

I escaped, dragged my brother out the door into fresh air. My father stayed in the dusty cave, pouring over pictures from the man's life. I watched, from outside in the cool breeze, as my father crept at a snail's pace along the wall, exploring details of paintings, photographs, revealing the spark of memory in the old man's eye with each question. I thought, amused, I can picture my father living here.

Reluctantly, my father pulled himself away. Up the path, through the orchard, back to the highway we climbed. The old man told us about his land. It wasn't really his, but, he said, he "claimed" it. He lived here, no one else. A seventy-year-old man by himself on a mountain in the middle of Nowhere, California. He gestured, his arms encompassing his whole mountain. "As far as I'm concerned, it's all mine. No one bothers me. Who cares?" His voice floated out to us, "Who cares?"

My father took pictures of the old man in his orchard, which we enlarged and sent to his P.O. Box. Weeks later, they came back, stamped in red ink, "UNABLE TO FORWARD-DECEASED."

Who cared? I thought sadly. Who cared?

At first she had steered away from writing long pieces because she was "afraid of losing peoples' focus, or maybe I'm afraid I'll lose my own focus." She discussed how "Melted Wax" came together:

> I was brainstorming all the positives and negatives in my life . . . trying to think of a way to write down what I thought of Linda's death. One of the things that makes the piece good is the layers of depth that people can find. Most people can come up with the point of the candles . . . but if they don't, they can still enjoy it. I changed the lead all around. My first lead was dull and didn't say much. Now it starts with a quote and pulls people in better.
>
> I think I'm learning more to do—as you say—showing, not telling. Before now I don't think I was really aware of the difference. My writing really changes a lot from first to last draft.

Nahanni also accomplished her third goal: to send a piece for publication. The poem she selected went through as many changes as her first poem.

THROUGH THE NIGHT WINDOW
I IMAGINE WHAT COULD BE HIDDEN

A delicious horizon,
   like smoked white-fish on deli-wrap,
   beckons to me.
A Great-Blue Heron breezes on grayish icy water.
Straggling, gnarled fingers struggle for a place
   to clutch the faulty ground halfway across the bay.
Houses scatter across the distant shore,
   bread crumbs for the birds.
Tiny diamonds of light pinpoint
   quickly darkening gray-blue shadows.
I turn . . . delicious.

Nahanni recounted what happened when she submitted the poem for publication:

> I like this poem, but it doesn't have that much meaning to me. I sent it to *Merlyn's Pen* and that's what they told me. I knew they would. I think I'll make it how they'd like it since if it's changed it's not a problem for me because I don't think it's perfect the way it is. It's not for me that I want to keep it that way. Like the poem I wrote for my friend, "Looking across rows of music stands." I wouldn't change that no matter what anybody thinks. It's for me—and my friend.
>
> One thing I'm not sure I will change in "Night Window" is the image of smoked white-fish on deli-wrap. The editor said he didn't think it fit. My dad and I think he must not be Jewish. If he was he'd know how well it does fit.

This year Nahanni started reading thirty books and finished twenty-nine. Her favorites were *The Little Prince* (Saint Exupery 1971), *One*

Child (Hayden 1980), *The Chocolate War* (Cormier 1974), *Beyond the Chocolate War* (Cormier 1985), *Night* (Wiesel 1960), and *The Princess Bride* (Goldman 1973).

She formed some definite opinions on the subject of reading:

> In order to be a good reader I think you must read a lot and think about what you are reading—how it relates to you, what the writer wants you to think, versus what you really get out of it. I think the responses I got to my reactions to books were written or asked in such a way that I feel my ideas are important and that makes me think more.

In responding to *The Runner* (1985) by Cynthia Voigt, Nahanni wrote:

> Sometimes reading this book really frustrates me. It's not that it isn't interesting, but sometimes I just don't get it. Bullet seems to have dealt with things in a strange way, burying himself. Burying himself from everyone else . . . Bullet and Katrin have learned to sort of remove themselves and not get too involved in things they care about, so they never get hurt . . . I think I'd rather live through some of the bad times than never see any good times. Sort of like in *The Little Prince,* the taming of the fox. I'd rather love, lose, get hurt and go away with memories than never love and never know the difference between happy and sad. What words! Happy? Sad? When I was little I thought happy meant a smile and going to the circus. Sad was a frown and sitting home on a rainy day.

Jay, a peer, responded to Nahanni, in her log confirming and extending what they both knew:

> I never thought of Bullet burying himself, I guess I thought of him isolating himself, in the boxes he always talks about. Isolated, being able to see out, but no one can see in. Do you think people, like Bullet and Katrin *really* know what happy and sad are? In their boxes? I guess you and me would rather have loved and lost than never to have loved at all. There is a point though where the lost overcomes the loved and you (collectively, not just you, Nahanni) end up feeling like cuckies. At least for me—Have you read *Sons from Afar?* By Cynthia Voigt. That, and I guess *Homecoming,* too, show how similar Sammy is to Bullet. Them and their boxes. Scot is like that too. I guess he has good reason. His parents both left him in the lurch. But he doesn't let himself get too involved, because he always got hurt. Whatever flics your Bic, I guess. . . .

Discussing her reading goals, Nahanni said, "I wanted to read faster. . . . I don't think I accomplished this, except that now I read more than I did before. I don't think that [reading faster] was a really important goal. I wanted to understand more, and I think I've done that."

Nahanni not only understood more, but she connected what she understood with her own life as she questioned, evaluated, criticized, and analyzed.

Of *The Little Prince* (1971) she said:

I love the part in this book about the fox who believes in taming something unknown. When the little prince sees all the roses that look exactly like his flower, he is angry. When the fox is finished with him, he returns to the roses and is happy. He knows that no other rose in the whole universe is like his . . . because he's cared for it . . . What is the point in life if you are afraid to get involved? People want to be strong so that they will not be sad when they have to leave someone. How do they think they can be strong? They have to be sad at one point in order to really learn . . .

From *the Chocolate War* (1974) she learned "what peer pressure and a crowd of kids can do to people." She wrote:

Archie, and people like him . . . are always in the darkness. They do things to other kids because it makes them feel superior and happy with themselves . . . For a second, at the end of the book I thought Archie won. But he didn't. He just thought he did . . . The vigils live in darkness. I thought vigil was supposed to mean watchfull? VIGIL—dictionary definition—a purposeful or watchful staying awake during the sleeping hours. Is this name appropriate? . . . I guess it is sort of appropriate. The vigils do think that they are watchful, sort of keeping an eye on things. Oh, here's a good analogy: The cord—I forget what it's called—that goes to the brain from the eye, is broken or just not there. So the image that is focused on the retina is upside down. There is no cord going to the brain so the image remains upside down. I think the vigils have an upside down picture of the world and people's place in it . . . in the last paragraph of the book Archie and Obie sit and walk around in darkness. They might think they are vigilant, but who can see clearly in the dark?

Through reading *One Child,* (1980) Nahanni not only discussed Hayden's influence on her choice of professions, but how the book opened her mind to diversity.

Reading Torey Hayden's books, I always think I want to do what she does. I would love to do something to help people. I used to think that maybe I'd be a psychiatrist but I don't think that I'd really want to help the people who could come to me. To make a real difference I'd want to help the people who really couldn't go to look for help themselves . . . I wonder if Boo really does live in another world. Actually, I guess we all do. We've all got separate ideas of what the world should be. It's like we're all sitting in a building looking into a circular field. Everybody has their own window and everybody looks out onto the same field but from a slightly different angle . . . you can never really see the field from exactly their angle.

Nahanni believes that if a book is really good, you can learn a lot about what the author thinks about life. In a good book, the meaning is made clear so that "I think I've discovered it on my own, not so it was told to me." Her responses to books showed she was wondering deeply about life and discovering how we all fit into the bigger scheme.

She knows too there are some books just to read for pure pleasure. "I loved *The Princess Bride* [1973] because it was so funny and a break from a book where you are expected to think!"

Nahanni doesn't think she consciously connects reading and writing, but listen to what she consciously did:

> I think I've been looking a lot more for metaphors and hidden meanings in my reading. This is a result of my change in writing—or vice-versa. I think that now I look for things that aren't so obvious. I've discovered that those things mean so much to me. The words that are unwritten teach much stronger than words on paper. . . . [In books] I can understand the author's point of view and think about my own views.

She not only reads as a writer, trying to find her own views, but she observes as a writer. While driving to New York, Nahanni was reading a book, yet decided to respond to what she saw, instead of what she was reading.

> At the side of this thruway is an Hispanic man looking into the hood of a pale green, rusty, dented old station wagon. In the lane to the right of us is a shiny black new Oldsmobile with shaded windows. It purrs along . . . Here we are in the middle, pretty neutral—a Toyota. Why do the wealthy people like to tint their windows so we can't see in? Are they embarrassed that we might find out they look exactly the same as we do . . . grafiti . . . why do people write on walls? Central Park . . . people on park benches. On rocks. In bushes. Their pantry is a garbage can.

By the end of the year Nahanni even recognized she had become the observer of everything around her. She wrote in her log:

> I'm just lying here in the grass with sun on my face. Outside the UNH library on the lawn . . . Monica is working with Dave on his MacBeth essay. Now, finally, just feeling like an observer, I can just listen and watch and realize how wonderful it is. Dave is perfectly able. He just needs Monica to help him hold his concentration and put his pen on paper. Dave sits there yelling and grumbling. But he's got a smile on his face . . . That's how it was with Jeff and me. He always had the ability. Sometimes he caught onto things faster than I did. What he didn't have was the patience to sit down and work on something. He needed the trust in himself and to believe that he could do it . . . One great thing about Jeff is his art. He always encouraged me in art, just like I always did for him . . . Every night I sit up and draw. I never showed anyone or told anyone but when Jeff comes back I'll show him so he can encourage me again.

Nahanni told me constantly—in her writing, in her reading responses, and in her evaluations of herself as a learner—that she learns from her own discoveries, not from someone telling her what she is supposed to know. Isn't that what real learning is all about? Isn't that what real teaching should be about?

SELF-EVALUATION, SELF-DISCOVERY

I don't have to be the sole evaluator of Nahanni's reading and writing. She, like the rest of my students, is far better at it than I am. With 125 students the only possible way of keeping such extensive notes on each student is to have them keep them themselves. And the better Nahanni, as with all the students, knows her own process as a writer and reader, the better she becomes at both.

But I *can* evaluate Nahanni's growth, as well as any of my students, as a writer and reader, if I have to. I have all the evidence in front of me in their drafts of writing from rough to final, in their response to what they're reading, in their self-evaluations of themselves as writers and readers, and in my responses to them on their writing and in their reading logs. As teachers, we must listen first to the perceptions our students have of themselves and address what they think they can and cannot do.

From what Nahanni showed me, I wrote the following narrative about her growth as a learner:

Nahanni has become an independent learner who reads and writes for her purposes because she wants to become better at what she does. Her reading and writing show me she is engaged in the excitement of learning. She is a keen observer of life around her, often finding topics because she is always looking. She has an acute sense of detail, able to see, hear, smell, touch, and feel things that many of us miss, all with a sensitivity to the human factor. She is a caring, sensitive young woman who leaves an impact.

As a writer Nahanni knows how to find a topic, how to play with words until they say exactly what she means, how to seek help for revision, how to use a variety of resources, how to ask questions, and how to answer them. She is not afraid to take risks with new genres. She has tried poetry this year, while still attempting a variety of prose pieces. There is always a meaning to her writing—a reason to read it. She has a message for her reader, because the message is always for her first.

Nahanni has an acute sense of audience. After receiving a rejection from one magazine I asked her if she wanted to revise the piece and resubmit it. "No," she said. "This wasn't for the magazine anyway." Another piece she will revise because it wasn't for her alone.

Her images are fresh and vivid. She searches for precise words. Her dedication is evident in her willingness to revise until pieces say exactly what she means, in the appropriate format. She grapples with big issues: friendship, control, love, prejudice, hate, fear, uniqueness. . . .

She is a thoughtful reader who reads a variety of books (historical fiction, nonfiction, adolescent fiction, classics, poetry, realistic fiction, etc.) for a variety of reasons: some to make her think, others just for fun. She knows how to take meaning to, and meaning from a book. She relates her own life experiences to the experiences she draws from books. She comprehends, analyzes, reflects, contrasts, compares, synthesizes, wonders, questions, criticizes, and enjoys literature.

I believe her writing has changed her perceptions as a reader. At first she wondered why authors did certain things; now she reflects on how she would have done it differently. Nahanni writes and reads to find out what she is thinking.

I wrote extensive narratives like Nahanni's for more than fifty of my students. (I gave up after two classes and three sleepless nights.) It took about twenty to thirty minutes per student. Of the more than fifty I wrote, I received response from only one parent, even though I asked specifically for feedback as to what this kind of response showed them about their son or daughter. Several students told me their parents were "too busy" to read the evaluations, let alone respond in writing to them. Several other parents asked, "What's the bottom line?"

Will I do such extensive evaluations again? No. But I know I *can* do them if I have to. I have more information about what my students can do as writers and readers than any number of standardized tests or writing samples could ever show.

I also know I can show someone very quickly and succinctly how any one of these students has grown. Simply by taking Nahanni's self-selected "most effective" piece I can see growth by looking at two areas I value in writing: verbs and leads.

Verbs in first rough draft		Verbs in final draft	
are	go	looking	hide
think	wish	see	issue
mean	were	know	fade
call	feels	laugh	crescendo
had	want	cheer	fill
be		cry	give
		raise	bring
		sway	laugh
		frown	heal
		carry	share
		dance	

Lead in her first draft: You're my very best friend and I think you know I don't mean that in an ordinary way.

Lead in final draft: Looking across rows of music stands I see an ordinary face—a quarter note on a sheet of paper.

Certainly the verbs chosen for the final piece are stronger and carry more vivid images than the first draft. The two leads are also very different—the first bland and nondescript, the final clearly metaphorical, rhythmic, and far more appealing even in its design.

As teachers, if we think about what we value most that our students can do, we can look at those areas as the students move from draft to draft or as they respond to literature in their journals. Simply looking at verbs or leads takes less than five minutes, yet I know that I can discover other strengths in a similar manner. I can look at metaphorical language, dialogue, topic choices, genres of books chosen, types and changes in reading response. I can use what I discover as minilessons in addition to evaluative information.

If students keep their rough drafts attached to their finals, all the evidence for showing growth is right in front of me. If students keep their responses to literature in some kind of journals, who they are as readers is documented for the entire year.

Searching for the perfect record-keeping system for 125 students has always been a cumbersome and impossible task for me. When I started looking at portfolios, working folders, logs, reading lists, and self-evaluation sheets, I realized all the information was there and the students were keeping the records themselves. It is far more comprehensive evidence than any checklist I have ever attempted to develop.

Reading, writing, speaking, and listening are the tools students work with to create meaning for their own purposes. I value students who are able to communicate, think, create, and reflect with those tools. Portfolios become the evidence for what we value in our classrooms. The act of putting together a portfolio is a reflective act in itself, as students choose what to put in there and why. That reflection on where they've been, where they are now, and how they got there is what real learning is all about.

BUILDING TOWARD PORTFOLIOS: WHAT CAN WE DO?

Will the portfolio concept work in every classroom? Yes, but certain conditions must be present. First, students must be immersed in reading, writing, speaking, and listening. Second, they need to be given time in large blocks. Third, they need to be allowed choice as to what they are writing and reading—for their reasons, their purposes. And fourth, they must receive positive response to their ideas.

Once these conditions exist, we can introduce the concept of portfolios as places where students collect evidence of who they are.

- as readers and writers (their best pieces of writing, their reading lists, and most effective responses to literature)
- as learners (all their rough drafts and ideas for getting from one draft to the next attached to their best pieces)
- as *reflective* learners (self-evaluations and reflections on what they've done and how they've done it)

And we have to keep and share our own portfolios. The more I discover what I can do, the higher my expectations are of what kids can do. They seldom disappoint me.

Each trimester I ask the students to arrange their writing from most effective to least effective and to evaluate it considering the following questions:

- What makes this your best piece?
- How did you go about writing it?
- What problems did you encounter?
- How did you solve them?
- What makes your most effective piece different from your least effective piece?
- What goals did you set for yourself?
- How well did you accomplish them?
- What are you able to do as a writer that you couldn't do before?
- What has helped you the most with your writing during this trimester?
- What are your writing goals for the next twelve weeks?

As readers I ask them to consider similar questions about the books they have chosen to read.

- What's the best book you've read this trimester?
- What makes this one of the best you've ever read?
- How did you go about choosing this book to read?
- What's the most significant thing you learned from this book and/or discovered about yourself as you read it?
- What were your reading goals at the beginning of the trimester?
- How well did you accomplish them?
- In the past twelve weeks, how have you changed or grown as a reader?

- What has helped you the most with your reading?
- What are your reading goals for the next twelve weeks?
- In what ways are your reading and writing connected?
  How does one affect the other?

THE KIND OF EVALUATION THAT MATTERS

Nahanni is not the exception in my class. She is becoming the norm. She is motivated and persistent, and she cares about learning. She reads and writes for real reasons. Through her portfolio and her reading log I know her as a reader, writer, thinker, and human being, not as a 5 or a 7. Through their portfolios of writing and reading, I know all my students. They, like Nahanni, are articulate learners because they continually *practice* discussing what they know and how they know it: by sharing with me, their peers, the community, and other grade levels; by teaching teachers at writing workshops; and by publishing locally and nationally.

Learning to make meaning in writing and reading is not objective, as our evaluation systems would seem to indicate. We must become more flexible in our assessment of students' work. When kids are given choices in what they read and what they write, and time to think about what they are doing, their writing and reading get better. When we trust them to set goals and to evaluate their learning in progress, we will begin to realize that they know much more than we allow them to tell us through our set curriculums, our standardized tests, our writing samples.

If our goals are to keep students writing and reading, to help them get better at both, and to help them become independent learners, then we *must* nurture self-evaluation of writing and reading in progress *and* as a final product. This is the kind of evaluation that matters because it is for Nahanni. Who else is evaluation for?

5

COLLEGE SOPHOMORES REOPEN THE CLOSED PORTFOLIO

ELIZABETH CHISERI-STRATER

My longtime experience with writing folders as an end-of-term assessment tool in my beginning composition courses blinded me from seeing other possibilities for portfolios. In fact, my initial use of the portfolio resembled its etymological root: the word *portfolio* comes from the Latin verb *portare*, meaning to carry, and the Latin noun *foglio*, meaning sheets or leaves of paper. *Portfolios* are cases for holding papers, prints, drawings, maps, or musical scores that are carried from place to place. Because of my long-time use of writing folders, I thought of portfolios mainly as physical receptacles for holding students' written work, a kind of dressy writing folder.

No wonder my first attempt at instituting portfolios in my writing courses was narrowly conceived, rigidly defined, and traditionally evaluated. Rather than reflecting on the theory behind the process of portfolio compilation—what Donald Schön would call "reflection in action"—I relied only on my past experience of using writing folders for evaluating students' most polished work. Schön critiques teachers and other practitioners for wedding themselves to pre-existing and overly comfortable ways of thought: "They have become too skillful at techniques of selective inattention, junk categories, and situational control" (1983, 69). Writing folders served almost as a "junk" category, preventing me from thinking of new ways of conceiving of students' portfolios, binding me to my previous knowledge and experience as a teacher. I

Thanks to all my students who allowed me to use parts of their portfolios for this chapter.

arrived at a way of transforming the writing folder into a literacy port-folio only after I had collected and analyzed my students' responses to their own experiences of portfolio compilation. Through reflective thinking with my students about new possibilities for literacy portfolios, I began to revise my classroom practices.

My earlier, failed attempt at using portfolios started with my an-nouncing to my sophomore college writing course that during the semester we would develop "literacy portfolios" that they would turn in at midterm and at year end. Working with Donald Graves' early con-cepts of range, depth, and growth, I outlined in scrupulous detail what I expected and wanted in my students' portfolios. Where writing folders had left the choice open for students to include their best written work completed in the course, the portfolio gave them structured categories for selection (to show growth, range, and depth). Such tight guidelines represented a regression in my classroom practices. However, my stu-dents readily complied with my request for what I now call the "Chinese dinner" approach to portfolio construction: take two from column A, one from column B, and possibly a special appetizer or dessert, and voila! A portfolio that combines all the styles and genres of writing undertaken by the student writer (range) with all the revisions of one piece of writing (depth). Then stir in the reflective essay or letter written to describe the student's overall development as shown through the portfolio (growth). While there is nothing inherently wrong with this approach, it focuses heavily on the teacher's setting the agenda and the criteria for evaluation and the students' passive compliance with the teacher's goals.

To give my students more credit than I will give myself, they spoke generously about two features of the structured midterm portfolios that they submitted: one, the portfolio implied more personal ownership or engagement than a writing folder; and two, my guidelines provided some structure for students who felt they would be unable to make such choices themselves. In their opening letters about their portfolios, stu-dents hinted at other ways of organizing portfolios that could take them beyond traditional assessment functions. These letters helped me open portfolios to the diversity of literacies among my students and helped me encourage them to develop portfolios around personally constructed (rather than teacher-directed) literacy goals.

STRETCHING THE SEAMS OF PORTFOLIOS

After reading that midterm set of portfolios from students in my prose writing course, I felt a vague sense of disappointment. While the stu-dents' work was well written and well organized and their introductory letters gave me some understanding of their writing process, the port-folios seemed more mine than theirs. My disappointment led me to look again at what students were saying to me in their portfolio letters. By attending to students like Meredith, I was able to re-envision the portfolio as something more elastic, a case that could expand to include a wider range of student literacies than only writing completed for my course. Meredith had included poetry in her final portfolio—poetry not written for my expository prose writing class; poetry I had not read before. In her letter, Meredith wrote that she had included all the required writing for the portfolio, but she felt that for me to really understand her literacy, I needed to know that she was a poet and songwriter. Clearly Meredith valued her experiences writing poetry and needed and wanted me to understand how that personal literacy defined her as I read her other written work.

David was another student who helped me enlarge my ideas about portfolios. In his letter, David wrote that if I was to really consider his writing in the same way he did, I needed to know that he was a visual thinker (John-Steiner 1985; Gardner 1983) and that the descriptive writing he had worked on during the semester, like our short in-class exercises on natural objects such as shells and other descriptive narra-tives, represented the writing he valued most in his portfolio.

Both David and Meredith had hinted that no matter what was included, their portfolios needed to reflect their own definitions of literacy, not mine. By thinking about what students wrote about their portfolios, I came to see the different criteria they used to evaluate their own work and I also came to understand what students personally valued in my writing curriculum.

For their end-of-term portfolios I asked the same students to deter-mine their own principles for organizing their portfolios and to provide a rationale for those choices. For example, students might decide to submit only one paper in the final portfolio but would also include all the brainstorming, drafting, and peer and teacher response that led to that final rewrite. In the reflective essay, they would need to state that revision was the criterion on which the portfolio was built, show why they value revision, and outline what they learned about their own literacy in the process of compiling that type of portfolio. In short, for the final portfolios in this prose writing course, I was expecting the unexpected.

Some students were wary of this new invitation to take risks; others were disturbed that they had to determine the criteria for the portfolio themselves. One student, Richie, visited and revisited my office many times after class to find out what I "really wanted"; clearly, he believed that there was a subtext to this portfolio assignment. And, of course, there was: I wanted to understand how students valued their own literacies. Taking the responsibility for figuring out what kind of writers and learners they were became a challenge for many of my students. Reviewing their choices and reflecting on them became a challenge for me as a teacher.

THREE LITERACY CONFIGURATIONS

After I rethought my ideas about portfolios, students in my subsequent writing courses began to organize their portfolios according to self-selected literacy criteria. While I still offered guidance, I no longer provided hard and fast guidelines. New literacy configurations were shaped by my students as they experimented with possibilities and taught me new ways of considering literacy as they learned. Not only did portfolios encourage my student writers to find new ways to reflect on their growth as readers, writers, and thinkers, they made me reflect on my own classroom curriculum. I began to see that the most powerful use of the portfolio for students was a yet-untapped source for teachers: portfolios for self-assessment.

After spending some time analyzing my students' portfolios, I found that they arranged their work in three distinctive ways, which reflected different pedagogical strands of my writing curriculum. Their portfolios displayed a primary focus on writing, learning, or self-reflection.

Writing Portfolios

Students who emphasized writing as a craft or skill included some of the following pieces in their portfolio:

- Multiple drafts of a single paper.
- In-class writing exercises.
- Essays on literature.
- Writing completed in other disciplines.
- Essays about the process of writing as self-exploration.

Their portfolios followed the most obvious of the stated goals of my course: to provide students with an opportunity to become more expansive and skilled writers by drafting, sharing, and revising within a wide range of genres.

Eleanor was a student who developed a portfolio with a strong writing emphasis. She included four different versions of her paper "The Haven," which documented her own recent experiences working in a shelter for homeless women. In her portfolio letter to me, Eleanor described how her voice changed in each draft, from being "free flowing" and "emotional" to becoming more "objective," to "blending the subjective and objective voices together," ending with a draft that added a "sociological perspective." The value of the final version of "The Haven," Eleanor suggested, is that she learned to employ "a more complex range of devices, using several voices, descriptive passages, weaving in and out of the voices of [her] composite characters, and ending with a barely contained journalistic voice."

As I read Eleanor's portfolio letter I was able to see how she interpreted the goals for my writing assignments into her needs as a writer. The development of her voice in writing matched many of the assignments of the course, which began with personal narratives (emotional, subjective), moved on to researched essays (outside sources, objectivity) and ended with collaboratively researched projects (adopting another person's perspective.)

In addition to her extensively rewritten paper, Eleanor also included a piece from her sociology course, a paper entitled "Economic Rights for Women," which Eleanor says represents "yet another attempt to come to grips with women's lives and the institutions that cause it to be predominately women who need shelters." Eleanor ends her portfolio letter by stating that "I am a more focused, confident, and stronger writer in December than in September, and I feel I have made some important steps along the path of my personal goal to become a good writer. Thank you."

Eleanor's portfolio reflects her own personally constructed goal to improve her craft and skills as a writer. Through her arrangment and discussion of her writing, I could see how she achieved some of her goals through specific assignments in my writing curriculum.

Learning Portfolios

Another type of portfolio assembled by many of my students focused on learning. Rather than viewing writing mainly as a craft or set of skills that lead to self-discovery, these students were more concerned with writing as a mode of learning that generates new meaning. Their portfolios included the following:

- Journal entries.
- Reader-response papers.
- Process papers.
- Collaborative projects.
- Expressions of mutiple literacies (videos, musical compositions, artwork).
- Reflective essays about the learning process as self-exploration.

Students who organized their portfolios in this way selected different aspects of my curriculum to explain their literacy configurations. Journal entries and process papers about either reading or writing showed how they valued the process of learning more than the product. Learning portfolios tended to include collaborative writing projects or extended the definition of literacy to encompass other modes of communication.

When students found the experience of researching, learning, and writing together successful, they often valued that writing over all other work completed in the course. Even when the collaboratively written paper landed short of their personal goals, students involved in group writing often realized that "the process is the product" and that learning holds value in itself.

Tim was one student whose final portfolio stressed the importance of collaboration. Skeptical at first about collaborative writing, Tim recognized that he had "a tendency to want to impose my [his] views on others," because he wanted to "remake the world in light of [my] own beliefs, values, and morals." After doing some research collaboratively, however, Tim found what he believed was the real strength of collaboration: in its ability to "de-mystify or unmask the knowledge within a culture and allow learners to see that knowledge really is a process of social and cultural institutionalization of dominant beliefs and values." Tim recognized that the values of collaboration are not the same as the values of the academy as a whole because when students collaborate, "we are not being rugged individualists," nor are students "engaged in the solitary pursuit of academe." Indeed another way of learning is in operation during collaboration, and that mode, according to Tim, is "how to deal with the world and share knowledge with learners." For Tim and others like him, the process of collaboration became a type of literate behavior that they valued and wanted their portfolios to display.

Just as portfolios that emphasized writing often included writing outside of my class, portfolios that emphasized learning might include some commentary about literacies besides reading and writing, such as dance, art, or music. Reading these portfolios showed me still another type of literacy configuration, one I had tried to include in my curriculum as well.

Sarah's portfolio, for example, included a videotape of her own dance performance and an accompanying paper, in which she compared the process of dancing to that of writing. Sarah explains:

> Dancing gives me the same feeling of release I get when I write or when I scream. It's control within a state of being out of control. Dancing is like being under water and not having to hold your breath, or like flying without being strapped into a seat. And there's always that shaft of energy that kind of propels you along and you have no idea where it comes from.

In her introductory letter Sarah asks that I don't "critique" the videotape of her dancing "or else I'll fail." She includes the video because she says that it will help me to better understand her literacies: "I am submitting a copy of the video because the dance is part of my portfolio in a way. It's another medium through which I enjoy expressing myself." Writing for Sarah is an important part of her literacy, but it is through the comparision of writing and dance that she can best show who she is as a learner: "Just understand that [dance] is just something I have to do, even though I'm not that good at it. It's like writing, I can't not do it and feel complete."

As Sarah's instructor, I needed to get inside her perspective of herself as a learner. Her portfolio helped me understand dance as another type of language, well described by dancer Katherine Dunham: "Alone or in concert man dances his various selves and his emotions and his dance becomes a communication as clear as though it were written or spoken in a universal language" (John-Steiner 1985, 171).

Students who focused on writing as learning or the relationship between writing and other literacies compiled their portfolios from entirely different aspects of my curriculum. It was interesting for me as their instructor to understand that, when invited, students take from our courses what is most valuable to them as learners.

The Self-Reflective Portfolio

A third type of portfolio, submitted by a small group of students, seemed different enough to warrant a separate category. These students constructed their portfolios as a kind of mirror of who they were and where they stood in their lives, emphasizing writing as self-development and self-reflection. Because each of these portfolios was so different, I cannot generalize what went into them; they can only be presented as particular cases. As anthropologist Clifford Geertz has suggested, individual cases form a kind of truth in and of themselves: "There is no ascent to truth without a descent to cases" (1973). This group of student portfolios showed me still another reading of my course curriculum, configured by stretching the portfolio into yet another shape.

All of the students who put together what I call the self-reflective portfolio were victims of some type of abuse: rape, incest, wife or child beating, drug or food addiction. Most, but not all, were women. Their abusive experiences and their literacies were described by these students as co-dependent variables. Their abusive experiences were central to defining their literacy, and their literacy was central to salvaging or rescuing who they were. Many students asked that the papers written about these experiences not be evaluated as part of their portfolio but be considered as the center from which all else about them as writers and learners could be understood.

Sasha was a student who put together a self-reflective portfolio, literally writing herself into an understanding of the various addictions that had shaped her life. Interestingly, Sasha's course writing did not center on these issues at all until it came time to complete her final portfolio. In an end-of-term portfolio conference where I expected to help her revise an early narrative, Sasha brought in an entirely new draft. This paper described an early childhood rape, her struggle with bulimia, her overdependence on drugs and alcohol, and the realization of her need for professional help. Overwhelmed by Sasha's problems and needs, I felt that all I could do as her writing teacher was offer my support and affirm her bravery for confronting these issues and suggest that she join Narcotics Anonymous.

Sasha, and some other students who faced similar abusive circumstances, used the occasion of portfolio development to look critically into themselves and compile a portfolio around their self-described goal of honest reflection. This took such students out of a neat portfolio design into the messy middle of writing for their lives. From this, I too was allowed to learn and grow by understanding the centrality of these abusive experiences in shaping their literacies and lives.

Sasha's final portfolio included only one other paper (her collaborative research project) aside from the many drafts of her paper about her abusive past, all written in an intense two-week period before the portfolios were due. In her earliest draft Sasha had merely outlined her drug abuse, almost using writing as a form of confession: "I have already touched on my experiences with drug use . . . it goes much deeper than just having fun and being a little out of control. . . . I am an addict. Because of my personality, I have problems with dependency."

As Sasha worked through her material, all of the skills we had discussed in our writing course came into play to help her render her experiences into a narrative called "Looking on the Inside," complete with detailed scenes and reflections:

> "James, hand me my bottle of Jeg!"
> "Alright Michael, but you'd better slow down. You've polished off a fifth and y'all are leavin in a little while."
> Yeah, Michael drank a fifth of Jegermesiter: He was also tripping on three hits of acid and had sniffed a line of speed a few hours earlier. Trip, a good friend from Memphis, was in town for a while and the two of them decided to go cruising around. From the guys' point of view, the situation was innocent enough. This is what you're supposed to be doing the summer after graduation, right?

Michael and Trip headed down the curves of Hixon Pike toward Taco Bell to get a bite to eat. They didn't quite make it the whole four miles. In an instant Michael's body was transformed into an eggshell, with only one limb remaining. By some miracle, the passenger side was barely touched and Trip got out and began wandering around, not even comprehending what had happened until the pain and blood jerked him back to reality.

We all needed a jerk back to reality. But the ten of us who constantly hung out at James and Holt's apartment were excited about the summer and we didn't allow time for deep thinking and sorrow.

I remember driving over to the junk yard to see what was left of the car. I couldn't stop clinging to the chain fence as the tears streamed down my face. I kept repeating the word, "why" over and over. I remember Heather saying, "Think about it, at least he must have been happy when he died." Maybe, but I doubt it.

Within this long narrative paper, Sasha shows how writing, even within the confusion of her drug experiences, helped save her life: "I went to a Grateful Dead show and had a very bad acid trip. I remember sitting on the bathroom sink, watching myself in the mirror. I saw the tears melt my face as they rolled down. I was writing because there was nothing else to do and my last sentence [before I passed out] was: 'I'm still tripping . . . I hope I never wake up.' "

Students who compile reflective portfolios are interested in both writing and learning, but most of all they have charged themselves to be searingly honest with important life issues. Fred said that the reason he wrote both his narrative and his research paper on wife abuse—about his own father's abuse of his mother—was that if he didn't understand the problem from all angles, "I might end up perpetuating this vicious cycle of abuse myself." Shelly suggested that if she couldn't share her rape experience in her portfolio, I wouldn't understand the center of her being and how everything in her life—school, friends, parents—had been affected by this event. She needed to write about and share this experience in order to understand it:

Sharing the pain and experiences that so many of us have kept under a tight lock and key can [be] a very powerful step in the healing process. Somehow when the dark secrets are put into words, the weight that they push on your back becomes lighter. But the risk involved in letting the secrets go is often very difficult. The pain has become part of the whole person, it is part of their identity.

Shelly asked that I read her account but not evaluate it. Her portfolio included a wide range of other writing submitted for formal evaluation.

These reflective student portfolios bring up the same problems for teachers that they face with journals: the writing may become too confessional; teachers aren't therapists; teachers have no way of evaluating such work. As I put these portfolios into a separate category, I wonder at the courage of these writers to take on such critical issues in their lives. And I also realize that if they don't use my class and their portfolios to write themselves into spaces for healing, where else will they do it? Portfolios offered this group of students a safe place from which to write. As composition and women's studies theorist Cinthia Gannett suggests: "While many teachers may appropriately feel they cannot take on the roles of professional healers, they should not deny the curative power of writing itself and its relation to knowing" ("Stories of Our Lives," 32).

EVALUATION OF THE OPEN PORTFOLIO

I ask students who work with an open portfolio design to assign a certain weight for each paper in their final portfolio up to a total of seventy-five points. (I reserve twenty-five points for class participation, attendance, library exercises, and journal writing.) The grade for their portfolio serves as the major grade in the course.

Evaluating on their own how much each paper will count towards their final grade is a big responsibility. Shifting this responsibility to students does not, however, mean that I must agree with their assessments but rather that I can better understand how students are valuing their work.

Figure 5–1 shows how one student evaluated his final portfolio submissions: my grades are listed alongside his percentages. This student made good choices for his portfolio. He included a wide range of writing styles, from an essay about Richard Rodriguez to a collaborative research paper on chemical warfare. He gives his three pieces of polished narrative writing—"A Night to Remember," "Hit By a Car", "A Day in Court"—the most weight overall; they total fifty percent of his grade. Although I found his researched essay on chemical warfare weaker than his narrative "Hit by a Car," this student's overall self-evaluation of the quality of his work matches my sense of it.

Not all students are able to make such good choices about how to weigh their work. Figure 5–2 shows another student's evaluation. She included only three papers in her final portfolio, two narratives and one response to literature. The narrative paper she gave the most weight to fell into the C plus range, but her reading response (for which she assigned only twenty percent of her final grade) was an outstanding piece of work. In addition to my finding a lack of range in her work (fifty-five percent of it is narrative) and my disagreement with her over the quality of one of her narrative papers, the student's overall lack of participation in the course contributed to her final evaluation of C.

TITLE	STUDENT WEIGHT	TEACHER GRADE
TITLE	A Night To Remember 25%	A
TITLE	Hit By A Car 15%	B+
TITLE	A Day In Court 10%	B
TITLE	Richard Rodriguez 10%	C+
TITLE	Chemical Warfare 15%	C
	CLASS PARTICIPATION 25%	B
	FINAL GRADE	B

FIGURE 5–1   One Student's Evaluation

TITLE	STUDENT WEIGHT	TEACHER GRADE
TITLE	Double Messages 45%	C+
TITLE	That Night 20%	A
TITLE	The Intruder 10%	B—
TITLE		
TITLE		
	CLASS PARTICIPATION 25%	C
Omitted Classes	Journal Incomplete	
	FINAL GRADE	C

FIGURE 5–2   Another Student's Evaluation

When students give far less credit to a final paper than I do, I try to adjust their own evaluation in favor of higher grades. In working with this system, I have found that student and teacher evaluations are usually quite similar.

Students' evaluations of their portfolios is important to me because I find out through the choices students make what parts of my curriculum are most useful to them. What I discover when reviewing all my students' self-evaluation forms is that they value personal narrative over all other forms. Narrative writing totals from fifty to ninty percent of the submissions in their final portfolios. Second to personal narratives, my students value their collaboratively written research papers.

Tallying this information allows me to see whether students' portfolio submissions match the amount of time I spent on various forms or projects in my course. Individual research essays, responses to literature, expanded journal writing, and in-class exercises rank lower in terms of final portfolio submissions; this has forced me to rethink how much space in my curriculum to give over to such writing. Like most teachers, some of my writing curriculum reflects the skills I feel that students must know to survive in school. Often those kinds of writing are the ones least prized by students themselves. Knowing that only a handful of students included their researched essays, which we spent more than three weeks doing, makes me look hard at that part of my writing course and see if I can change my way of teaching this form. Knowing that students value narrative writing also shows me that I have spent enough time on this form and that students will continue to work on personal narratives out of self-interest and satisfaction. Portfolios help me adjust my classroom curriculum.

When I look at how my students have chosen to organize and discuss their writing portfolios, I see how far they have helped me stretch my ideas. I have come a long way from writing folders to these open portfolios. I have also come a long way from using portfolios for assessment of students to using portfolios for assessment of myself and my own writing curriculum.

6

TEACHERS EVALUATE
THEIR OWN LITERACY

JANE HANSEN

S ince 1989 I've experimented with portfolios in my reading/ writing classes at the University of New Hampshire. The teachers in these courses have evaluated themselves, their work, and their plans for what to learn next. I've asked students in those classes to create portfolios.

In this chapter, I'll share what I learned from the portfolios created by the students in my spring 1990 "Foundations of Reading" course. This is a Master's level course that includes experienced to novice teachers, interns, and pre-interns. They work at all grade levels, from preschool through adult literacy programs, but the interest of the majority is elementary education. There were twenty-seven students in this class; we met once a week for fifteen weeks for two and a half hours per session. We conducted a reading/writing workshop for the first part of each class, during which we wrote, read, shared in small groups, and held an all-class conference. For the last part of each class we related our workshop to the settings in which the class members teach, or I showed a video, slides, or overheads of children's writing and reading in order to share what I've learned in classrooms.

I started the first class by arranging all the chairs in a circle and placing on each chair two or three books from my collection, mostly adult literature, but some children's books as well. We spent that session sharing these books, which got the students started on reading or gave them new ideas for books to read. They could read my books throughout the semester, and they did, but they mostly brought their own books from then on. I expected them to read and write in all genres as much as possible.

Also in that first meeting, I gave them the syllabus, in letter form. In it, I told them about myself and I outlined the course. I required reading from professional books as well as trade books, but I did not have a required text. I gave them an annotated list of books, all of which were in the university bookstore and library, and required them to read at least two professional books during the term. They could, if they wanted, read books not on my suggested list. Many read more than two books.

I also required students to read some articles from "The Box," a container that holds about forty articles, which I constantly add to and subtract from. I gave them an annotated list of the contents of The Box and asked them to read at least six; but, as with the books, many read more.

In addition to writing what they wanted, I gave two assignments, both interviews. One was to conduct an interview with three students of any age, to ask these four questions: What do you do well as a reader? What's the most recent thing you've learned to do as a reader? What do you want to learn next in order to be a better reader? How do you intend to go about learning how to do that? The questions could also be asked about writing. My students were to write a paper based on the interviews.

The second assignment was to learn the stories of a reader and a nonreader. They were to find their reader and nonreader by asking people a single question: Are you a reader? An unqualified yes gave them a reader; a no identified a nonreader. The nonreader was someone who knew how to read, but who considered himself or herself a nonreader. The interviewers in this second assignment had no set questions. They were simply to find out what the interviewee's current reading habits were and how those habits evolved from the person's early years through the present.

I didn't care which of the two assignments my students did first, but they were to include one in their portfolio each of the two times they handed in their portfolio.

These assignments placed my students in the position of listening to others reflect on their literacy. Not only was this interesting in itself, but these reflections gave my students insights into their own literacy. For example, some students who did not consider themselves readers identified with other nonreaders as they recounted childhood experiences in which reading was not valued. The interviews enriched my students' pictures of themselves.

To bring all their work together, I asked each student to create a portfolio. In their portfolios they were to do two things: compile a portrait of themselves as a reader, writer, teacher, and learner; and evaluate themselves as literate individuals.

The first attempt at compiling a portfolio was difficult, rewarding, and revealing—for me and the students. In the summer of 1989, the first time I asked a class to create portfolios, they kept asking, "What do you want?" I could only reply, "I don't know. I've never done this before." Students struggled with the open-endedness of the assignment. At the end of the course, I asked my class, "Now that I have a better idea of what a portfolio contains, should I give guidelines to the students in my fall classes? *No!*"

The students found trying to figure out who they were an agonizing process, but afterwards they realized it was a necessary part of creating their portfolios. Most of them had never given serious thought to who they were as literate persons and found it painful to admit this.

After listening to the groans of that summer class, three fall classes, and a spring class, I decided to give some guidelines. During the summer of 1990, I started the portfolio process by sharing mine and distributing to the class copies of a letter in which I explained my portfolio, how I felt about the artifacts in it, and what my plans were. I told them I was worried that by doing this I might constrain their thinking about their portfolios, so I emphasized that this was a portrait of me, and that their portfolios would be very different from mine and from each other's. I needn't have worried. Their low level of anxiety compared to my former classes relieved me, and their portfolios were not carbon copies of mine. Someone in that class could easily have made the comment that Peggy in my fall 1989 course offered after the first time they'd shared their portfolios in class: "You really see what someone's like when you look at their portfolio!"

Even the outward appearance of their portfolios gave a glimpse of the individuality of the students: a leather folder with gold trim rescued from a trunk; manila folders; an accordion-pocket portfolio; plain pocket-folders like my green one; a three-ring binder with tabbed sections; one covered with wallpaper; and a shiny folder with merry-go-round horses on it.

Inside, I found cartoons, pamphlets about the environment, an underground rag, goal charts of high school runners, and all kinds of writing: journal entries, letters, poetry, short stories, papers from other

classes, and notes written to little children. I found remnants of teaching, such as articles the high school biology teacher's students brought
to class each Friday, and a collection of poetry written by an intern's
class. I found evidence of learning in journal reflections on teaching and
personal narratives about family events. For reading, many portfolios
contained lists of books, some charts, excerpts from books and poems,
and short or long reflections about some readings. Clearly, my students
led full lives.

Students evaluated themselves through three "Dear Jane" letters.
They wrote the first letter about one-third of the way into the course,
both to begin to evaluate themselves and to tell me about their literate lives. They included the second and third letters in their portfolios
when they handed them in, about two-thirds of the way through the
course and at the end. In these letters they told me about the items
in the portfolio, why they had included them, and the significance
of each.

I wrote about a one-page response to each letter. I responded to their
chit-chat and included news about my own weekend activities. I
responded to their writing and told about my own, as well as their
reading. I commented on their teaching and learning. It took me about
one hour to respond to each letter, so I staggered the due dates. One-
third were due at a time. The previous fall, when I required portfolios of all three of my classes, I was swamped, so I wrote shorter
response letters, and one of my students complained that she'd put
enough work into the portfolio to warrant more of a response from me
than she received. So, in the spring of 1990 I decided to stagger the
submissions and give myself a more reasonable workload—although
reading portfolios is not work. They fascinate me. The following examples are typical.

AN EXPERIENCED TEACHER
BECOMES A WRITER

First, I'll share the writing experiences of Sue Murphy, an experienced
elementary teacher. About one third of the way into the course, Sue
wrote to me, "I hope this course will inspire me to set some personal
writing goals for myself. . . . I do want to be a writer, a good writer, so
I should begin. . . . Someday I will write a children's book. . . . One of
my very favorite stories is A Chair for My Mother by Vera Williams
[1982]. I recently heard her speak and found out that she did not start
to write until she was 43 or 44. 'WOW! There is still hope for me.' "

About two-thirds of the way into the course, Sue shared her portfolio with me for the first time. In the letter that accompanied it, she wrote, "I have enclosed two poems. . . . I do like to write but have not disciplined myself."

In her third letter, written at the end of the course to accompany her revised portfolio, a new Sue emerged. "I am pleased to see that I do have much more writing than last time. . . . I am really enjoying writing poems. None are finished that I have included but are on my computer so I can keep adding and changing as I want." Here is part of one of Sue's poems:

Two small children stand at a window.
Their mother comes up the walk with a new baby.
They see it for the first time.
They join hands, stand closer in silence.

A little girl is sent to camp for the summer.
Her mother has left, she doesn't know why.
There is no place for her at this time.
She feels alone, frightened.
She doesn't speak.
Her brother is not with her.
She cannot hold his hand.

The girl is on a train,
she is alone.
She is taking a long trip to a grandmother in Michigan.
She holds tightly to a doll with a porcelain head
that her mother gave her.
She sits quietly, stares out the window.
The train stops, she stands
clutching the doll to her breast.
A sudden jolt
The doll drops.
The head breaks into a million tiny pieces
that are gone forever.
She stares and stares
but no tears fall.

Sue has become a writer. She was determined to do so and set this goal for herself, but she needed two-thirds of the course to think and fret. If I had averaged her grades for the three parts of the course, she wouldn't have fared well, but she wrote, "I would give myself an A for the course." I did.

One of the most striking things I and others (Seidel 1989) learned from studying portfolios is that learning doesn't travel in a straight, gradually ascending line. No. Learning goes through many seemingly dry periods and a few spurts. The accomplishments come after much thought and time, during which the learner is trying to decide what to do and planning. Complex behaviors develop gradually and call for instructional environments that differ from the present organization of schools, which are inhospitable to long-term goals (Airasian 1988).

Learners need as much choice as possible to find the best way to grow, and to show that growth to themselves and others. My requirement was that they show what they learned, and because of the pressure created by this requirement they struggled to make progress. Within the course structure I tried to foster divergence as the class members evaluated who they were and who they wanted to become as literate educators.

AN EXPERIENCED LEARNER WILL BECOME A TEACHER

Larry Gray wrote and read, but the part of Larry's self-evaluation that I present here shows who he is as a learner. In his first "Dear Jane" letter he said, "Wouldn't you know it—now is the time PBS has begun showing classic silent films, which is a growing interest for me. . . . Then there's my insistence on seeing every episode of the new 'Eyes on the Prize' series, my constant need to expand my musical listening horizons (latest favorite is 1950s Frank Sinatra albums), my growing list of penpals, and my recent inexplicable desire to learn world geography. . . . I am eager to learn all I can to be as good a teacher— and person—as possible."

In his second letter he responded to my plans to visit the USSR. In accordance with his interest in geography, he wrote, "I promptly looked up Murmansk to see where you are headed. Up by Finland! I hope you have a warm overcoat—that place is above the Arctic Circle!"

In his third letter, Larry referred to a copy of The Fishwrapper, an "underground rag" he included in his portfolio. He had accepted the position of Arts Editor for it, but wrote, "I warn you. 'Tis not censored in thought or language, so keep out of the reach of children and easily-offended adults. . . . I'm doing a lot of work for Earth Day, and doing respite for a mother of a special-needs child, and working at the record store on weekends."

Also during those last few weeks, Larry spent a great deal of time finding his internship placement for the following year. At UNH, a year-long internship is required for the Master's in teaching, and finding a classroom for that internship is like looking for a job. Larry found the grade level he wanted: first grade. "I'm really looking forward to it."

Larry's interesting life will help him as a teacher. That's something else these portfolios taught me. As teachers, we need to lead multi-faceted lives. To be literate means we have control over several litera-cies and can set up our classrooms so that our students can acquire new discourses (Gee 1989a). Larry closed his letter to me with, "It is a very busy time, but a good one, and I am learning a great deal every day! Be well, Jane." For all of us to be able to say, "I am learning a great deal every day. . . . "

EXPERIENCED READERS LEARN ABOUT READING

Ellen O'Neil taught high school English but at the time she took my course was a full-time graduate student who intended to return to the classroom the following year. She had started her graduate studies about a year before and since that time had researched and read several black women writers. She included in her portfolio a list of all the books she'd read since starting graduate school—a long list. She continued this interest throughout the semester of my course, but didn't say any-thing in particular about her reading in either her first or second "Dear Jane" letter.

Then, in her third letter, she wrote about rereading *The Color Purple* (Walker 1982) three times, and rereading Toni Morrison's *Beloved* (1987). "Though I'm not one who goes to the same movie twice, or reads a novel more than once, I think I had to, and may have to again, reread to gain a clearer understanding. . . . I thought about *The Color Purple* this time in relation to *Sojourner Truth* (Krass 1983), which has brought me to a much different understanding." Ellen, already an avid reader with a specialty, had a significant experience with books the semester she took my course.

Sue Murphy had a similar experience. She also entered the course as an avid reader. However, during the first two-thirds of the course she didn't find a book that truly engaged her. Then one week, when Judy Fueyo taught the class in my abscence, Judy read aloud from *Fried Green Tomatoes at the Whistle Stop Cafe* by Fannie Flagg (1987). Sue searched it out, read it, and wrote, "What a wonderful book!! It's the best book I've read in a long time. It makes you laugh, reflect, cry . . . a great book. I highly recommend it." Sue also had a significant experience with books that semester.

That's the challenge: to find worthwhile learning experiences. And that is something else I learned from the portfolios. "Assessment cannot stop with a review of work. Learners must be asked to articulate their hopes for the coming months and year" (Levi 1990, 271). Learners must strive to learn, to find experiences that allow them to feel movement and growth. They constantly keep their antennae out as they look for an opportunity to capitalize on, a book to read, or a reason to reread. They need to put themselves in learning situations where they have the flexibility they need and the time they must have to find something of interest and to pursue their quest.

EVALUATORS LEARN ABOUT TEACHING

Besides reading, writing, and learning, my students shared their teaching. They included artifacts to show who they were as teachers and explanations of things they tried because of this course. Because a focus of our class was evaluation, many of them tried new evaluation ideas, which teachers must do in order to seek credible replacements for the out-of-date assessment systems that they usually work with and that inhibit rich educational experiences for students (Brown 1987a).

For example, after receiving my response to her first "Dear Jane" letter, Sue decided to write letters to her students after their dinosaur projects. Because she had appreciated a letter from her teacher, she thought her students would also. She included a letter she wrote to one of her students in her portfolio.

Ellen, who was not teaching at the time, shared plans for the following year, when she was to return to the classroom. She is a runner and a high school women's track and cross-country coach. In her portfolio, she included Goals Sheets for two of her runners and explained that her runners become more proficient at filling out these sheets over time. "Helen has filled out sheets in past years, thus her goals are concrete. . . . Jean was a rookie, so her goals were obscure, yet they became clearer once the season progressed." Ellen's runners learn what a realistic goal is, as do my students, over time.

Ellen continued, "In writing, my runners must state their objectives. This is so important for high school athletes to do, especially in a physically enduring sport that emphasizes the individual's mental powers. It's amazing what kids will do once they put in writing what they want to accomplish. It is very common at the conclusion of races for athletes to tell friends, family members, and each other, 'I got my goal!' " Ellen's comments go beyond high school women runners, to adult teachers, learners, readers, and writers. When they state their goals in writing, it's amazing what they will accomplish.

In her last letter to me, Ellen wrote, "I'm definitely going to integrate portfolio evaluation into my curriculum next year, somehow, someway!" That's our challenge. Each of us to figure out how portfolios, with self-evaluation as their core, can become part of our classrooms. Our own portfolios give us many cues and keep the portfolio notion alive as we constantly add to and delete from our own collections, for our own reasons.

A teacher thinks . . .

As I see it, three components make up [the portfolio] process: self-study, self-definition, and self-disclosure. To begin, I must ask myself what objects or documents represent who I am as a reader/writer, or, more broadly, as a literate person, or, even more broadly, as a learner. . . . Self-study is good . . . Know Thyself 101. Some students, particularly the many who are not yet aware they exist, may need just this: "I have a portfolio, therefore I am."

But self-definition comes next. This is harder. . . . One cannot become a literate person alone. One is responding when one reads and one is also, perhaps less immediately, responding when one writes. . . . [A portfolio is] a frustrating mosaic with many pieces and most of the grout missing. But now, self-disclosure. Oh, I must share the thing! . . . The better job I do of assembling it, the more precious, the more sacred it becomes. Let us not have talk of scrapbook portfolios as alternative assessment.

Sharon Lundahl
Teacher, grade 8
Washington, DC, and Silver Spring, Maryland

II

EXAMINE POSSIBILITIES, RETHINK DIRECTIONS

"Are we there yet?" ask children when, hot and tired, they are miles from [their] destination. . . . Exploring and displaying our unique backgrounds as literary people gives us common ground on which to start building the foundation of trust we need in the writer's workplace. . . . My portfolio is still in three sections: my personal history, my professional life, and my life as a learner.

Marta M. Snow
Special education teacher
Epping, New Hampshire

Elizabeth Coatsworth writes: "Some writers say they hate writing and only do it because they hate *not* writing even more." I can see myself moving in that direction. I have discovered the portfolio to be a big impetus for my writing. It fished out memories submerged in the ocean of my mind. Many more will surface, if I can just keep scuba diving.

Initially, I felt uncomfortable about doing a personal "me" portfolio. We were taught in high school English Composition class that no one ever uses the word "I" or "me" in stories. "No one cares what you think or feel." Teachers would remark. "Just show us how skillful you can be with the topic." The trend continued in college, and became more clinical. "Always write a report about a student in the third person." How could we share the joy of living and learning if it was masked in the third person? . . . I'm intrigued with Elizabeth Chiseri-Strater's notion of using the portfolio for assessment of oneself as teacher. The challenge remains, not only *if* to use portfolios, but *how.*"

Pat Thivierge
Teacher, grades 2 and 3
Suffield, Connecticut

7

HELP STUDENTS LEARN TO READ THEIR PORTFOLIOS

DONALD H. GRAVES

Students need to learn to evaluate their own work. When I first began to teach writing thirty-five years ago I allowed my students just one day of writing a week, corrected the daylights out of what they wrote, and knew I was the only one with enough sense to judge their work. They wrote for me, and I was proud of my standards. They feared my red pen; I called their fear respect. Worse, I called their fear learning. Not once did I ask them to evaluate their own work. Consequently, they developed little skill in reading their own work.

There's a danger that portfolios may be evaluated the way I evaluated the writing of my students all those years ago. We'll evaluate the students' portfolios, curse their lack of ability to judge and improve their own work, then choose what work they ought to include. Fortunately, some professionals believe that students can learn to evaluate their own work effectively and make good choices for their portfolios. An emphasis on student evaluation, however, is slow going and tough work.

The portfolio movement has uncovered just how much help students need in order to learn how to evaluate their own work. Even when students are allowed to decide which work belongs in their portfolios, the reasons for their decisions often seem casual: "I'm choosing this one because it is about the Boston Celtics." "I worked hard on that one; it's my longest one." "This is better because it's about dogs, not cats." "This is my research paper on the Civil War. My teacher gave it an A."

If students are to become more proficient in making good judgments about their portfolio selections, they need to become acquainted with the criteria that characterize good writing. To do this, we need to help students learn to read like writers.

In this chapter I offer four approaches to help students become better readers of their own work. In each, you work to acquaint students with the elements that make good writing. I begin with simply encouraging students to experiment with new ways of writing and looking at their own work. The next two approaches focus on how students become more sensitive to good writing when their writing is shared. The fourth approach helps students become aware of the range of feelings they have about various pieces of their writing. Each of the approaches helps students make better decisions when they finally choose work to place in their portfolios.

NUDGE STUDENTS TO EXPERIMENT WITH THEIR WRITING

Sometimes someone chooses just the right verb to capture the right teaching practice. Mary Ellen Giacobbe did that for me when she chose the word *nudge* as an important part of the writing conference. The word implies just a little shove, an encouragement for the student to experiment with something he or she may not have tried before. I think Lev Vygotsky, the famous Russian psychologist, would have approved of Mary Ellen's choice of word. The word implies a knowledge of where the student is at the moment, as well as the new "zone of proximal development" (Vygotsky 1962) or the new area of learning the child ought to enter. The teacher senses the moment as well as the area for new learning by the student.

Carry some "nudge paper" with you when you walk through the classroom responding to student writing. By "nudge paper" I mean a small piece of paper on which a child can try a five- to ten-minute experiment with writing. The paper may be lined or unlined, but it should be similar to the kind of paper the children are used to using in class (this is especially important for very young children). You may even use the back of paper that has been written on. The small size of the nudge paper is meant to suggest "temporary, experimental, under construction."

The nudge itself is a general invitation to experiment. Ideally, the student will act on the nudge without further instruction, but in some cases you need to be more directive by saying something like, "I want you to. . . . I'll be back to see how you are doing."

The following are some examples of nudges (note that not all nudges require paper).

Teacher: John, I see you have a new character here. What does he look like?

John: I'm not sure. I want him to be about sixteen, kind of big.

Teacher: Tell me some more about him. What kind of person is he? If I were to meet him, what would he be like?

John: He gives people trouble. He picks on smaller kids.

Teacher: I get a feel for him now. He is kind of big and he picks on others, especially people smaller than himself. Tell me about his face when he picks on someone.

John: Oh—hmm—he has kind of snaky eyes. He squints when he looks at you.

Teacher: I see him. Take this piece of paper and experiment quickly with what he looks like, John. He's important to your piece. Just experiment for about five minutes. You may not want to use this, but experiment anyway.

Teacher: That's a hard word you've tried over here, Tanya. You've almost got it spelled just right. I see it's an important word to you because you use it quite a bit. Take this piece of paper and experiment with it a few times just to see if you can get all of it.

Teacher: Mark, look over the verbs here on your first page. What do you see?

Mark [after a pause]: Hmm. Got, got, was, went.

Teacher: What kinds of pictures do you get from those words?

Mark: Not much.

Teacher: Okay, take this small sheet here [the nudge paper] and try this [writes each of Marks verbs on separate line]:

1. got—"picked up"
2. got
3. was
4. went

Experiment with some different verbs that will create a clearer picture for you and the reader of what is going on here in the piece. Try the first one: *got.*

Mark: How about *picked up* the newspaper?

Teacher: Do you get more of a picture from that?

Mark: Yup.

Teacher: Experiment with these others for a little while. See how it goes.

Teacher: Heidi, I know you want this to be an authentic piece on the early dame schools. You have something here on hornbooks, but I'm not sure you have accurate information about how they were used. You'll want to double-check it. Take a few minutes to do that now.

Teacher: Ben, you've got two important characters here in Willy and Popo. But they don't really talk with each other. I'm just wondering if you think there is something they'd ever talk about that would be important to your story. For example, when Popo came over to Willy's house and Willy's dog, Brendan, tore Popo's pants leg, they must have said something to each other. Tell me about it.

Ben: Popo yelled, "Pull him off! Pull him off!" He was afraid Brendan would really bite his leg.

Teacher: Then what happened or what did Willy say?

Ben: Willy said, "Hold still. He's just a puppy."

Teacher: Okay, you've got a start here. I think you know what they might say after that. Just take this piece of paper and experiment with a conversation for about five minutes. You might want to use it; you might not. Do you think you are ready to handle something like that?

If students are ultimately to make good choices for their portfolios, I have to nudge them into trying new approaches to writing. I try to sense during the conference if a student can handle a new experiment. I don't want the student to feel that the experiment has to go into the piece, but I do want the student to stretch a little. The stretching, however, should not be unattainable or unreasonable, or take too much time. That's why I nudge the student to make a quick sketch.

Notice how, in the examples above, the students are helped through the conference. I need to have some assurance that the student will use the five to ten minutes well. In addition, if a student wants to use the experiment in the main piece, he or she may need further help with transitions or with the mechanical aspects of putting two pieces of work together.

RETHINK THE WAYS STUDENTS SHARE THEIR WRITING

For some time now I've been concerned that when students share with larger groups their work gets only thin responses and generalized questions that could have been asked of any piece that might be read. I'm referring to such questions as "What's your favorite part?" "What will you write about next?" "Do you think it is exciting?"

Sharing should also encourage new experiments and new thinking. Done well, it can keep students in daily contact with new criteria and new ways for evaluating and improving their work.

Here are some questions that might be asked of the class at share time:

- *Did anyone create a new character in their fiction today?* This question deliberately focuses on character formation, the heart of writing good fiction. If someone answers this question positively, the other children may want to ask some follow-up questions:
  - What is the character's name? How did you choose the character?
  - What is going to happen to him/her? How come?
  - How old is he/she?
  - What does he/she look like? Read that part.
  - Read the part where he/she talks.

  Children ask these questions because you have helped them develop fictional characters in a workshop setting (Graves 1989). You also demonstrate with your own questions how to develop the writer's characters.

- *Did anyone try a new form of punctuation today?* Children should keep track of when they use new forms of punctuation. They can keep track of their first use of the punctuation form on a sheet that records their use of conventions along with the title and page of the piece in which it was used. This helps them keep their own reference book on punctuation. It also helps them notice how professional writers use punctuation. That way, when children share their reading, they can also point out which new conventions they've noticed the author use. (See Figure 7–1.)

- *Did anyone try an experiment—, that is, something new for you— today? It may not have worked, but you tried it.* This is a general kind of question to open up the discussion about anything new the

FIGURE 7–1   Record of Conventions

Convention	Date	Page	Piece
comma (serial)	10/2	1	Dog to the Vet
colon	10/30	2	Whales
cap - name	11/6	1	Trip to New York
apostrophe (contraction)	11/21	3	Space Story

children tried. There is no way to anticipate all the different kinds of new things that might come up.

- *Did anyone try a different form of writing today—a poem, a piece of fiction, or a personal narrative?* I'd suggest the same when children share books. If they try a different kind of book it ought to be shared with the class.
- *Did anyone use some words today that they liked? Maybe it was just the right kind of verb.* You might also say, "Let's read some of your new verbs aloud." This kind of question can lead to a mini-lesson on the importance of precise word use.
- *Did anyone struggle with spelling a tough word?*
- *Did anyone experiment with something that didn't work today? Maybe it was an experiment that didn't quite turn out the way you'd hoped.* This is a good time for children to be interviewed about their experiments—what didn't work, what they learned, and how they might change the experiment to make it work the next time.

You can use these questions at various times during class sharing. Rarely will more than two be used at any one time.

The basic question underlying all of these questions is "What's new?" In time, students will get a better sense of how and when to share their experiments. Obviously, our sharing with the children what we have tried in our own writing is an important part of the sharing as well. In short, we show how we read.

No doubt you can add many more questions of your own to the ones listed here. As you move about the room and talk with the children, you will become more aware of their experiments and the ways in which they are trying to improve themselves as writers. (Remember to share your own writing experiments, too.) This type of "What's new?" sharing allows the class to share in the victories and the learning of other class members and is a natural extension of your nudging. But in the end, the victories are individual ones. One child may be trying to spell a word that another child knew how to spell two years ago. Make the tone of your class one that supports all kinds of individual growth.

LET STUDENTS PRACTICE EVALUATING

Students usually know when their writing is good, but it is hard for them to know *why* their writing is good. They usually can't say why because they don't know what elements make up a good piece of writing. Once they know the elements, they need practice with them in order to get the feel of what makes their work good.

One of the places to apply these elements is at share time, when two or three children read their writing aloud to the entire class while the class receives the work and then asks questions to help the author.

Here is a variation on traditional share time:

Teacher: We're going to try a new way of listening to pieces this morning. I'll need help from quite a few of you. And this is going to take some practice. Here's the help I'll need:

I'll need two children to listen for *good words* when Lisa reads her story. Okay, Mark, you and Randy listen for words you like. When Lisa finishes reading we'll ask you for the words.

We'll also listen for one more new thing. I need two people to listen for pictures the words create in their heads. For example, if I read the words "The red Subaru smashed into the green pickup truck," do you see a picture? Tell me what is in your picture. Who will listen for some pictures in Lisa's piece? Okay, Alison and Nancy.

After children have demonstrated that they are able to handle these elements, gradually add to the list so that as many as six to seven elements are being handled at a single reading.

Other elements may also be considered. For example, if a piece of fiction is read, students may listen for the following:

- How the main character is first introduced.
- What good dialogue is, and how the author handled dialogue.
- The details of setting—time, place, color, weather, and so forth.
- The problem, conflict, or driving force to the plot.
- How the ending was handled in relation to the main conflict or problem.
- Overall impressions of the selection.
- Other stories—their own and in literature—that the piece reminds them of.

Here are some specific questions you may ask when fiction—a professional author's, a piece of your own, or a student piece—is read aloud:

1. Listen for when the character appears. Try to remember when a character appears. What are the characters like? Can you see them? Can you hear them? Did they say anything? What did they say?
2. Did the author give you any pictures about where this takes place?
3. Listen for any problem. Any tension—like you could feel in your stomach?

4. Did this piece create any other stories in your head? Ones that happened to you? to your friends? in anything you'd read?
5. What's the one thing this is about?
6. How did the author start and finish the piece?
7. How did the author try to keep you reading (or listening)?
8. What's the one thing you think the author wanted you to get from this story?

The children themselves will probably suggest other elements to listen for. In fact, when sharing one of their own pieces, they might say, "These are the things I want you to listen for when I read. Bill, you and Pete listen for the language. . . . "

As for nonfiction, try these questions when sharing a piece of writing:

1. What is this about?
2. Does this remind you about other things you know? If so, what? Does it remind you of other stories or experiences?
3. How does the author start and finish the piece?
4. How did the author keep you reading (or listening)?
5. Listen for something that you didn't know about before, and now you do.
6. Overall, how did this strike you?
7. What's the one thing this author wanted you to get from this piece?
8. Were there any points at which you felt a little tension? reading or listening to this?

HELP STUDENTS BECOME MORE ACQUAINTED WITH THEIR RANGE OF VALUES

I've found that students need to approach their choices for portfolios from a variety of angles before making their actual selections. Every piece has a particular value to them, but these values may be hidden. Our job is to help students become acquainted with their feelings about their work.

Ask the class or a small group of students to take out their writing folders and remove the contents, placing the pieces in an array on the table or desk in front of them. Give them four to six minutes to familiarize themselves with their collection. Young children may work best with no more than six to eight pieces at a time. Then, ask the children to take out a pencil and be prepared to write single words at the top of each of their pages. (If they're reluctant to make notes on a finished copy, you may provide them with small pieces of paper about three by five inches, which they clip to the top edge.) Then, give the group these instructions:

- Pick out two pieces that you just like. Your gut feeling is, I just like that one. Maybe you know why, maybe you don't. Label "Like" at the top of each of those papers.
- Pick out a piece that was just plain hard to write. Label it "Hard" at the top.
- Pick out one piece where you might have said to yourself, "I think I'm getting the hang of this." Label it "Hang of it" at the top.
- Pick out one piece where something surprised you during the writing—that is, what you had was new information. Before you wrote it, you didn't know this new thing; now you do. Label this one "Surprise" at the top.

At about this point a hand will be raised. "I have two words on the same piece. Is that all right?" It certainly is. Some pieces will have as many as three or four labels on them. Students frequently choose those pieces for the portfolio.

Others may say, "I don't have any where I was surprised." That's all right, too. They don't have to use that label if nothing seems appropriate.

The directions continue:

- Pick out a piece that, when you were writing it you might have said something like this to yourself: "Oh, I'm the same old writer I've always been." You wanted the words to be better, the piece to be better, but you were aware that the piece resembled your old way of writing. Label this piece "History" at the top.
- Pick out a piece in which you felt you were learning something as a writer. That is, you were aware that some things were happening in your writing that you'd wanted to have there as a writer. Label this piece "Writer" at the top.
- Pick out a piece where you actually learned something about the event or information you were writing about. Maybe you gained an insight into a person, or you put together some facts, or you clarified a relationship. Label this piece "Learn about the subject" at the top.
- Find two places where, if you read the piece aloud to people who had their eyes closed, they would be able to see a picture. Put brackets around those lines and write "See picture" at the top.

- Find two pieces whose first line you like. Label these pieces "First line" at the top.
- Find a piece you'd just as soon forget you ever wrote. Write "Burn" at the top. Now write for three minutes about why you want to burn it. This writing is just for you; there's no need to share if you don't want to. Or write for three minutes about why you want to keep two pieces.
- Pick out two pieces that you just wanted to keep writing even though you'd run out of time. Label them "Keep going" at the top.
- Pick out two pieces where you'd like to go back and rework the lines. The piece had promise and you'd like to make the writing more precise. Label these pieces "Promise" at the top.

Some of these labels may not be appropriate for very young children. You will sense which ones will apply to your class. Use what you feel is right for your students.

FINAL REFLECTION

Students don't suddenly become good readers of their own work. Ask them to choose their own good or important work without help, and their choices will probably reflect their feelings of the moment. Further, if they are not taught the various elements that make up good writing (both in their own work and others), their criteria for making portfolio selections will be limited.

Specific intervening, teaching acts are required if students are to make good choices. I begin with nudges while students are writing. Nudges extend the work students are already doing and lead them to try new things: rethink verbs, reconsider information, experiment with dialogue, and examine the plausibility of characters in their fiction. Further, the resulting experiments, successful or unsuccessful, can become part of the class' sharing.

Students must learn to read their own work as well as work on their writing. When students recognize the qualities that make good writing as they read, and apply these criteria to their own work, revision can be truly productive.

These interventions are also diagnostic. When I nudge a student, I also get a glimpse of that student's ability to handle a particular task. Or if I introduce various elements for students to attend to when I read a story aloud to the class, I can see which students understand the various elements.

For years we've assumed that students knew how to read their own work. I used to think, "If they cared, they'd work harder and I'd have less to correct." They do care. Once students become aware of what constitutes good writing, and get help with the elements that make it better, they work hard to make the quality of their writing match their original intentions. The portfolio offers a fine opportunity for students to care about their work, especially if they know how to read and select their best pieces.

8

PORTFOLIOS FOR LARGE-SCALE ASSESSMENT

JAY SIMMONS

Writing assessment has changed over the last several years, somewhat for the better. Test designers have actually asked students to write. This has resulted in tests with more content validity. Teachers of reading and writing have organized classrooms to empower students to find their own voices, to take charge of territories that provide them with information and enable them to grow in their conscious control of language (Graves 1983; Hansen 1987). Evaluations, however, still tend to assess learning skills.

This skills orientation to the evaluation of writing ability drives us to create testing situations that can be broken down into component parts and to construct evaluative scales that enumerate factors that contribute to writing success. This skills orientation hearkens back to stimulus-response theories of human psychology, stage theories of human development, and production-line models of educational management. Teachers and students alike feel—and *are*—controlled from the outside by these testing situations.

Boards of directors control managers who control workers, just as school boards direct principals who supervise teachers who manage students. This top-down approach drives us to construct superficial measures. We tell students what to do, but never ask what they think about it as they do it. We then rate their products, sorting them into piles of normally distributed responses that appear in predictable sequence. Our society has believed that we can rate our outlay of capital, both financial and personal, against normal curves.

Management and assessment models based on exterior control may have been fine in an economy based on the production line. But today's information/service economy requires a new sort of worker. Current business leaders in Britain (Broadfoot 1988) and in America (Berger, Dertouzos, Lester, Solow, and Thurow 1989) are calling for actively involved workers who *evaluate* the nature of incoming information and their actions to it and then *communicate* to others about that information and those actions.

Similarly, in process classrooms, teachers no longer conceive of themselves as people who apply the knowledge in texts to passive receivers of information. Rather, they seek to transfer the locus of control to the writer and to take control of their own curriculum.

Assessment of students' work has been the last function to change. Lately, though, we've been hearing calls for more "naturalistic" methods of evaluation—methods that are less standardized and more in line with the day-to-day activities of teachers at work (Teale 1988). Teachers need to be given, and to take, a leading role in the construction of these new models. Glickman (1990) argues that the "twin pillars" of the new educational reform movement will be the 1960s' and 1970s' principle of equal access to education and the 1980s' notion of public accountability. Teachers and schools, he says, will be given the freedom to manage their own affairs as long as they are willing to demonstrate results.

In Vermont, where a statewide system of portfolio assessment of writing is being developed, teachers dominate the steering committee. Exemplar schools will develop the process, and in-service training will be provided to help teachers learn how to use portfolios in their own classrooms (Rothman 1990). Still, Vermont leaders feel they must demonstrate progress, or lack of it, across the state's various systems and compare their work with national standards. Accordingly, they plan to collect "benchmark" papers against which to compare future papers as evidence of development of writing ability.

But variation from, not congruence with, a benchmark may be the true hallmark of writing abilities. And I purposefully use "abilities" in plural. Individual patterns of behavior, the habits, preferences and judgments that create a piece of writing, are important indicators of ability. Moreover, the value of any good writing rests more in its effect than its form, and effects are harder to measure and prescribe than forms. Because of this, we have settled too often in the past for measures of written products and called these measures of writing abilities.

LEVELS OF PORTFOLIO INFORMATION

Student-constructed portfolios can help teachers focus on process as well as product. Table 8–1 shows the three levels of information portfolios can present.

At the product level, students include the best pieces they or their teachers have chosen or the best examples of their work in required forms or subject areas. Traditional evaluation approaches, such as analytical or holistic scoring, typically examine finished pieces, measuring stable, normally distributed, external forms of human behavior

TABLE 8–1   Levels of Portfolio Information

Level of Information	Purpose	Traits	Contents
Product	Assessment of written products	Ideas Organization Wording Mechanics Flavor	Best pieces • Student choice • Teacher choice • Joint selection Required pieces
Process	Assessment of writing abilities	What I do, know, think How I do it, know it, think it What I feel How I see myself How I approach work How I use/give feedback How I challenge myself	Ordered pieces: • Student ranking • Drafts Notes, journals, logs Labels Conversations Experiences Readings Teacher notes Self and peer evaluations Conference logs

Program	Assessment of development of writing abilities	Chances to:
		• Discover topic
		• Use many forms
		• Confer
		• Keep task open
		• Vary length
		How do students and
		    teachers:
		• Agree on standards
		• Understand the other
		Change over time
		Impact on ability,
		    socioeconomic status
			Assignment lists
			Conference logs
			Interview data:
			• Length
			• Duration
			• Range
			• Evaluations
			• Expectations
			• Socioeconomic status
			Scores

(individual papers) on as absolute and differentiated a scale as possible, using at least the five traits shown in the table.

But the products of writing are not the only things educators should evaluate. Writing abilities and programs must also be examined. Students must be screened for future instruction, remedial or advanced. School systems or states must rate the productivity of individual schools or districts in how well they produce students who can write. In both cases, writing abilities, not written products, need to be examined.

Need to Reflect Process

In *The Reader, the Text, the Poem* Louise Rosenblatt (1978) says that analysis of a text tells us almost nothing about the habits of the writer who created it. Before Rosenblatt, Lev Vygotsky, in *Mind in Society* (1978), had pointed out that product examinations do not illuminate process. Rosenblatt goes further, however, and insists that no "work itself" exists in the text. Works are created by readers as they experience and are guided by the texts. Therefore, each reader is responding to a different work in any attempt at text analysis. Don Graves added to the discussion in *Writing: Teachers and Children at Work* (1983) when he pointed out that skills are developed in the pursuit of information, not through isolated practice dictated by the need for examinations of curriculum-based product. Finally, Howard Gardner contended that, to assess abilities, we must ascertain not only the learners' actions, but also their preferences and judgments (Brandt 1988).

Portfolios help us evaluate writing abilities because they provide insight into the development of the thinking that generates written products. This thinking is reflected (see Table 8–1) in the order in which students rank their works; the development of drafts into finished pieces; the notes, journals, and logs students keep while writing; and the way they label their portfolios. If students keep journals for the writing class, they may record conversations, experiences, and readings for later reflection. Portfolios also typically include teacher notes, self and peer evaluations, and conference logs as evidence of what people thought as the pieces developed. Gardner and Vera John-Steiner (1985) have used the same materials to trace the intellectual development of artists, scientists, mathematicians, writers, and musicians.

Table 8–2 indicates how assessment and instruction change when we focus on abilities in addition to products. It incorporates the ways suggested above to describe what writers do as they create papers that experienced readers find to be effective. Thus, process-bound assessments can be constructed around the idea of multiple abilities (Gardner

TABLE 8–2   Focus of Writing Assessment: Products Versus Abilities

Focus on Products	Focus on Abilities
Monolithic	Multiple
Text-bound	Process-bound
Examination of:	Examination of:
• Ideas	• Habits:
• Organization	• Length
• Wording	• Duration
• Mechanics	• Products
• Flavor	• Preferences
	• Modes
	• Strengths
	• Judgments
	• Expectations
	• Self-ratings
	• Matches
	• Range
Leads to/derives from:	Leads to/derives from:
Skill Instruction:	Programs that enhance:
• Five-paragraph essay	• Habits:
• Leads and clinchers	• Keeping the work open
• Diction	• Producing "skillful" text
• Grammer and usage	• Preferences:
• Style	• Choosing varied modes
	• Seeing strengths of work
	• Judgments:
	• Predicting adult ratings
	• Being able to self-rate
	• Matching adult judgment

and Hatch 1989). Whereas in the past we rated papers based on text features such as ideas, organization, wording, mechanics, and flavor, we now can also examine the habits, preferences, and judgments of the writers in order to determine what they think as they produce. If we conceive of evaluation as research rather than a horse race, we can free ourselves to study those habits, preferences, and judgments of writers.

Portfolios for Program Evaluation

We have all heard that portfolios offer detailed portraits of individual growth. But school systems, regions, and states all need to evaluate the effectiveness of their writing programs across larger populations.

Traditionally, we have done so by holding a horse race. We have lined up students at a starting line called a writing topic or multiple-choice test, given them a time limit, and collected their products at the end of the testing period. Those schools whose students brought back the largest pile of highly rated products won.

But this has taught us precious little about the writing abilities of our students or the writing behaviors our curricula shape. If we can rid ourselves of this horse-race mentality (and convince the president, the nation's governors, and many testing professionals to do the same), we may avail ourselves of the information that portfolios can tell us about our writing programs.

Because portfolios contain more than one piece of work by each student, they are more time-consuming to assess. Because portfolios include drafts, notes, journals, and the students' own evaluations, the information is hard to categorize consistently and inexpensively with large populations.

But because portfolios consist of exactly these components exterior to the finished product but central to the developing processes, they allow valid assessment of writing programs (see Table 8–1) as well as abilities and products.

Once we abandon superficial, global testing, we can sample random subsets of our school populations, generating profiles of the writing behaviors our curricula foster (Table 8–1, Program Traits).

Some groups, however (including the state of Vermont and the southern New Hampshire school consortium Seacoast Educational Services) have found that teachers and administrators worry that random selection will not be fair. Typical concerns are: "Only our worst (and/or their best) students will choose to participate" or "In small schools random selection may focus by chance on one ability group."

I believe these fears are unwarranted. In both my pilot study with one school (Simmons 1990a, 1990b) and more current data drawn from eleven school unions, more than 70 percent of the invited fifth graders, and an equal percentage of eighth graders, chose to participate. (Far fewer high school writers—46 percent—submitted work, however. Clearly, high school teachers and students do not regularly save students' written work, as do their elementary and middle school counterparts.)

Vermont chose to begin its statewide portfolio assessment of writing with grades four and eight and mandated the keeping of writing portfolios in all classrooms statewide for those two grades. But they, and all of us who wish to use naturalistic assessment at the high school level, need to develop procedures for saving student work in the secondary schools. (One way to do this may be to save a student's best pieces each year and pass the developing portfolio along to the student's teacher the following year.)

Concerns about the representativeness of samples may be solved more simply. Schools can require (as researchers cannot) participation in testing programs to insure adequate numbers. Random samples may be grouped by standard ability level to insure fair distribution.

A LARGE-SCALE PORTFOLIO ASSESSMENT

In the spring of 1989 teachers from eleven New England school administrative units (SAUs) approved a March–April 1990 sampling date for portfolios and a general prompt for an extemporaneous writing test to be collected at the same time (Simmons 1991). In the fall, representatives of participating SAUs met to plan collection of the prompted test piece and three student-selected "best pieces." We collected 263 portfolios submitted by students in grades five, eight, and eleven: 115 from grade five; 87 from grade eight; and 61 from grade eleven. SAUs were rated by socioeconomic status (SES) based on counts of free and reduced-rate lunches.

In order to examine student judgment in portfolio construction, we had each subject select three best drafts done during the 1989–90 school year that would show how good a writer he or she is. Each writer noted on a cover sheet (Figure 8–1) the month of the school year during which the piece was begun and the month during which the final draft was finished, as a gauge of duration of work.

To measure students' evaluative thinking, we asked them to specify qualities for each piece that they felt made that piece good enough to be in the portfolio.

As a test of the effect of writing context, subjects were asked to write a fourth sample during a ninety-minute writing period. (Dictionaries were available.) The general writing prompt, devised by the teachers and intended to allow response in many modes of discourse, was "Write about something you know and care about. Make sure your reader knows how much you know and how much you care."

A complete portfolio consisted of:

1. The test piece.
2. The mode of discourse of the test, the writer's gender, the genders of the scorers, and their ratings.
3. Three pieces chosen by the student to show how good a writer he or she is.
4. A cover sheet for each piece listing mode of discourse; three reasons why the paper was chosen; the month the work began; the duration of the writing; the length of the paper; the student's own rating (2–8) of the piece; and the rating (2–8) the student would expect from a teacher.

In the spring in three separate sessions, scorers met at an area junior high school to score the portfolio pieces and test essays holistically with a method that duplicated the writing-sample scoring in the region over the past ten years.

FIGURE 8–1   Portfolio Paper Cover Sheet

Student number _____   Gender: Male   Female
Paper number   1 2 3   Grade: 5 8 11   Mode: N D E A P

Three reasons this paper shows how good a writer you are (use back if needed):

_____
_____
_____
_____
_____
_____
_____
_____
_____
_____
_____

Month you started or got the assignment (circle one):

Sept.	Oct.	Nov.	Dec.	Jan.	Feb.	Mar.
1	2	3	4	5	6	7

Number of days until you finished _____

Length of the paper in words _____

Compared to the writing of <u>other people your age</u>, how would <u>you</u> rate this paper? (circle one):

    2   3   4   5   6   7   8
Among the worst   Among the best

Compared to the writing of <u>other people your age</u>, how would you expect <u>a teacher</u> to rate this paper? (circle one):

    2   3   4   5   6   7   8
Among the worst   Among the best

Raters listed three strengths of each paper at the time of scoring so that I could compare their criteria with those of the students. Experienced teachers of writing sorted the student comments into categories used by the teachers, based on Diederich (1974): ideas, organization, wording, mechanics, and flavor. I added a category—experience (referring to the experience of the writer in writing or sharing the piece)—in an attempt to capture the students' tendency to focus on the experiences surrounding the piece of writing, but not included in it (Newkirk 1984; Benedict 1989).

NEW ANSWERS TO OLD QUESTIONS

For a decade the participating SAUs had received reports of average scores on prompted writing tests and lists of qualities raters found to be present in both effective and less effective pieces. Some schools suffered recriminations from administrators when average scores, say a 4.8, fell below a neighboring school's 5.2. In some schools teachers met to discuss how to improve word choice in below-average papers. In most areas, however, results were routinely ignored. Teachers resented the intrusion into their curricula; students were bored by the ninety-minute exercises on canned topics.

Nobody, of course, mentioned that ordinal values, such as those generated by holistic or analytic scoring, should not be averaged; nor did anyone apply inferential statistics to the results to see which, if any, differences were significant.

Applying such steps to the data collected in March–April 1990 shows that only in the grade five test scores, the group with the largest gap from low group mean (2.67) to high group mean (6.65), did significant differences appear. Since no other grade level demonstrated significant differences in test score among SAU, and since the measure of actual classroom performance, the portfolio score, produced no significant differences at any grade level, this finding seems to hold little importance.

Since SES correlated with test score, richer schools might have been expected to outscore poorer ones, as happened in four cases. It is more surprising that SAU F of the poorer SES group significantly outscored SAU H, also of the poorer group. Most striking, however, is the difference in duration of work. SAU H students worked about half as long on their pieces (7.6 days) as other fifth graders (overall average: 14.8 days), whereas writers from SAU F worked on their writing about twice as long as average (26.3 days).

This comparison suggests that students from SAU F may be able to achieve results similar to those of richer schools by keeping their work open to revision longer. Since duration of work did correlate with score, the below-average figure of SAU H may indicate a need for students in that school to be encouraged to go back and review work for possible revision, or for the system to ask teachers if they determine when a piece is finished, rather than leaving that choice for the writer.

The much longer than average duration of SAU F students' work nearly matches that of the eighth graders. Since students from richer districts also kept work open longer, it would seem SAU F may have been able to offset, in part, the effects associated with the lack of wealth by providing a program in which students have more incentive to keep their work open longer.

Clearly, evaluating portfolios can lead us more quickly to questions about the writing process in our classrooms than more traditional evaluation methods can do. Sadly, the superintendents who received the results took a different view. Partly because past results had been misinterpreted and misused, and partly because teachers resented the intrusion of isolated testing, but mostly because the results produced a call for substantial program reform, not a list of winners and losers. Faced with this, the superintendents suspended all assessment.

ANSWERS TO QUESTIONS WE NEVER ASK

Public officials calling for assessment of educational programs do so, purportedly, to improve those programs or to devise new, and better, ones. In fact, analysis of the student-selected portfolios in the study just described yielded both a confirmation of a decade of efforts in elementary and middle schools and a call to action for high schools. Patterns of student performance, preference, and judgment repeatedly demonstrated that students progress from grade five to grade eight in their ability to make the choices adult writers make, but that such growth is erased by high school practices that emphasize testing, rather than the development of writing abilities.

Table 8–3 shows that students in all three grades clearly preferred to write narratives, even in a timed test situation. However, previously marked coursework constituted the majority of eleventh-grade portfolio papers, not narratives. This could signal a greater degree of teacher influence in the selection of papers, and a corresponding lessening of student choice.

High school raters complained that the portfolio pieces lacked "personalization" and actually preferred reading the test papers. Yet the raters themselves, as high school teachers, gave the assignments that produced such deadly portfolio writing. It would seem that high school teachers value one set of qualities when they read student papers as samples of writing ability, but use another set when they construct writing assignments to transact their daily classroom business. (These results confirm predictions by Freedman 1983 that forced-choice tasks may produce duller writing.)

High school raters also complained that the portfolio pieces were often handed in with significant teacher comments left unaddressed. But why would a student rewrite a piece, created only to complete an assignment, after it was already graded? By way of contrast, many elementary school teachers kept their students' work, photocopying covers, illustrations, text, and all, in order to preserve the treasured originals in the classroom.

Table 8–3 clearly indicates that students choose very different writing tasks to represent their abilities when provided with choice, time, and a supportive community. Whereas poems accounted for only two percent of the test papers, sixteen percent of the portfolio selections

TABLE 8–3   Distribution of modes of discourse used in the test and in the portfolio by grade level

TEST

Grade	Narrative	Description	Exposition	Argument	Poetry	Total
5	55	40	15	2	1	113
(%)	(49)	(35)	(13)	(2)	(1)	
8	30	17	16	20	3	86
(%)	(35)	(20)	(19)	(23)	(3)	
11	22	3	19	17	0	61
(%)	(36)	(5)	(31)	(28)	(0)	
Total	107	60	50	39	4	260
(%)	(41)	(23)	(19)	(15)	(2)	

PORTFOLIO

Grade	Narrative	Description	Exposition	Argument	Poetry	Total
5	206	62	19	7	36	330
(%)	(62)	(19)	(6)	(2)	(11)	
8	102	38	38	20	57	255
(%)	(40)	(15)	(15)	(8)	(22)	
11	38	23	64	18	25	168
(%)	(23)	(14)	(38)	(11)	(15)	
Total	346	123	121	45	118	753
(%)	(46)	(16)	(16)	(6)	(16)	

were poems chosen from pieces written in the classroom during the course of the year. And the writers seem to have exercised good judgment by limiting their poetry writing to the portfolio. Although poems ranked lowest in the ratings for grades eight and eleven test papers, they did not differ significantly in score from other modes of discourse in portfolio rankings. Since grade eight shows the biggest increase in poetry from test situation to portfolio, and eighth graders matched adult judgment in both paper score and strength of paper (see page 108), their more frequent inclusion of poetry seems based on mature awareness of both the writing context and the values of their readers.

Distribution of narratives relative to exposition and argument as reflected in Table 8–3 also supports Moffett's (1981) definition of growth as doing more things and the old things better. Narrative, a form learned earlier in school, declines as a percentage of the sample in both the test and the portfolio from grade five through high school, but the decline is more pronounced in the portfolio selection. At the same time, argument and exposition, later emerging forms, consistently increase through the grade levels. According to Crowhurst and Piche (1979), Lunsford (1981), and Flower (1981), these figures indicate increasing ability to use less narrative and more argument and exposition when time demands it (on the test), or to select (for the portfolio) the forms requiring more abstract thinking, greater distance between writer and audience, and more cognitively developed syntactic structures.

Therefore, student choice, either in the form of more general prompts for essay tests or control of portfolio construction, provides a measure of growth over time that is abrogated by systems that require pieces from certain genres or that give selection to the teacher.

Higher scores generally reflected students' ability to use and value more types of writing (Simmons 1990a, 1990b). Significant correlations occur in the more recent study with scores for grades eight and eleven. The inclusion of more types of writing predicted a higher portfolio score in the grade eight students especially. Those who wrote and valued a range of modes of discourse demonstrated the ability to produce more highly rated classroom writing. In grade eleven the reverse obtained. There, those who scored poorly on the test but chose a variety of pieces for their portfolios actually got worse scores. Those who scored well on the test tended to choose fewer modes to represent their talent in the portfolios.

These results support Moffett (1981) and can be used to argue against requiring certain types of writing in a portfolio, since the requirement would rob students of the chance to demonstrate the predictive power of choice. The appearance of the predictive power in grade eight may indicate growth over grade five, but the reversal of the trend in the high school sample would indicate an erosion of that ability by grade eleven.

WHAT SCHOOLS LET STUDENTS DO

Because portfolio assessment yields scores for more than one paper and provides more than ratings of superficial traits of students' texts, we can see not only what our writers do, but also infer what our programs let them do. For instance, consider the data on time spent on work. Length of duration of work increased from grade five to grade eight, but decreased for high school writers. Fifth graders worked an average of two weeks (15 days) on their papers, as opposed to 29 days in eighth grade and less than a week (6 days) for high school juniors. At the same time, the month of work, portfolio scores, and test scores remained constant across grade levels. Since the judgments of teachers, as reflected in the ratings, and the judgment of the students, reflected in the choice of papers on average from the same point in the year, remain the same, the program differences indicated by duration of work are probably reliable. Our schools seem to provide younger students more time to develop pieces, but ask high schoolers to crank out work more quickly.

WRITER AND AUDIENCE

In a traditional product-only assessment, raters can only guess at the writer's sense of audience, based on the reader's response to the work he or she creates from the student's text (Rosenblatt 1978). In the spring 1990 portfolio study, students rated their own work and predicted the scores teachers would give them. The better writers predicted their readers' responses more reliably. Again, however, the high school group proved to be the exception.

Middle and high test score groups in grades five and eight predicted their graders' ratings with significant accuracy, but their grade eleven counterparts did not. In grade five, student expectations correlated highly with teacher ratings of portfolio pieces, while in grade eight both student expectations and the students' own ratings paralleled teacher grades. (In all cases, to no one's surprise, students tended to overestimate their teachers' grades.) Since the lower test groups in grades five and eight were the ones less able to predict teacher ratings, the high school juniors' similar lack of success might indicate some lack of ability on their part.

Increasingly, individual students' portfolios include journals or tea-cher notes of conferences, indicating what students think about their work and how those judgments match those of peers and adults. The portfolio study measured the degree to which students and adult raters both chose the same categories of comments as strengths for the portfolio pieces, and whether agreement predicted higher scores on the papers.

If both rater and student marked the ideas or organization as a strength of a piece, then they agreed on the *conception* of the paper. If they both chose wording or mechanics, they matched on *language.* And if both reader and writer listed the flavor of the piece or the experience of the writer producing or sharing it, I recorded a match on the *emotion* involved in the writing.

In grade eight, emotion significantly predicted portfolio score. That is, average and above-average portfolio writers tended to agree with their raters on the emotional strengths of the writing, while those who scored poorly did not. Combined with earlier findings on the students' expected scores and self-ratings, these figures indicate growth in maturity of judgment between grade five and grade eight, since more nonagreement on emotion occurred in the earlier grade, but the lack of agreement was not localized among low scorers. By grade eight, such disagreement has dropped in magnitude and does predict a low score. In the high school sample, the percentage of agreement dropped and the nonagreement is no longer localized to low-scoring writers. This finding indicates a return to the grade-five pattern of judgment.

Matches on language and conception echo this pattern of progress from grade five to eight followed by regression in grade eleven. Many fifth (66.1 percent) and eighth (72.4 percent) graders agreed with the raters on quality of wording and mechanics in the portfolios, while fewer than half (45.9 percent) of the high schoolers agreed. Mean-while, the percentage of raters and writers who failed to find language a strength dropped from 9 percent in grade five to 1.6 percent in grade eight, then rose to 13.1 percent in grade eleven.

Agreement on ideas and organization (conception) in grades five and eight remained high and stable across score groups, but high-scoring grade eleven writers agreed less with adults than did their lower-scoring peers. In fact, no high school group matched adult judg-ment as well as any of the fifth graders.

As for the emotional factors, agreement reverses among high schoolers, the weakest writers agreeing more than the best, who barely surpassed the weakest fifth graders.

Emotional agreement between adult readers and student writers demonstrates growth in writing abilities from grade five to grade eight, and an apparent lack of growth in high school (Boy 1990; Eisner 1990a; Corey and Corey 1987).

Boy (1990) argues that an inability to deal with the emotional content of experience often prevents us from exercising skills and cognitive strengths. In grade eight, both the language and emotional agreement increased with score. Boy also points out that, as a culture, we tend to focus on the conceptual content of experience due to a lack of emotional vocabulary. Consistently high agreement on conception confirms this assertion.

Boy also relates the inability to reflect client feelings with three common failures of counselors. First, such counselors tend to analyze immediately, explaining the meaning of client behavior too quickly. Second, they often tend too quickly to offer a solution to the client. Third, they frequently move too quickly toward the solution of a less important problem without giving the client time enough to focus on another, more serious problem.

Writers and the teachers with whom they confer are akin to clients and counselors striving to effect change in human behavior. The pattern of judgments and choices made by teachers and students in my study indicates that high school teachers may be subject to the same failures as some counselors. First, in the high school sample, agreement on conception, or analytical features of the work, remained high, while agreement on the emotions dropped. Second, several factors (the number of assigned class papers appearing in the sample, the requests by raters for the original assignments, the differences in writers' choice of modes between the test and the portfolios, and the raters' preference for the personal flair of the test pieces) indicate that the high school teachers tended to define students' problems and solutions for them in the classroom writing. Finally, duration of work in the high school was short, which suggests that teachers made assignments with quick turnaround time, failing to give their students time to warm up and address more serious problems they may have discovered themselves.

Eisner (1990) and Corey and Corey (1987) find traditional measurements intended to assess growth inadequate because they omit key emotional and attitudinal factors. Both the bias and ineffectiveness of test writing in predicting classroom performance, as well as the prominence of emotional agreement above language and conceptual agreement as an indicator of growth, support their calls for assessment that includes these aspects of human learning.

Certainly, as teachers of writing we need to address the apparent shortcomings in high school instruction. On the other hand, as evaluators of writing abilities we can appreciate the insight into writer and reader attitudes at work in our writing programs. Such findings do not result from traditional writing tests.

THE DANGERS OF TRADITIONAL TESTING

Timed writing tests are worse than shallow. Most students who score the lowest on timed writing tasks do significantly better when classroom writing is graded, while most average and above-average scorers do not (Simmons 1990a, 1990b, 1991). In Table 8–4, column 1, we can see that only 4 of 20 low test scorers also scored low in the classroom writing included in the portfolio. Meanwhile, 16 of them achieved average scores or above. That is, if we had failed those 20 low scorers on the test and shunted them off to remedial programs, 80 percent of them would actually have been able to pass the classroom work that we denied them the opportunity to attempt. In contrast, however, columns 2 and 3 show us that just 16 students of a total of 240 scored low in the portfolio but average or above on the test. That is, less than 7 percent of those who performed adequately on the test were unable to handle the class work. Therefore, prompted-essay tests hurt the weakest test takers more often than they benefit the best.

Test writers might argue that screening devices ought to be conservative. It is better for a test to exclude a few candidates from a program who might actually have succeeded than to admit too many who fail, thereby "wasting" the resources spent on them. But prompted writing tests don't meet this standard, either. Row 1 of Table 8–4 shows that 20 students did poorly in the classroom writing selected for the portfolio, but that 16 of them, or 80 percent, had scored in the middle or high test groups.

TABLE 8–4 Observed frequency of test score groups (columns) and portfolio score groups (rows) across the entire sample

Portfolio Score Groups	Test Score Groups			
	Low	Middle	High	Totals
Low	4	12	4	20
Middle	14	114	45	173
High	2	20	45	67
Totals	20	146	94	260

Prompted test pieces, therefore, unfairly downgrade our weakest students and fail to discriminate actual failures effectively. They should not be used in isolation.

And what of socioeconomic standing? The socioeconomic level (SES) of the schools' population at all grade levels significantly predicted the test score. This finding had particular impact in grade five, where students' classroom work clearly exceeded the test work in both length of piece and duration of work.

Socioeconomic status predicted 45 percent of the test score of the weakest fifth-grade writers, but less than 1 percent of the middle and average score groups. Since SES was directly correlated with test score, this means that poorer schools are hurt most by essay-only writing tests. Rich schools' test scores significantly surpassed those of low SES grade five schools, while portfolio differences for the same schools were only marginal.

In grade eight, the SES of the lowest test score group fell dramatically below those of the more successful groups, or below the SES rating of schools in any group at any grade level. Richer middle schools significantly outperformed poorer middle schools in the test essays, but no significant differences appeared in portfolio scores.

Programs at low SES schools seemed to make a difference: students from poorer schools were permitted to keep their classroom work open to revision for nearly two months (54 days) versus three weeks (19 days) for the richer schools. Both wealthy (16 days) and poor (13 days) elementary students worked about two weeks on their portfolio pieces.

In grade eleven, however, the effect of social status takes a strange twist. First, although richer schools gave their students longer deadlines than poorer ones (8 days versus 3), even the longest average high school work fell far short of that of either their middle or elementary school counterparts. Thus, the testing context—a writing session limited to ninety minutes on one day—was less different from the normal writing behavior of high schoolers in general, and of the lowest SES group in particular. Second, neither test nor portfolio scores of rich and poor high schools produced significant differences. At the high school level, then, we may have erased the effect of SES on test-taking ability by constructing all writing tasks as if they were tests, whereas in grade eight, teachers provided students from the poorest schools the longest time to keep their classroom work open, thus erasing the effect of SES on portfolio scores (which were average), while biased test results continued.

In a society that reacts to poor test scores by denial of funds, promotion, or job tenure, testing bias against low SES groups must be eradicated as quickly as possible, regardless of cost.

CONCLUSION

Classroom teachers have long bemoaned the waste, inaccuracy, and bias inherent in traditional measures of academic achievement. Holistically scored, prompted writing samples ten years ago constituted an improvement on indirect, multiple-choice tests of language usage as vehicles for evaluating writing ability. Portfolio assessment has now developed sufficiently at the individual level to be adapted to large-scale settings. To fail to do so, or to settle in the process of change for only the most superficial or highly constrained forms of portfolios, can only perpetuate the inequalities and inaccuracies of the past.

9

PORTFOLIO DEFINITIONS: TOWARD A SHARED NOTION

F. DAN SEGER

The term *portfolio* has long been used in the worlds of fine arts and financial investing. A quick survey of language arts journal citations, the ERIC system, and professional conference program booklets, however, shows that *portfolio* has been a viable term in language arts instruction only in the last five or so years. In that short time, literature on portfolios has proliferated, portfolio newsletters have sprung up, publishers are entering the scene, and school districtwide portfolio support groups have been established. The aftermath of this explosive beginning has left many teachers wondering just what portfolios are and what they might mean for language arts instruction.

A FEVERED START

Several factors stimulated the urgent entry of portfolios into public schools. During the mid-1980s, the writing practices of professional writers began to influence language arts instruction. Novelists, technical writers, journalists, poets, and other writers had long been familiar with portfolios and shared their ideas with educators and students. Since writing folders as places to keep daily writing had already been established (Graves 1983; Calkins 1986; Atwell 1987), portfolios seemed a logical next step.

At the same time, education was undergoing significant changes. Classroom instruction was shifting gradually from individualized approaches that fostered autonomy toward more collaborative ones

114

that fostered connectedness. Also, teachers were conceptualizing literacy more as an emerging process than as a set of skills to acquire (Hall 1987). These changes forced teachers to look beyond the standardized test when they measured student progress.

Still another factor was the attack on the quality of American education from several fronts. Business leaders were saying that high school diplomas no longer guaranteed that graduating seniors had the literacy skills necessary for entry-level jobs. Government leaders were saying that our students couldn't compete with foreign students in math and science. And the public was saying that it was not getting its money's worth out of public schools.

This was the climate in language arts instruction when portfolios entered, one of fevered demands for accountability and broader-based assessment. At the Atlanta NCTE convention in 1990, Dan Kirby quipped that the term "*portfolio* transformed into *portfolio assessment* within hours" of its introduction into language arts. The "assessment" concept has nearly pre-empted other ideas about the purpose or potential of portfolios.

MULTIPLE NOTIONS

Even within the definitions of assessment, portfolios emerge with multiple images as educators stretch the concept to cover more and more issues. For example, evaluation issues might stretch portfolios to be used for assessing readers and writers in situated contexts rather than on tests, assessing accomplishments personally rather than in comparison to other students, or transcending the limitations of report cards or the large gaps in standardized tests. Accountability issues might stretch them into being used for record keeping over time—what skills have been taught and which show up in students' reading and writing. And affective issues might stretch portfolios into being examined as personal accounts that reveal students' motivations, aspirations, and feelings about literacy.

Each of these issues establishes a different purpose for keeping portfolios. Each purpose modifies the parameters for selecting their contents. So each implementation would cause portfolios to take on a different look, one that reflects the purpose for which the portfolio is kept. Thus, we are left with a plethora of examples, each claiming a piece of the loosely defined territory represented by the word *portfolio*. Defining *portfolio* from such multiple notions would be like an early biologist trying to define *mammal* when presented with a whale, a human being, and a bat.

Like *mammal* was at one time, *portfolio* is a linguistic placeholder whose meaning will develop through examination and reflection. Unlike *mammal*, we have acquired the term *portfolio* before its linguistic territory has stabilized in our field. But the term is still new enough to have a plastic quality that allows us to test it and reshape it to see how it fits best into language arts instruction. Perhaps from this we will learn its potential and limitations. But there is also the danger that we may stretch it too thin, or bind it so tightly to evaluation that it becomes an impotent label for a fad of the nineties.

In the pages that follow, I first connect portfolios to their counterparts in art and finance in an attempt to explore the parameters and dynamics that operate within each. Second, I compare three reading and writing portfolio situations to show how different purposes affect those parameters and what results from each.

FROM CONCRETE TO ABSTRACT

For artists, the most concrete definition of a portfolio is a case or binder in which loose papers, paintings, drawings, photographs, and the like are kept. Artists collect their work with an eye on gaining entry into art schools, gallery shows, or jobs. For an investor, the portfolio is a collection of papers representing an array of assets purchased with an eye on their potential increase in value. Despite their very different purposes, both portfolios present evolving personal portraits drawn from continued self-evaluation of the portfolio's contents. Thus, on a more abstract level, the portfolio keeper is the one in control, calibrating the range of contents and the depth of representation in the portfolio in order to achieve personal goals.

Investment Portfolios

Harry M. Markowitz, professor of finance at Baruch College of the City University of New York, defined the concept of investment portfolios in the 1950s (Prokesch 1990). His research showed that investors measured the risk of various potential investments and then mixed high- and low-risk assets into an "optimal portfolio" that would achieve the maximum return with a minimum risk of loss. This approach is common today, but thirty-five years ago it broke new ground in economic theory. For his pioneering work in portfolio theory as well as subsequent contributions, Markowitz was one of three recipients of the Nobel Prize in Economic Science in 1990. His illustration of the interplay between return and risk is like the relationship of range and depth in a language arts portfolio.

A Portrait: Range and Depth.

Investors' portfolios may include such things as life insurance, securities, real estate, stocks, bonds, and so on. If investors wish to build assets for retirement, they may invest in a wide-ranging mixture of slow-growing, stable securities and a few faster-growing but riskier ones. If, on the other hand, the investor has a short-term need for a quick increase in value and can manage a potential loss, he or she may increase the depth of investment in the riskier fast-growers. Range and depth act here as variables that calibrate the portfolio to specific financial goals.

Investors can also consider the nature of the businesses in which they invest. They can then invest in those companies whose policies and practices are consistent with their own personal values and avoid the ones that violate them. Considering where and how much money is invested, the investor colors his or her portfolio portrait with shades of what is personally important.

Self-evaluation: Revision of Range and Depth.

At the same time, investors evaluate the performance of their investments. They balance their portfolio assets against their financial liabilities to determine their net financial worth. This should show an increase over time. If not, the investor revises the contents of the portfolio, realigning the range and depth of investments to increase the potential for financial growth. Through this continuing process, investors build their financial security on personally selected businesses that reflect personally held values of moral choice and ethical practice. Together, self-evaluation and the subsequent realignment of range and depth of investments continually redefine the investor's identity in the portrait that results.

Artist's Portfolios

Where the investor's portfolio remains largely a private matter, an artist's portfolio bears a more public purpose. It bridges the self to the outside world. Artists use their portfolios for admission to art schools, for employment, or for entry into gallery shows. These three uses share some considerations. Harlan Hoffa, associate dean in the College of Art and Architecture at Pennsylvania State University, finds that preparing a portfolio can be a learning experience (1987). He claims a high school art teacher can learn "whether a student has the 'fire in the belly' that is needed to succeed in college as an art student" (17).

A Portrait: Range and Depth.

Hoffa describes the portrait feature of portfolios:

> A portfolio tells the college faculty more than simply whether the student can draw or not—important though that is. It also speaks volumes about attitude, about work habits, and about those most necessary qualities of drive, inner discipline, commitment of art, and the compulsion to succeed. (17)

The artist's portfolio consists of photographs, or originals if the size is appropriate, of current or recently completed works. These are mounted and bound together in a flexible case or hinged presentational folder and are labeled with short summaries of pertinent information. Removable pages allow the artist to update or revise the contents from time to time as new works are completed. Rough copies or early sketches of works included indicate speed of production and artistic instincts, two dimensions of particular interest to prospective employers.

In a vocational school's curriculum development report, Janet Bourque (Bourque et al. 1983) also emphasizes the need for a "professional looking" portfolio. To prospective sewing professionals she cautions, "The portfolio represents you even before they see the contents." She recommends a "tailored style" and "safe" colors (black, brown, or navy) for the business world.

As in investment portfolios, range and depth operate in artists' portfolios to create personal portraits. Katherine Lammon (1985), in an article about jobs for artists, suggests that student artists include works that show talents as well as interests. The works showing special talents make a portfolio memorable, and the wider range of interests prevents stereotypes (13). In both school application and employment portfolios, artists should be "utterly ruthless" (Hoffa 1987, 18) choosing their best representative works and arranging them to highlight the depth of their strengths and the diversity of their skills.

Self-evaluation: Revision of Range and Depth.

An outside audience ultimately decides who is admitted to an art school or a gallery show. But this audience is not actively involved in creating the portfolio. It is the artist's self-evaluation that creates it. Both Hoffa and Lammon stress the importance of knowing as much as possible about this audience. Such knowledge helps the artist refine his or her portfolio selections according to the evaluator's needs and expectations. The artist makes personal selections, adjusting range and depth to mesh the self-portrait with the evaluator's interpretive frame. Hoffa notes, "Strange as it may seem, colleges are not all that interested in what an applicant has done—*except* insofar as it reflects what a student is capable of doing" (18). This audience looks beyond the works themselves. Their interest lies not so much in a technical analysis of the specific works as it does in finding the promise and potential in an artist's current technical mastery. In this way, the portfolio connects past and future: the past summarized in the portfolio's contents at a point in time; the future held in the potential that the audience discerns from examining the contents. The artist may revise the range and depth for different audiences, or in view of newly produced work. But, as in the investor's portfolio, portrait and self-evaluation interact to represent externally the artist's identity.

Stance

Both the investor's and artist's versions of portfolios point to the important stance of the portfolio keeper—that is, where the keepers stand in relation to the artwork or assets they choose to include. Who controls the contents? There may be advice from a broker or expectations of an admissions committee to consider, but the keepers make the final decisions about what is included. They evaluate their own artwork or available investments according to a blend of personal goals, purposes, and external audiences. Then they choose items that harmonize. When the keeper's stance is central, portfolios become tangible extensions of thinking. They are at once profiles, as well as indicators of progress toward personally set goals. More than a simple tool for assessment, portfolios become, over time, as personal as signatures.

PORTFOLIOS AND LANGUAGE ARTS

These concepts are also compatible with what readers and writers do. They, too, develop skill and artistic sensitivity in the practice of their craft. Professional writers generate manuscripts and reading lists with which they gauge a range of genres and depth of representation that highlight personal strengths and interests. Chosen from a central stance, the contents of their portfolios provide the evidence of their literate selves.

When the purpose of a portfolio shifts from self-evaluation to an outsider's assessment, the keeper's stance moves to the side, or even outside the portfolio. A concept other than the self occupies the central controlling position, and this in turn realigns the parameters for range, depth, and self-evaluation. In the three examples that follow, I look at how different purposes affect the portfolio keeper's stance, affect the range and depth of the contents, and produce very different portfolios.

A Central Stance

Linda Rief (chapter 4 in this volume) uses portfolios in her middle school English classes. For her, portfolios "have become the students' stories of who they are as readers and writers—rich with the evidence of what they are able to do and how they are able to do it." She sets what she calls "external" criteria, minimum numbers of works—including drafts and written self-evaluations. The students are in charge of the "internal" criteria: which pieces of work and for what reasons they've chosen them. One student, whom Rief considers typical, kept the following in her portfolio: three poems, a personal narrative, a character sketch, a letter, a pen-and-ink drawing, a play, an essay, and a picture of her final project of the year, an acrylic collage stimulated by a novel she had read. This student also noted in her portfolio that during the year she had started reading thirty books and had finished twenty-nine of them. Titles ranged from *The Little Prince* (Saint Exupery) to *Night* (Elie Wiesel).

With an eye on her curriculum guide, Rief exposes her students to the required genres, reading and discussing professionally and personally written pieces. She expects her students to set goals and then practice reading and writing daily in various genres. The students then choose what they feel is their best work for their portfolio. They include drafts that led up to final pieces as well as a written history or evaluation of each piece. Thus, the contents are generated and owned entirely by the portfolio keepers.

Rief's external criteria are guidelines that help to make concrete the notion of portfolios for her students. The internal criteria, however, keep her students central in their creation. The portfolios form an integral part of the instruction plan for her classroom. The students share their portfolios with Rief and with one another and discuss what they've chosen. The contents change over the year in response to changes in the keeper's skill level and ability to self-evaluate. This results in a portfolio that evolves organically from within each student. The classroom environment provides the nutrients in models, discussion, and shared portfolios. What emerges is agility and accomplishment in a very personal portrait representing range of genres and depth of involvement in reading and writing.

With the wealth of final copies, drafts, and self-evaluations in her students' portfolios, Rief says, "I *can* evaluate [a student's growth] as a writer and reader, if I have to," but she keeps her teacher's evaluation and assessment in second place to theirs. With a central stance, the students' portraits and self-evaluations remain linked by the range and depth of items as they choose to show what they know.

This is but one teacher's use of portfolios in a classroom setting. For Linda Rief, the portfolio seemed an appropriate way to collect evidence of students' thinking. It grew out of their experiences. A very different picture emerges when the concept of portfolio falls into a context of assessment and accountability.

Standing on the Side

Kathryn Au, Judith Scheu, Alice Kawakami, and Patricia Herman write about portfolios within the context of the Kamehama Elementary Education Program (KEEP) in Hawaii (1990). They note that the teachers within the program had moved away from "traditional" approaches of teaching reading and writing that included "basal reading programs, curriculum guides, and criterion-referenced tests intended to support skills-oriented approaches" (574). They found that the teachers were comfortable with their new ways of teaching reading and writing, but "they missed the security provided by earlier systems of curriculum objectives and tests" (574).

So they designed a curriculum framework that included portfolios as a part of its assessment and accountability system. The portfolio's purpose in the system is to provide developmental information on six aspects of literacy defined by the curriculum framework. These dimensions are: "ownership, reading comprehension, writing process, word identification, language and vocabulary knowledge, and voluntary reading" (575).

Citing a strong administrative and state reliance on standardized testing, the program designers coupled this curriculum framework and portfolio assessment to common standards. Thus, they "anchored portfolio assessment to grade level benchmarks reflecting expectations for the hypothetical average student" (576). They took these expectations from a state language arts curriculum guide, a standardized achievement test, and basal text scope and sequence charts. Ironically, "average" was derived from the materials that had been abandoned in the classroom.

Teachers summarize a student's progress in six literacy areas on a profile sheet, which is kept in the portfolio. The data are generated from five major "assessment tasks and procedures":

1. A questionnaire on attitudes towards reading and writing.
2. A response to literature task, which uses a "story frame" and checklist.
3. A sample of the student's writing.
4. A running record (after Clay's *The Early Detection of Reading Difficulties*, 1979).
5. A voluntary reading log, listing book titles and genres. (576)

On the profile sheet, for each literacy area the teacher indicates whether a student is performing at the benchmark average expectation level, above it, or below it.

The student's stance is more on the perimeter of this portfolio design. In the center is the concept of the hypothetical average to which teachers compare their students. The students produce work for the portfolio, but there is no provision for self-evaluation of the work. Tasks are prescribed rather than generated from personally set goals. Students and teachers use forms or follow procedures that create literary behaviors under fairly standard conditions.

This procedural approach to portfolio limits the usefulness of range and depth for creating a personal portrait of a learner. The student's range of performance is defined by the five assessment tasks and procedures. Protocols from each of the five tasks comprise the depth of representation. The data when summarized on the profile sheet yields a portrait best described as a distance above or below the central concept of average. And that assessment derives from behavior samples rather than observed demonstrations in reading and writing. The students are called in from the sidelines to generate the comparative data that fits the assessment and accountability purposes defined for portfolios in this school program.

Standing Outside

James Flood and Diane Lapp (1989) describe another version of the portfolio used in grade one. It is also based in assessment and accountability, but in this case, the purpose is to report to parents. Responding to their perceived need to give a fuller description of student progress than a single standardized test score, the authors suggest the use of a "comparison portfolio" (508) as a way of showing growth over time.

The authors note that problems arise when parents misunderstand or misperceive what a test score or grade actually represents. To address this, a teacher assembles items taken from different times of the year into a portfolio "to show parents a picture of their child's progress (or lack of progress) by showing them a comparison of their child's performance at the beginning of the year and at the end of the year or from one time to a later time" (510). This contrasts to the KEEP program's comparison to a grade level average. The earlier and later work will essentially speak for itself; the teacher becomes an interpreter, explaining factors that contribute or detract from the student's progress.

The contents of the portfolio include standardized and criterion-referenced test scores, informal test results, writing samples, voluntary reading program reports, self-assessments, and samples of the school materials used by the student at different times of the year (511). These items are gathered by the teacher, although the authors suggest that "once the children are capable" they can join the teacher in preparing the portfolio. Choosing representative items from early and later parts of the school year could be adapted to other grade levels.

With respect to this portfolio, the student stands outside. In the center is the concept of quantitative progress. Even when the students join the teacher in selecting work for the portfolio, their attention focuses on the changes apparent in completed products rather than on the child as a learner. This purpose redefines range and depth again. An external framework prescribes the range of items in the portfolio, as in the KEEP program, but the items are all paired with work or test scores from a different part of the year. Thus, the range is limited to several prescribed categories of data mixed with the variable of time.

Depth of representation is limited to two items in each category. The responsibility for showing depth lies, therefore, in the teacher's ability to interpret rather than in the works themselves. The self-assessment that is included may add some depth to the portfolio, but in contrast to Rief's students' self-assessments, it is written when the portfolio is being assembled rather than as part of the instructional plan. These self-assessments function more as a data source for the teacher than a means for students to develop critical thinking and goal-setting ability. The students may therefore remain somewhat inexperienced at self-evaluation.

The portrait that emerges from this portfolio is one of the child as producer. For example, the authors suggest that the numbers of books read in the voluntary reading program be charted with two lines: one line to indicate the number of books read per month; the other to graph the accumulating total. The books per month would fluctuate slightly, but present a relatively flat profile, while the accumulating total would show a fairly steady incline. Comparing the two, the teacher would point out that the flatter profile does not really indicate a lack of progress, but merely small, expected variances. The authors suggest graphing other reading behaviors, too, such as reading in class versus reading out of class, silent versus group reading, and so on. Without knowing the titles or genres of the books that are graphed, the picture of the student that emerges from graphs of this sort is one of product defined by quantity achieved rather than by quality or range of work. Samples of school materials can round out the picture. However, limiting the depth of representation to two samples misses the reader/writer's versatility.

TOWARD A SHARED NOTION

These are just three of the many versions of portfolio keeping that have appeared in the last few years in language arts instruction. There are districtwide and statewide implementations; there are interdisciplinary, crossdisciplinary, and multidisciplinary portfolios; there are portfolios as measures of revision strategies; and more. It is not surprising that teachers are confused. What helped me gain perspective was to step briefly into two other fields that have a longer history of using portfolios. While there, I learned about the dynamics at work when artists and investors keep portfolios. Their stance is central. They engage in a process of self-evaluation and constant adjustment. Their portfolios are ever-changing reflections of who they are, what they value, and their progress toward personally set goals.

When I brought this perspective back to my own field, I could see how assessment and accountability issues have skewed the stance of our young portfolio keepers. Literacy is complex, and evidence of it is as varied as the number of students in a class. It is difficult to reduce literacy to checklists and charts. Portfolios provide a sensitive structure to tap it as long as their keepers stand in the middle and choose the contents as evidence of the range and depth of what they know. Then a portfolio can be an instructional vehicle rather than an elaborate test.

A teacher thinks . . .

After the first week:
If I choose wisely the selections for my portfolio, I reveal to you, and particularly to myself, who I am as a reader, writer, speaker, thinker. I am reluctant this time around to impose an order or to assign categories. I prefer instead to toss selections into the portfolio at random, like vegetables boiling down to a thick winter soup, testing and savoring the . . . flavor.

After the second week:
This is a reflection on my literacy portfolio, the second time around. My vision of portfolios is expanding. . . . I know people who would consider reflection to be an act of indulgence. I would argue . . . that reflection is necessary for growth, and necessary for the soul. It is new for me, however, to use a portfolio as a frame for my reflection. This is an exciting concept.

After the third week:
If there is a problem, it is that I want to include too much in my portfolio. . . . Since it is flexible, I have the option of adding to it whenever I wish. These are my current categories: Giving (what goes out from me to others). Receiving (what comes from others to me), and Being Me (what I keep/create for me). I'm still not entirely satisfied with these, but I prefer them to categories that separate my personal and professional selves.

Donna Beveridge
Teacher, grades 2, 3
Bridgton, Maine

III

PORTFOLIO KEEPERS: FOUR PORTRAITS

I constantly ask myself, does this really show my literacies? I believe I am a "blended" reader and writer. I cannot separate the two. I often ask students, "Are you a reader and writer?" My own answer would be, "Both, but it depends on what time of day."

I have thought about what's not in my portfolio. My family pops up in my writing all the time, yet I do not directly make any reference to them in my portfolio. There is nothing in there on my schooling from kindergarten through my B.S. degree. Wondering about this, I realize I did not view myself as a thinker until I graduated from college. This is where my real learning took place. In all honesty, it has taken years to see myself as an intelligent person. I read in high school and college. I was awake, but sleepwalking through school. As Annie Dillard would say, "I woke up in the early eighties." . . . I am not sure that a portfolio will ever give a complete picture, but it does represent more than a test score or a one-page essay. . . . It is an extension of me now. What is in it is of my choosing. It is how I want to paint myself.

Kim Boothroyd
Teacher, grade 5
Ithaca, New York

10

STAYING THE COURSE: ONE SUPERINTENDENT

BONNIE S. SUNSTEIN

Whitehen he moved into his new office, Ken Greenbaum gave away a huge desk, "a legacy from the ex-superintendent . . . the size of a president's desk. We wanted to design our offices so we could talk to people. I don't want to meet them across a big desk." Ken and I talk at a small round table across from his desk, sipping coffee. His bulletin board is heavy with schedules, but his talk is heavy with teachers and students, parents and taxpayers—the inside and the outside of his school system. Ken is superintendent of the Moultonborough School District, a rural New England town nestled at the edge of New Hampshire's mountains, on the shores of Lake Winnipesaukee. The population is a blend of families rooted for generations to the town and obliged to the tourist industry and of summer homeowners or retirees with little connection to the schools. Ken's new office is housed inside the town's elementary school. It is a metaphorical reminder of the relationship he has with his faculty, staff, and students.

I already know the central office is not a typical one: I have been working with Ken for well over a year. Our long distance project includes a year-long course in the teaching of writing, taught by a team from the University of New Hampshire. We have combined on-site visits in classrooms with speaker-phone conferences and exchanges through fax and mail. With other colleagues, Ken and I have done a lot of planning together.

As we sit down to talk about his portfolio, our project is at the end of its first full year. For the second year, we are considering a portfolio project at all grade levels. Everyone involved would keep a literacy portfolio. Ken wanted to experiment as we considered it for his schools. He didn't want to ask his staff or his students to do anything he hadn't tried. So this spring, at my request, he assembled his own portfolio. Two months after he began collecting materials for it, we are sitting in his office with my tape recorder and his portfolio.

Would it be useful for superintendents to keep portfolios? Would it help them reflect on themselves as professionals, as figures at the juncture between the school and the public? Would it help in their own self-assessment, policy-making decisions, their role as educational leaders? I wondered.

Democratic reform cannot come without participation from its leaders, and Ken understands that. It was his idea to try keeping a portfolio before bringing the idea to his schools. In *Educational Leadership*, Ron Brandt asserts that "leaders can, over time, create a culture in which the quest for improvement becomes the norm" (1990, 4). But leaders cannot expect to create a culture for change without participating, without reflecting. Israel Scheffler (1990) argues that the education of policymakers should go beyond technical knowledge into the realm of reflexive self-awareness. Policymakers need to learn the languages of those their policies affect.

I wondered if a portfolio would be a way for Ken to reflect. I did not give him an assignment or limits when he decided to create one. I only asked that what he collected be what he considers representative of his reading and writing. Two and a half hours into our interview, I feel as if I've completed a course in educational administration, curriculum, and philosophy, with Ken and John Dewey as classmates. Together, we decide that my interview with him ought to be part of his portfolio, too.

"I learned that a portfolio doesn't have to be just *things that you like*," says Ken. "It's *things that you do*. . . . Putting it together made me see all the different ways I'm involved with writing. When you think of writing, you think of things that are publishable. But in this, I was able to see that most of the ways I'm involved with writing are *not* the publishable ones." On the surface, his portfolio represents a cross-section of the genres that he works in, but a closer look reveals his personal and professional convictions. These are the pieces he chose, with the reason he chose each one:

- Three newspaper columns titled "Your Public Schools," which he writes for the town paper. They are a special mix of his public and private selves. He included them because each deals with one educational issue he's been thinking about. So far, two of the columns have been published.

- An observation/evaluation of a junior high school teacher—because it was difficult to write.
- A letter of recommendation for an elementary school principal—because it was easy to write.
- Three speeches: one for an elementary school graduation, one for a junior high school honor society induction ceremony, and one for a Rotary club in a neighboring town—because although he hates to give speeches, it is an important part of his job.
- A letter to a delinquent parent detailing school bus procedures—because it was an opportunity for him to take a strong stand.
- A formal case study of his six-year-old daughter Abigail and her emergent literacy, a paper he wrote in the writing class—because it is special to him as a teacher.
- A personal journal entry, from his vantage point as a parent, about writing the case study of Abigail—because it is special to him as a parent.
- A course paper, in his words, "discussing the organizational dynamics that have influenced Moultonborough's acceptance of the writing process approach"—because it articulates his perspective of deep change and emergent transformation inside one school system.

Ken's roles harmonize his four voices: he is parent, teacher, private person, and superintendent. Right away, his portfolio shows me that being a superintendent means constantly shifting between roles. He notices that his choices reflect his thinking more than his professional chores: "I think your portfolio pieces are the pieces that become really a part of you, a part of your thinking. I *think* about the pieces that I've written that are important to me, and the others I really don't think about."

As he talks and we look at his choices, I hear some recurrent themes: a belief in collaborative school leadership, a personal ethic of self-improvement, and a commitment to reflective practice as a means toward change. He is sensitive to the balance between the languages inside and outside his school. Ken explains his pragmatic approach to school leadership with a metaphor. "Stay the course, that's what I tell my administrators when we run into a brick wall and we're frustrated, but we feel ultimately we know where we're headed. We may have to take a different detour, but I just say 'Stay the course.' " He explains: "It's a dynamic view of the world, rather than a static view, that things are constantly changing, and you're not going to get to a point where everything is all right—it's never all right, you're constantly moving and changing, and that's why you stay the course, because that's what it's all about. It's not about reaching the harbor. I mean, it's a great experience when you finally do reach a landmark, but it's not a daily experience, and sometimes it's five years out."

As superintendent, Ken serves as balance and ballast. His sailing metaphor, balancing in a shifting wind, is a lovely reflection of Dewey's (1938) philosophy that "teaching and learning is a continuous process of reconstruction of experience, (87). With a debt to William James, Dewey taught us that change is grounded in history. It happens as we grow over time, to "make acquaintance with the past a means of understanding the present" (78).

WRITING TO THINK

Together, we look at Ken's piece called "The Myth of Grade Level," one of Ken's "Your Public Schools" columns. It begins:

> On the average, an unprotected human could survive the temperatures on the moon! Temperatures on the moon range from +300F to −300F. This places the average temperature around 0 F. . . . If NASA had relied on the average as a measure to determine the needs of its lunar landing team, catastrophe would have resulted. . . .
>
> Grade level is an average! It is a measure used to determine at what achievement level students can be expected to perform during a given year in school. . . . Yet grade level is no more reliable for a school's use than average temperatures on the moon are for NASA's use. A brief examination of how "grade level" is determined reveals the fallacy of this long accepted approach. . . .

"Pretty diplomatic," I remark, for an audience of citizens, but Ken disagrees. "*You and I* may look at it as diplomatic, but if you're a heavy traditionalist, it's hotter than a two-dollar pistol. . . . We could take the position of blaming our citizens. . . . If they believe a certain way, it's out of a tradition of what educators have told them for so long. . . . We make people believe that there's something wrong if everybody doesn't fall at the grade level point or higher, which completely contradicts the whole concept of what grade level is all about. *It's an average.*" Ken considered running this piece in the local paper at the beginning of the school year, just when the results of the state achievement tests were made public, but "it might still create more questions than it does answers." Ken is passionate about wanting to temper the value the public places on testing: "The tiny dogmatic points are only consequential to us as adults, they don't even matter to the kids," he says. "They're asking, 'Why aren't we testing as high as the Japanese?' But the critical question is—Does it matter?"

Ken may never publish this piece. He wrote the first draft eight years ago, and "every time I read it I revise it because either my thinking has changed or when I read a sentence, I think 'That doesn't really convey what I want to convey.' I imagine this article will never be done. . . . When is your editing done? . . . My experience with myself is that I want to edit it again. I don't want to ever stop editing it." But reworking this article for eight years has helped Ken clarify his thinking. Whether or not he ever publishes it, this article keeps him an arbiter between the pressures inside and outside of school.

The two published "Your Public Schools" columns grew out of his metaphors. He begins with the idea, he tells me, something he's been feeling strongly about. What about those metaphors, I wonder? Does the thought come first through an image? He thinks so. He's currently working with blueberry picking—the hours and hours it takes to do it well—wanting to connect it with something about the schools. He never goes out looking for a metaphor but, like a good journalist, he looks for an interesting angle, and that's when it comes. "I use a style where the lead is out of line from what people are expecting so they'll read on. If they see it's the superintendent writing it, they'd just put the paper down otherwise. I have to keep the reader interested." In one column, he discusses building consensus using fishing as his lead and central metaphor:

> Don't let anyone tell you that the bass fishing in Lake Winnipesaukee is anything but great. . . . The amount of fight in a smallmouth bass undoubtedly makes it, pound for pound, the best game fish there is. . . . Each fish puts up such a valiant struggle to get away when it alone is being caught, yet when placed on a stringer with other fish, all of whom want freedom, they all struggle in different directions with the net effect that the stringer goes nowhere. . . .
>
> There is no shortage of people with opinions about how to achieve the goal of educating our children. . . . Placed in a group in which consensus has to be achieved, the result is often the same as the bass on the stringer. . . . Is it any wonder that little progress is made in upgrading our schools? . . . [We need to] place the greatest priority on building a basis for consensus. It requires that each of us attempt to reach beyond our own perspective in order to understand the needs of others. . . . Let us learn from the Winnipesaukee smallmouth bass. Their inability to achieve common purpose keeps them on the stringer even when they have the freedom to escape.

In his other column, an elderly woman's negative perspective on the "old days" leads to an argument for solutions to schools' new problems. He begins by describing the woman, a member of the Historical Society with whom he boarded when he first came to town. A romanticized view of "the good old days," she thought, was nonsense:

She began to reflect on how she remembers cold, drafty houses, slavery to wood stoves, day-long trips to shops, and the terrible isolation caused by winter weather. . . . When we are tempted to reflect upon "the good old days" in education . . . a brief review of the historical data paints a much different picture of reality. . . . In 1870, only 2% of Americans received a high school diploma. The average education was at a fourth grade level. In the 1950's, still only 59% of Americans graduated from high school. . . . If we allowed today's high schools to operate with only the top 59% of the students, it would be much easier to attain the high standards attributed to schools of the past. . . . Yesterday's solutions will not solve today's problems. . . .

Draft for draft, image for image, Ken gets a lot out of his ideas. He enjoys writing these pieces; he is not under pressure for time or topic. When an idea comes, he plays with it. When he shapes a thought, he writes it. When he polishes a column, the paper prints it.

EVALUATION AS DRAFT

Unlike newspaper columns he chooses to write, Ken is forced to evaluate his staff members. "It is rare . . . that it really turns out exactly the way I like it, and this one didn't either. I think the key when I finish an evaluation . . . is that I've really been able to be helpful, not effusive. A lot of administrators write *love notes* . . . that's a way they can keep out of trouble." The two hardest genres he says he writes are teacher evaluations and public speeches, and he's included samples of each in his portfolio. He's chosen an evaluation of an English teacher who has left the system. It notes, "Pupils seemed generally attentive to worksheets; however, some confusion was evident in regard to subjects and predicates in unusual positions and sentence fragments." For this teacher, he details three strengths and three recommendations. In his summary he states that the teacher is "having a successful beginning to her first year," that her "instruction is well planned and contains all the elements necessary for her to develop into an excellent teacher. She deserves much credit for her openness during the evaluation process, is anxious for suggestions, and seems to appreciate constructive criticism."

As a student, Ken hadn't liked English or English teachers, and he still fights his anger: "They didn't care what it was that I had to contribute, they cared about this sort of summative evaluation about how much student I was, not what kind of contribution I could make." For Ken, it is crucial that the evaluation process be a growth experience, that the teacher contribute to it.

"Now I do evaluations in drafts. One of the things I haven't been happy about is the static nature of an evaluation. And it seems to me, in a post-conference, that you shouldn't hand somebody a final piece. . . . I deliberately mark it up." He speaks with passion, and he scrawls the perimeter of the table with his arm and an imaginary pen. "Because what I think I have seen has to be consonant with what they feel that they were doing." His voice gets louder as he tells me that he always, always has at least one post-conference, "because the evaluation is really not my piece—it is something that I've written, but it's about another person, and they really have to have input. Lots of input. Until they're ready to sign it . . . our evaluation approach is formative." Ken views evaluation as collaborative, and that is clear here in his portfolio.

Often he is asked to quantify the quality of a teacher's performance, and he says he has no checklists. "Especially school board members," he chuckles. "I always reflect back to them. I say, 'Well, how good a pharmacist are you? How good are you compared to that guy over there? Are you a 2? Or a 3? And how would I know it anyway?' "

A PRIVATE SELF, A PUBLIC VOICE

Ken's commitment to formative growth in education and his belief in fairness and hard work show up in his speeches, too, even though he hates to give them ("One of the banes of my existence"). There are three speeches in his portfolio. Ken tries to make his speeches "more than clichés." He observes that when the superintendent stands to take the podium, there are audible moans from the audience. "Think about it—the last person that any group wants to hear from is the superintendent . . . so I try to share a little bit of myself in a speech."

Of everything in his portfolio, I've learned more about Ken's personal history from his public speeches than from any of his other writing. That seems ironic, since it's his least favorite genre. "I've always liked the opportunity to share with people at a genuine level," he tells me, and mentions that he had a fantastic teacher for a public speaking course in high school. In each speech he blends a clear public objective with a personal message.

At the Rotary club, he asks people to set aside their specific concerns and think about broader questions: "What evidence will we consider to be a valid measure of our schools' effectiveness? What messages do we want our schools to send to children? What mission should our schools have for pupils?" He talks about increasing academic rigor, standards set by SAT scores, and inadvertently adapting an arrogant attitude— "Educate the best, shoot the rest." Without realizing it, he warns, we are disenfranchising a large group of students, stigmatizing them as second-class citizens. He gives a few statistics, reads a paragraph from *Education USA*, notes in the margin to "talk about people in the room."

In his conclusion, he urges, "We must embrace all pupils with a sense of pride about what it is they do best."

Ken tells me about this speech. It was in an "upwardly mobile community," and he was "trying to decenter people" from "focusing all their resources on their kids who are going to college, and then *abandoning* the rest of the population. . . . Many of those people were tradesmen who had become contractors, and I was able to touch them and say, 'Well, was that the only path to success? . . . What would *you* have liked done for *you?*'" It was not enjoyable, he admits, but he feels he accomplished his objectives.

In both graduation speeches, he balances quotations and confessions. He speaks to parents and to students, to the successful and the less than successful. The recurrent themes of hard work and fairness emerge in both speeches. For the honor society, Ken tells me, "I was trying to drive home the point that kids today are the same as kids always were." As he says in his speech:

> Today is important because it gives us an opportunity to celebrate what is right about our young people. Let's face it, at times people get fed up with kids. In fact, I was reading an article by a famous author, and I'd like to read part of it to you: "The children of today are too much in love with luxury. They have awful manners, flaunt authority, and have no respect for their elders. They no longer rise when their parents or teachers enter the room. I can only fear what kind of awful creatures they will be when they grow up." The article is signed Socrates and was written in 399 B.C.

With Ken's characteristic nod to collaboration and egalitarianism, he goes on to mention each student by name, notes that their achievements were not made alone, and recognizes their parents. Then he speaks to the other students:

> I have a confession to make. . . . I was never inducted into the National Honor Society. . . . I remember at ceremonies like this one that I always envied the inductees because they were "the smart kids." . . . I needed a way to excuse my own lack of effort.

He quotes Thomas Edison that "genius is one percent inspiration and ninety-nine percent perspiration." "If you were to ask any of these inductees whether this achievement was easy to attain because they were 'smart,' I'm sure they would share with you that they worked hard, made sacrifices, and at times expressed anxiety and self-doubt." His conclusion honors teachers, parents, and the students who will share the inductees' accomplishments.

The elementary school graduation speech begins with words to parents, celebrating "the landmarks in our lives and the lives of our children." Ken jokes that his role as a father had come into sharp focus recently when his son bought him a bottle of English Leather cologne. This seemed particularly appropriate, he said, because "to him I will always smell like a wallet." He acknowledges the financial and emotional investments that parents make, and then turns to the sixth graders with three messages: "Believe in yourself: you are each special people," "Success takes time and patience: part of it is being able to fail," and "We all grow and change: prepare yourself to be flexible." Each of the three messages is dotted with examples from *Fortune* magazine's poll of millionaires, and Connie Chung and Goldie Hawn, two famous women with whom Ken went to junior high. Ken's public self echoes his private self with drive, humor, and honesty.

SUCCESS AND THE SYSTEM

"I never called it a portfolio before, but I have a folder I call 'Speeches and Other Things That I Have Liked,' Ken tells me, "because you're constantly calling on your old material to redefine and resynthesize." He collects quotations in this file, like the ones he used from Edison and Socrates. His interest in defining success runs to presidents: "You know, we talk about some of our favorite presidents, and we're attracted to the Lincolns and the Kennedys as people who were very important, and philosophically they certainly were, but neither one of them really was able to follow through. The single president who really effected change was Lyndon Johnson, who got through more legislation and did more for the civil rights movement than any other president in history. . . . He's a guy who understood how the system worked. . . . He knew how to use the system to get the job done." I look around at the space where once sat the "president's desk" that Ken gave away to make room for the round table where we are talking.

"The successful people are the copers in this world," he says, "the people who weren't the cheerleaders." At one point in our talk, Ken mentions that he "was one of those late-developing little boys. . . . When other guys were men, I was still a little boy. . . . I went to school with women. . . . While I hated it at the time, that has served me far better in my life than all of the social things I would have enjoyed so much. . . . I look at some of the people who were more successful than I was, and when the glitz disappeared, so did their self-worth." He talks about developing the skills of introspection: "You say to yourself, do I have some worth as a person, and what is it that I can do?" It is these self-evaluative skills, he thinks, that direct his speech writing and his leadership style. "If you really look at the people who've made a difference, it hasn't been the flashes in the pan, but the people who, day in and day out, hit that wall—bloodied themselves, muddied themselves, got up, dusted themselves off, and said 'Let's go on.' "

He tells me that he loves to read self-improvement books, "how to make yourself a better person." He notes, "When you boil them down, all the messages say, 'Be true to yourself, don't make excuses, you are in control of your life, and all you have to do to be in control is to *just do it.*' " He calls himself "a student of people." He remembers books from the seventies, among others, *Games People Play* ("Superintendents love to play 'Woe is me' and 'Nobody knows the trouble I've seen' ") and *Body Language* ("I will not fold my arms in an observation. . . . I try to show an open body position, and I smile"). Does he feel successful? "I'm a pretty happy adult. Except for school board meetings."

The root of anybody's success has to do with personal qualities, Ken asserts. His recommendation letter for Chele Miller, the new elementary school principal who had been working as interim principal for several months, is his choice of an easy piece to write. His purpose was to have "an outpouring of how I really felt" about her. It is "those qualities that are unteachable, so when I look for an administrator—or a teacher—first I look for the personal qualities and then I look for the person to want to be a learner. Chele is all of those things, and I hope I conveyed that. The only problem that I had with that piece was being able to put it together in a format that conveyed both sides." His final draft is a formal three-page letter, divided into five sections with detailed examples: school business management, educational leadership, personnel management and evaluation, conflict resolution, and public relations. He writes, "Only a very special person can consistently lay her own pride and investment aside in an effort to create a solution for the common good. Ms. Miller is that kind of person." He concludes: "I don't often feel compelled to elaborate on an individual qualification to the extent that I have done above. . . . I hope that readers of this recommendation will take notice that Michele Miller is not only an extraordinarily capable administrator, but she is also a very special person." Ken's sincere words about Chele echo his background; he taught fifth grade for ten years as a teaching principal. With this perspective, he says, "I could face the same problem from two different perspectives in the same day." He led by what he calls "referent power," with the support of colleagues in order to function. "It was beyond democratic—it was by collegial rapport."

Ken has a strong identity as a professional educator based on those years as a teaching principal. But unlike a principal, he feels, "The superintendent has no [specific] role. . . . There's no role left for the superintendent. . . . Each group has a certain expectation of advocacy —for the board, for the teachers, for the taxpayers. And if you choose not to [be an advocate], then at a minimum, you will be a nonpartisan. If you're nonpartisan about everything, who are you?" He struggles with seeing his job as a tool through which other people exercise their power. He tells me he's been criticized for his need to have contact with teachers. "That's a piece of me that I need to have professionally."

Ken sees evaluations as drafts and his own job as ill defined and politically delicate, so he isn't often able to assert himself. He is lonely: "My office is a very alone place." One of his portfolio choices shows a strength of voice he cannot usually exercise. In a letter to a parent who has refused to drive his children down his own unpassable private road, Ken writes:

> I feel compelled to share with you that it strikes me as somewhat ironic that the Moultonborough School District is willing to make a commitment of $8,000 a year in order to transport your children, yet you are unwilling to spend ten minutes each morning to drive your children to a point in the road where our driver feels comfortable in transporting them.

He isn't often able to speak with such conviction: "I've got to be the peacemaker most of the time, sometimes so diplomatic that nobody knows what it is that I'm saying. I felt no compunction to do that in this piece, and that's why it's there in the portfolio." For a year now, I've seen him work with strong conviction, and I tell him I'm surprised. He grits his teeth and says, "I feel every day that I'm the biggest wimp that ever lived. I'm constantly holding back, constantly saying 'Geez, I'd like to say that now, but I better not.' . . . I'm not at all satisfied with my performance in that regard. . . . I beat myself up for that regularly. Just regularly."

THE PROFESSIONAL STANCE

It is not as a wimp, but as a strong professional voice that Ken analyzes his daughter Abigail's emergent literacy. In his portfolio, Ken has coupled the analysis with a personal journal entry about writing it. In the journal, he reflects on the influence of both Don Holdaway's and Marie Clay's work and his previous knowledge about emergent literacy. But "it wasn't until this case study that much of what they've said has become real to me." In his journal entry, Ken shuttles between teacher and father: "She often 'retells' a familiar book from memory while pretending to be reading the actual text. She reads to her dolls, her mother, her father, and her brother. . . . Her writing is parallel to her reading inasmuch as she often retells her story because she cannot actually read the text that she has written. All that I've described absorbs an enormous amount of her time. . . . Abigail believes in her own ability to read and write. Consequently, she is reading and writing."

Ken's nineteen-page case study is clear, strong, and detailed, written in the voice of a master professional. Ken writes a clinical description of Abigail's physical, social, emotional, and cognitive development, then a thorough description of her reading and writing. He includes four examples of her writing with detailed analyses of each:

> This latest example represents an interesting and surprising development in Abigail's writing. It consists of several pages of print without any pictures. In this example, words are represented in every form. One can find words represented with only initial consonants as well as words spelled correctly. When writing in this fashion, Abigail appears to lose her sense of wordness. All print is run together. Oddly enough, there appears to be the beginning of paragraphing. These can be seen as places where Abigail has chosen to stop in the middle of a line and then start again on the next line. These places seem to correspond with logical breaks in her story. This development is surprisingly advanced and seems out of place in the context of the rest of her writing.

Ken mentions that this example took Abigail two hours to write, in which "she was very focused on capturing her thoughts in print . . . less on form than content . . . a surprising period of time for a child who is only six years old. This writing confirms that Abigail sees writing as a means of communicating her ideas to others and capturing her thoughts for herself." His conclusion summarizes his observations as an expert professional, and it echoes his thoughts as a delighted father:

> Increasingly more print is evident in Abigail's work. She demonstrates an understanding of wordness, of one-to-one correspondence between print and words she reads, of sound symbol relationships, of correct spelling as opposed to invented spelling, of beginning paragraphing and ending punctuation. Most of this has emerged in less than 3 months! . . . More importantly than what Abigail will achieve is what Abigail has become. She is presently a child who is deeply involved in the writing/reading process. . . . It is an important part of the way in which she chooses to communicate and record her thoughts. . . . Because this is now a part of who she is, her literacy skills are likely to grow as she grows.

With deep passion and professional confidence, Ken proves that Abigail, at six, is already using writing to think, as he has discovered just recently in his own writing. I am impressed by his careful detailing, and I ask him if he sustains his objectivity because of his passion for teaching. "Most of my voice there was as a teacher . . . although there were places where I slipped back into the parent's role in talking about how my daughter uses her tininess and her apparent immaturity to charm people. I tried to tie into the clinical profile what her behavior really was. I was pleased with that piece, because I really do think that it captured who Abigail was. It's a very special piece to me because I think it accurately describes the advantages of a process, whole-language approach."

His case study mentions the large collection of books Abigail has at home and that her parents read to her regularly. When I asked him about his own reading habits, Ken told me that he reads *Education Week* because it encapsulates what's going on in his profession, and he loves self-improvement books, but his first choice in reading is children's literature. "I love to read children's literature, and I love realistic children's fiction. It has wonderful, wonderful messages—for adults." His children's literature course in college produced one of his dearest mentors. One of his closest friends is a teaching principal who gives workshops on children's literature: "We're like choir boys who preach to one another."

Sustaining his role as a passionate educator helps Ken handle his job. The superintendency, he has told me, "is not a position of educational leadership." Its voicelessness is a challenge and a bother: "When you're right, no one remembers, and when you're wrong, no one forgets." But by exercising careful balance, listening to all the languages outside and inside, using his many voices, Ken has been responsible for helping to effect some deep, institutionalized change, to feel some rewards of educational leadership. "You have to get yourself out of the traditional role in order to be effective as a leader."

THE GENIE OUT OF THE BOTTLE: DIMENSIONS OF EDUCATIONAL CHANGE

This year, Ken has positioned himself at the junction between the outside community's pressures and the inside community's experiments, and his stance is strong in the final piece he has chosen for his portfolio. Ken has completed the writing course with thirty teachers, a principal, a librarian, a reading specialist, and a learning disabilities specialist. It was an experiment for all of us. As educational theorist William Torbert (1990) has observed, when it is involved in careful self-study, a "true community of inquiry" experimenting together "can accept fundamental change within itself" (253). It is in this social setting, Torbert writes, that theory and practice can mutually reform one another: "Reform from the center, or self-reform, requires an integration of ongoing action and ongoing inquiry amidst real-time organizational pressures" (256).

In our long distance project, Ken has "joined the ongoing action" with his staff, instructors, and students, shared it with the public, and kept it for himself as a writer, too. At the end of the course, he writes: "I need to spend more time writing in order to clarify my own thinking. . . . It's useful even when there's not an audience. I've learned that writing serves a purpose other than to complete the teacher's assignment." His goal for himself is to write in a wider variety of genres. His goal for the school system, he writes, "is to learn how to incorporate a system of accountability into a strong process program."

Ken's final portfolio piece reflects both of his goals. His penchant for metaphor is strong in "Magic Lamps, Process Teaching, and Moultonborough Teachers":

> The genie is out of the magic lamp. . . . Students are committed to the use of print to both convey their ideas and to learn about the ideas of others. Because of this, few want to put this genie back. However, like any newly unleashed power, it has caused considerable discord among those who are attempting to learn how to martial its energy. What follows is a discussion of the organizational dynamics that have influenced the acceptance of writing process by Moultonborough teachers.

The piece is an overview of the course's effects on students, teachers, and administrators, written as his final project for the course. "The purpose of the piece was a view of changing practice as a superintendent; the assignment was to write about some kind of change." Between the lines, I read the themes I've learned are Ken's by studying his portfolio: an acknowledgment of his multilinguistic stance and a commitment to growth and reflection, collaboration, hard work, and self-improvement. Ken spends a lot of time thinking about the characteristics of change. In our interview, he says: "An effective change, if you're fortunate enough to be able to institutionalize change, is a three- to five-year commitment, probably on the five-year end. . . . Needing to take so long begins to frustrate the change itself, and that's why there are very few institutionalized changes. . . . When there is no dissonance, there is no change."

In his paper, Ken captures dissonance with his metaphor of the genie and the winds of change. Lower elementary teachers, he writes, had been preparing for four years, by reassessing their work in reading and writing and experimenting with more whole language approaches. High school teachers were trying more writing, too, and a major staff turnover had set the stage. But the upper elementary and junior high teachers, he writes, "were truly caught in a whirlwind." High school teachers gave mixed messages: "More writing, please, but prepare those kids for a traditional program." And elementary teachers were pressuring them to change: "They're waiting to see how the secondary school wind blows," he writes. "The course has intensified the conflict. This is testimony to the effectiveness of this project. . . . What has changed is that almost everyone, K–12, is aware that change is happening and that there must be an effort to accommodate this change. . . . It is doubtful that process students will ever allow their teachers to return to a traditional approach." His conclusion looks at the beginnings of institutionalized change as Ken understands it:

> To date, the Long Distance project has helped by providing a forum for the discussion of how to best implement this changing practice . . . [how to provide] the structure for guiding teachers in the use of this powerful genie. Moultonborough teachers look to the University of New Hampshire instructors for answers and are sometimes upset when they find that pat answers are not available. Perhaps that's because they're too interested in controlling this genie. After all, a genie's power is magical. If more energy were spent in learning how the genie works his magic, control might no longer be an issue!

Ken tells me about the dissonance that comes with making changes: "We seem to vacillate between two points. The first point is that as educators we're always looking for a pat prescription, the idiot-proof method. On the other end, we recognize and are reluctant to say, 'Well, there is just this one way of doing it,' and we create insecurity in our teachers—and this happened in the course—they're not getting the answers they need, and the answers that they need are inside them."

I ask Ken what kinds of deep changes he'd make if he could. He doesn't hesitate to suggest them: "The first thing I'd do is to do away with grade-level concepts, and form schools around developmentally based units, where students might spend a variable amount of time in each unit, not moving through at the same time. The second thing is curriculum. It's deductive; as adults looking back, with the whole picture in our minds, we analyze a task and say . . . what does it take in order for a child to get from the beginning level to an end point? The mistaken assumption is that everyone moves from A to Z, then—voila!—whatever we're trying to produce is formed. The problem is that not all learners go from A to B to C to D in order to get to Z. Learners go from A to H and back to B. . . . The underlying structure of our schools is our accountability system, so . . . two of the greatest issues that contradict the way human beings learn are grade level and the linear structure of the way we build curriculum . . . wholly inaccurate, in my estimation."

Through our interview and between the manila leaves of his portfolio, Ken's language glitters with metaphors. It is his art. Through his metaphors he learns and thinks. Dewey (1934) linked art with human experience, suggesting that art is not initially created for a museum, that it happens in the shop, the marketplace, and the school as well as the studio. Almost fifty years later, Eisner (1982) argued that there must be a place for art in curriculum. The interaction of individuals' environment with their "internal conditions" affects the kind of experience they have. Eisner contends that people choose artful forms of representation not only to convey their experience to others, but also to represent the ideas to themselves.

In the personal curriculum inside Ken's portfolio, his metaphors convey passion about education. Textbooks, he says, are "false idols," their scoping and sequencing a teacher's security—"Linus' blanket." The common notion of curriculum is "a cookbook approach." Our grade-level structure is "an industrial model where you can move students along like widgets . . . we check off kids as we go." He believes that textbooks go beyond the marketplace and "cut to the core of a district's insecurity." When a superintendent begins to burn out, "his agenda is to survive." Longtime superintendents have "been through wars." I ask him whether he's aware that he uses metaphors so artfully; I wonder if he likes poetry. Aristotle wrote that metaphor was crucial for sophisticated thinking, that "an acute mind will perceive resemblances even in things far apart" (1984, 191). Janet Emig (1983) suggested that metaphor is a necessary feature in coping with new concepts. And Ken Greenbaum tells me, "When you hit people with a lot of red-hot jargon about the way education can be, it tends to turn them off. If you hit people with a powerful metaphor, sometimes they develop more understanding about what you're talking about."

I am intrigued with the balance of Ken's many voices, the value of his reflection as it comes through in the choices he makes to represent himself in his portfolio. His belief in gradual, reflective, progressive educational transformation makes me wonder if he's read Dewey, if he counts him among his mentors. No, Ken says, not recently—only in an education course a long time ago. It occurs to me that the threads I've traced through Ken's writing and talk are all fibers of our American democratic tradition; it is the Deweyan cord that connects us as conscientious educators.

Late in his life, Dewey wrote poetry, his seeking, as he put it, to "catch life's inner speech" (1990, 259). Torbert writes:

> Dewey gradually came to feel how . . . thought occurs within context, always of one's daily practice, how true thought is not general, context-free philosophy or science, but rather poetry, thought reformed from the center by an awareness of its relation to one's current breath, passion, and action. (1990, 258)

Ken's portfolio, like Dewey's poetry, glows with "thought reformed from the center." It is thought related to his passion and his action. He writes to think, he evaluates to draft dialogue, he writes and speaks carefully to the public. In the process, he exposes his artful thinking and his private self. He studies his daughter to see himself better as a teacher. He watches, with joy and patience, as his staff engages in dissonance in order to move ahead. His poetry is in his metaphors. "Staying the course" is exactly what he and I have learned about him in this interview. Ken's growth is steady over time, shifting with gentle motion, as he looks around constantly, heading toward a floating distant marker of reform and he watches the compass as the needle wobbles. That is the job of a superintendent, as Ken sees it. And that is what we see in his portfolio.

11

MULTIGENRE RESEARCH: ONE COLLEGE SENIOR

TOM ROMANO

> *What we need in America is for students to get more deeply interested in things, more involved in them, more engaged in wanting to know; to have projects they can get excited about and work on over long periods of time; to be stimulated to find things out on their own.*
>
> *Howard Gardner*

Meg was involved in the kind of long-term project that Howard Gardner speaks of above during the final semester of her senior year at the University of New Hampshire. An English major who planned to teach middle school students one day, Meg had opted to do a senior honors thesis, and she had asked me, a teacher of hers the previous semester, to be her thesis advisor. To earn four hours of academic credit in the Honors English program, Meg researched a topic of her choosing and completed a project.

For the final assessment of her work, I suggested we employ a kind of portfolio evaluation that required her to review her decision-making processes, to reflect upon the body of her semester's work in order to come to explicit perceptions about what she had done. I knew that I would learn a great deal from Meg's reflection. I believed that she would, too.

For her honors thesis Meg chose to research nineteenth-century English novelist Mary Shelley. Out of her learning Meg wrote a multi-genre research paper.

THE MULTIGENRE RESEARCH PAPER

Melding facts, interpretation, and imagination, the multigenre research paper, as its name suggests, is a blend of genres. Canadian writer Michael Ondaatje's *The Collected Works of Billy the Kid* (1984) is perhaps the best example from the literary world of the multigenre style.

146

Ondaatje's recreation of the last few years of outlaw William Bonney's life is neither biography nor historical fiction; instead, it is a work that combines poems, monologues, character sketches, photographs, drawings, songs, newspaper interviews, narratives, stream-of-consciousness, and fiction generated from biographical fact. Each genre reveals a facet of Billy the Kid or of the characters who moved in and out of his life. Each piece is self-contained, making a point of its own, and is not connected to any of the others by conventional transitional devices.

Meg was eager to write a research paper in such a style. The previous semester her interest in Mary Shelley had been aroused in a children's literature course when she read a children's biography of the novelist. During that same semester she had learned about the multigenre research paper in "Teaching Writing," a class I taught to English majors who planned to go into teaching. Meg contacted me early in the second semester to ask if I would be her thesis advisor for her multigenre research paper. I agreed.

"As I will not be restricted by formal prose," wrote Meg in her honors thesis proposal, "I shall be able to show Mary Shelley's experiences and emotions through short prose pieces, poems, dialogues and fictional newspaper articles. This multigenre report will not detail her life from beginning to end, but will instead serve as a collage of bits of information which when pieced together will provide a feel for Mary Shelley and the way she viewed and experienced life."

Meg wanted to learn more about Mary Shelley, a woman she had begun to admire. But Meg had another ambition, too. She wanted to write well. And she wanted to write in a style other than the expository one she had used for dozens of papers in high school and college. She wanted to write in a multitude of genres, trying her hand at many of the forms she had been reading as an English major; she wanted to become a maker of literary artifacts, choosing to write in genres she deemed appropriate for revealing important aspects of Mary Shelley's life. She wanted to combine what is so often pejoratively called "creative writing" with scholarly investigation. Meg wanted to make art.

Dennie Palmer Wolf writes that "like other demanding cognitive activities, the arts involve people in symbol-use, analysis, problem solving, and invention" (Wolf 1987, 26).

Notable endeavors.

Researching Mary Shelley for fifteen weeks, selecting topics to write about from that research, and writing about those topics in various genres would involve Meg in the very cognitive activities that Wolf cites as so demanding: symbol-use with language, the creation of texts both as writer and reader, analysis, problem solving, and invention. Although Meg had chosen a nontraditional way to demonstrate her knowledge, members of the English department at the University of New Hampshire thought her proposal had merit and approved her multigenre research project.

The second semester Meg immersed herself in Mary Shelley. She read the neglected novelist's fiction, criticism about that fiction, and, most notably, biographies, the best of which, according to Meg, was *Mary Shelley: Romance and Reality* by Emily Sunstein (1989). Meg and I met for an hour each week, at which time she updated me on her research, sharing with me the notes she had taken on her reading and telling me stories of Mary Shelley; her husband, poet Percy Shelley; her father, the moral philosopher William Godwin; her feminist mother, Mary Wollstonecraft; and roguish Romantic poet Lord Byron. Each week for an hour Meg's talk transported me to early-nineteenth-century literary England.

Over the course of the semester, I was in on Meg's learning and invention. She read me the poems, narratives, and various other genre experiments she had been writing as she engaged in her extensive reading. I was also in on the tangles of her research. During one brief period, for example, I saw Meg fall into such infatuation with the mystique of Percy Shelley and Lord Byron that she temporarily lost the focus of her research. I saw her thinking emerge, transform, and find shape.

I did my part as a teacher, too, during our weekly meeting. I listened to Meg's writing as a curious reader, responding and asking the real questions that came to me. I passed along handouts to Meg of anything I came across that might be pertinent to her project. I gave her multigenre papers that high school seniors had written about Tennessee Williams, Jim Morrison, and Lady Jane Grey (she'd already read ones about John Lennon and Marilyn Monroe). I gave her prose poems by Judith Steinburgh (1988) to use as possible composition models. When I saw that Meg was logjammed in her writing during one stretch, I gave her an interview with Bernard Malamud. " Write your heart out," Malamud advised young writers (Malamud 1983, 46).

I gave Meg suggestions for writing, too. You might try some expository passages, I told her. How about an interview with Dr. Frankenstein's creation? Why not vividly describe Percy Shelley's charred heart that Leigh Hunt removed from the poet's funeral pyre?

The suggestions I made grew out of our conferences, when Meg divulged so much information. She had plans of her own, however, so she ignored most of my writing suggestions. Still, she said she was inspired to work after our weekly conferences. "I could have never done this independently," Meg wrote later. "I really needed the encouragement and interest of others." I was one of the others; so also were Meg's friends, whom she consulted frequently about her writing.

As the semester's end moved closer, Meg writing ever more consistently, adding pieces to her growing stockpile of writing about Mary Shelley, we began talking more about the final assessment of her work. I had told Meg at the beginning of the semester that although I was keenly interested in her final product, the multigenre research paper, I was just as interested in the processes of her thinking, in the development of her critical skills as she sought to shape literary artifacts out of the life of Mary Shelley. As a teacher I wanted to know about the decisions she made and the problems she solved.

Meg wanted to find out about Mary Shelley; I wanted to find out about Meg. Moreover, I wanted her to find out about her own processes of thinking, writing, and learning. To obtain such information, Meg compiled a portfolio of her work.

THE PORTFOLIO: ONE DEFINITION

Two weeks before her portfolio was due, I gave Meg a memo to explain my conception of a portfolio. I wanted her to have guidance in her portfolio preparation, and I wanted to have a place from which Meg and I could begin talking about the concept of portfolio:

> What is this portfolio I speak of?
>
> In a portfolio I want you to present your best face. I'd like you to make choices from all the genres you've written in conjunction with Mary Shelley. These pieces should be what you consider your best work.
>
> I'd like you to write about why you think these pieces are your best, why they well represent both the *range* and *depth* of what you can do as a writer. I'm interested in both. I want to get a picture of your versatility *and* your skill.
>
> I am also interested in your writing process. Not that there is one ideal process that you will be measured against. No. But I want to see that you have a writing process in place that enables you to get writing done that you are proud of. So include in your portfolio all the notes and drafts that went into making one piece of writing. I'd like to follow that piece from embryonic stage right up to the final typed version.

A week before Meg turned in her portfolio to me, I gave her this more specific memo:

> Meg:
>
> 1. Prepare two folders:
>   A. a folder of all your final products.
>   B. the portfolio of your choices that will represent you as a writer, reader, thinker, and learner, that will show the breadth and depth of your work, this accompanied by a cover letter.

What I want to do, Meg, is read folder A—all of your finished multigenre pieces—and make my own determinations. Then I want to read your portfolio—folder B—that contains your choices of the pieces you want to represent you and the reasoning behind those choices. I'm looking to discover if there are things a teacher can gain by having students self-assess their work with a portfolio, instead of simply grading blindly without considering the learner.

2. Prepare a cover letter to accompany your portfolio.

This is one of the major pieces of your work. The letter is your opportunity to explain, specifically, why you chose each piece to represent you. What made the pieces you chose stand out?

In your letter I also want you to take me through the one piece that represents your writing process. I, as a reader, want to get inside your thinking processes at every stage.

A week later Meg gave me the folder containing all the final products of her multigenre writing and the portfolio of writing that she chose to represent her. It was then that my learning began in earnest.

MEG'S PORTFOLIO AND SELF-ASSESSMENT

Howard Gardner has written that assessment of artistic work should involve production, perception, and reflection. The acronym PROPER (Gardner and Greenbaum 1986, 20) is a good reminder of this triumvirate. *Production* is the activity in the artistic medium—painting, playing music, taking photographs, acting, writing. *Perception* "means learning to see better, to hear better, to make finer discriminations, to see connections between things." *Reflection* "means to be able to say, 'What am I doing? Why am I doing it? What am I trying to achieve? Am I being successful? How can I revise my performance in a desirable way?' " (Gardner, quoted in Brandt 1988, 32). Production and reflection upon that production reveal perception.

This seemed a proper way of assessment: it comes from the learner, Meg, who had both struggled and delighted in her independent study all semester. Although there isn't room here to discuss each aspect of Meg's portfolio and self-assessment, I want to highlight some of the things she revealed.

One piece that Meg included in her portfolio to represent her "best face" was a prose poem in the form of a rhythmic "labyrinthine sentence" (Weathers 1980, 16). In the cover letter accompanying her portfolio, Meg reflected upon the production of this prose poem: "By making it one long sentence filled with information, I wanted to show the speed in which they made the trip. Their journey, like this piece, was short and packed."

ROAD TRIP

Their flight from the tyranny that wished them apart took Mary, Percy (and Mary's step-sister Claire) eight-hundred miles (through Paris, Lucerne, Basel, Strausbourg, Mannheim, Mainz, Cologne and Rotterdam) by donkey, by foot (with Percy carrying the weak, old donkey that he had purchased out of pity—Mary walking barefoot in her long gown on the dusty roads), by carriage (and running after the carriage when the driver, who thought them odd for wanting to stop so often to admire the landscapes, would leave without them), by canoe and by boat, in forty-eight days (July 28 through September 13, 1814) on thirty pounds.

I asked Meg if she had consciously written "Road Trip" as a labyrinthine sentence or if, instead, she had realized she was writing one during its composition. "I realized I had a labyrinthine sentence because I didn't want to stop it," Meg said. "I wanted to show haste. They just got up and went to all these places on thirty pounds. I didn't want to say, "They went 800 miles. They traveled through. . . . ' I thought the labyrinthine sentence gave you a sense of ecstasy."

Another piece Meg chose as one of her best was "Guilty of Too Much Innovation: An Interview with Mary Wollstonecraft Shelley." In the imaginary interview Meg travels back in time to 1818 Italy to talk with Mary Shelley about her first novel, *Frankenstein.* Just over four double-spaced pages long, this interview turned out to be the longest single piece in Meg's multigenre paper. It also proved to be the most difficult piece for her to write.

A major concern for Meg in writing this interview was voice. "It was so easy," she explained, "to slip into Meg talking with Meg as Mary rather than Meg talking to Mary." Meg didn't want to slide into casual, twentieth-century undergraduate speech for herself, nor did she want to attach a phony sophisticated British accent to Mary. She sought a subtle difference between the voices. Here's an excerpt of Meg as the interviewer from 1990—well prepared, just as a good interviewer should be—talking with the author, then twenty-one:

Meg: I read that although *Blackwood's Edinborough Magazine* and *Edinborough Magazine* praised your demonstrative powers, they found the content of *Frankenstein* too shocking.

Mary: Too shocking—too different I should say. The *Quarterly Review* condemned it for being "guilty of too much innovation" and said it wasn't "truly gothic." It was praised, however, as a piece of "very bold fiction" by *La Belle Assemblee,* a magazine for upperclass women.

Meg was also challenged by the great amount of information she included in the interview. It is loaded with specific details about *Frankenstein* and the events surrounding its creation and publication. Readers learn about the genesis of *Frankenstein,* the negative reaction to the novel by many critics, Mary's indignation with that criticism, and her strong moral stance in the novel. Meg tells Mary how her tale of man's meddling into the secret of creating life has been bastardized in the twentieth century and how contemporary critics consider *Frankenstein* "the progenitor of a genre called science-fiction."

Lastly, Meg was proud of the interview because it had been difficult to write. The voices, the difference in time, the great amount of information to be included, the locale of the interview—all these challenged Meg with problems she had to identify, analyze, and solve through language and invention. The task had prompted Meg to make an outline before she began writing a draft, something she rarely did. In addition, although Meg was not averse to revising, her revisions of "Guilty of Too Much Innovation" were many and extensive. "Usually," said Meg, "if I really work on something, I overwork it, and it just loses everything."

That had not happened with the interview.

Meg had written a half-page introduction to her conversation with Mary Shelley, a strategy she had learned from reading the Bernard Malamud interview. In the introduction Meg set the circumstance and scene and told how almost immediately Mary had asked how her husband was regarded in the twentieth century. In the interview itself, no mention is made of him. I asked Meg why she had dealt with Percy Shelley in the brief introduction instead of in the text of the interview. "I knew Mary would ask about Percy since she was so devoted to him, but I didn't want to go on and on about that. I wanted the interview to be about *Frankenstein.* I didn't want to clutter it up."

Increasingly, I was forming the picture of a young woman who worked hard on her writing, who developed definite standards before and during her work, who made rhetorical decisions based upon those standards. And the picture I was forming wasn't of Mary Shelley.

I learned even more about Meg's uncompromising standards of composition through the piece of writing she included in her portfolio to reveal her creative process. The piece was one I'd seen Meg working on for weeks, one she had considered opening her multigenre paper with. In the end, although she included this poem and all its drafts in her portfolio, she had decided not to use it in her multigenre paper.

But the poem was important to her nevertheless. It had gone through five drafts before she abandoned it. The first draft was in pencil and featured Mary talking to herself about her full name—Mary Wollstonecraft Godwin Shelley, a name that wasn't really hers, Meg pointed out, but was instead her mother's, her father's, and her husband's. In Meg's fourth draft the dialogue shifted dramatically, taking the form of a poem with Mary as the persona. "I wanted to be more concise," said Meg. "I thought the poem would probably be my first piece, and I didn't want to have Mary talking back and forth to herself, so I thought that Mary could ask these questions about her name." Once Meg had the conciseness she was after, she revised the poem one more time, casting it in the third person:

MARY WOLLSTONECRAFT GODWIN SHELLEY

Who was she that the poet Percy Bysshe Shelley delayed a journey to Wales to meet her and later left his wife Harriet to love?

Who was she that, if it was not for the opportunity to meet her, Lord Byron would have never agreed to see his former lover, her step-sister, again?

Who was she that ran off with a married man at seventeen?

Who was she that married that recently-widowed man, having already borne two of his children?

Who was she that is associated with bastardized movie versions of her most noted novel?

The daughter of William Godwin.

The daughter of Mary Wollstonecraft.

The lover of Percy Bysshe Shelley.

The wife of Percy Bysshe Shelley.

The author of *Frankenstein*.

BUT WHO WAS SHE?

In the end Meg set aside even this. "I had the worst time phrasing it," she said. "I had three different people read it to see if it made sense, and they got confused. So that was why I didn't want to use it. I liked the idea, but I didn't like how I had done it."

Instead of opening the multigenre paper with the poem, Meg began with the lead from an actual obituary published in the *Athenaeum* on February 15, 1851. She thought it showed that even an outside source viewed Mary in just such a troubling, identity-denying way:

MRS. SHELLEY

After having some years since disappeared from the world of literary occupation, the daughter of Godwin and Mary Wollstonecraft, the relict of the poet of "Adonais," died the other day—we believe in her fifty fourth year. Her health had long been on the decline.

THE INTERVIEW

Several researchers have stressed the importance of a follow-up interview with the student as an important part of portfolio evaluation (Budnick 1984; Thompson 1988; Wolf 1988). I found such an interview indispensable. After reading Meg's portfolio and learning so much about her as a writer and thinker, I was curious to know more. The interview satisfied that curiosity. It also showed me that asking a student to reflect upon her best work, her best face, will not necessarily reveal all of her ways of working or her aesthetic development.

After reading her portfolio, I jotted down questions, which I gave to Meg a few days before our interview. I didn't want to spring these on her; I wanted her to have time to reflect. I asked Meg to tell me about the pieces of writing from her project that she definitely would *not* have chosen to include in her portfolio. Often students are reluctant to associate unsatisfactory pieces of writing with their portfolios. They need reassurance that "both successes and 'failures' demonstrate writing growth and development" (Howard 1990, 7). Meg didn't mind sharing what she considered her failed pieces of writing with me, as long as she had the opportunity to point out that she'd had trouble with them just as she had with opening unused poem. The stories of these "failed" pieces revealed so much about Meg as a thinker and writer that in the future I will ask students to include unsatisfactory pieces, or failures, in their portfolios.

One piece Meg spoke of was a poem she had written about the *Don Juan*, the small boat Percy was sailing that capsized in a storm, drowning him and a companion. I had remembered Meg working on drafts of this poem early in her study, during her time of lost focus and infatuation with Percy and Lord Byron. This had gone on for two or three weeks, until she realized the trap she had fallen into. "I had been getting books about Mary, but reading really interesting things about Byron and Shelley. I didn't know what Mary was doing or where Mary was. I thought, 'I'm doing it, too, just like everyone else seems to.' " This realization, said Meg, shocked her back into the "Mary mode."

Neither in her multigenre paper nor in her portfolio did Meg use the *Don Juan* poem, which she had been so fond of. "If I was doing my paper about Percy, I'd put it in, but the *Don Juan* [poem] wasn't pertinent to Mary. The poem dealt with how Percy died. It wasn't Mary looking at Percy's death."

Another piece that Meg had much personal investment in was "Mary Wollstonecraft Shelley and Me," an expository piece that contrasted what she and Mary had each accomplished by the age of twenty-two. Although Meg hadn't published a novel, or borne three children, or traveled the European continent, she hadn't done badly in twenty-two years. She held a steady job, working thirty hours each week, and she was just one month away from college graduation with a B.A. in English. "Mary Wollstonecraft Shelley and Me" was almost everything for Meg. She had planned to include it in her portfolio as one of her best pieces; it was also going to figure prominently among the works of her multigenre paper.

She used it in neither.

"I felt like it was bringing me too much into the paper. I didn't want to do that. What are people going to think about me when they've read that? Nobody really knows me. They're going to say, 'So what? Who cares what this *me* did or didn't do in contrast to Mary?' "

Repeatedly, I learned through the portfolio and the follow-up interview that Meg was willing to put the integrity of the multigenre paper as a whole above her personal attachment to specific pieces she had written. Many experienced writers grapple with this kind of decision. If I hadn't interviewed Meg about the pieces of writing she had worked so hard on, but had set aside, I'd have been blind to the tough-minded editorial decisions she had made about her own work. What writers consider not their best work—and the reasons why—can be just as informative about their aesthetic growth as their best writing and the stories about that writing.

Dennie Palmer Wolf maintains that, through the process of interviewing, "teachers can assess just how self-aware students are" (Wolf 1988, 28). This was certainly true of Meg's work. Had I merely evaluated her final product, stamped a grade upon it, and written her a succinct note—had I not asked her to gather her significant work and reflect upon it through cover letter and interview—I would have missed learning about Meg's critical skills and writing standards.

THE IMPORTANCE OF PROJECTS

Doing a multigenre paper about Mary Shelley was Meg's choice. It was her project. If she carried it through in good faith, the English Department would grant her four credit hours. She had ample time to do her work, a full semester. She had regular response from a teacher and peers, people who were interested in her work. Ownership. Choice. Time. Response. All aspects of work imperative to the growth of writers (Graves 1983; Atwell 1987).

The project provided Meg with a topic she could become absorbed in. In his book *Flow: the Psychology of Optimal Experience*, Mihaly Csikszentmihalyi (1990, 71) writes about the experiences of people who become so involved in something that they lose track of time, they forget any self-consciousness they might otherwise feel, they are challenged yet have the skills to meet those challenges, and they get clear, frequent clues during the activity about how well they are doing.

Meg's project became such an experience for her. She described the time she found the Sunstein biography and sat down at a table in the Concord, New Hampshire, public library, fairly sinking into the pages, not stopping her reading until the lights flicked on and off to signal the library's imminent closing. She told of leaving her weekly conferences excited and inspired, and returning to her writing afresh. She told of entire days spent studying and writing, unaware of the passage of time until her friends arrived to take her to supper. One of Meg's most optimal experiences, however, she noted in her portfolio cover letter: "I've never been so confident in my conversational skill than when I've been telling people about this project."

In the interview that followed my perusal of her portfolio, I asked Meg about this newfound confidence in her conversational skills. Meg revealed a critical link between her personal identity, her past, and her plans for the future.

> The project gave me a lot of self-confidence. When the teacher of my women's lit class asked me to talk about Mary Wollstonecraft, I wasn't nervous. Normally, I would have been. I want to teach, and I want my students to do multigenre papers. I wanted to do one myself so I knew what I was talking about. I didn't want to say, "Hey, kids, do a multigenre paper" and I've never done one before. I wouldn't know what to do. I want to have experience with it. I can see how students would benefit from doing work such as this. They become authorities. I could see that if I had done this in seventh grade—when I didn't talk to *anybody* unless I had to—. . . . If you had put me at a table with somebody else to workshop our writing, I would have felt okay because I would have felt like I knew a lot.

PROJECTS, PORTFOLIOS, AND TEACHER SUPPORT OF STUDENT LEARNING

Meg described the day after she turned in her portfolio and her multigenre paper:

> I went down to the Bagelry where I work. A friend of mine there, Michael, is doing his senior thesis on the search for the Grail, so we're always talking thesis while we're working. "Michael," I said, "I've done my thesis! It's this thick and it's done and I turned it in!" An old woman sitting at one of the tables next to us started laughing. "Excuse me," she said, "but I was a professor. When students turned in their theses to me, all I ever heard them say was 'Here's my thesis. Thank you very much.' I never saw this excitement. I'm so happy."

Meg's end product, the culmination of her semester project, was worthy of exhilaration. But the story behind that work was even more exhilarating. And it's a story I wouldn't have discovered if I hadn't asked Meg to reflect upon the body of her work and to gather together samples of it in a portfolio.

I followed one student for fifteen weeks. I remembered teaching high school with a typical teaching load of 150 students. I couldn't have followed each of them the way I followed Meg. But I wouldn't have needed to. Students learn whether a teacher is aware of it or not. The teacher's job, as I see it, is to set up the classroom so that students may pursue, through reading, writing, talking, and listening, what they passionately care about, what they can become blissfully lost in.

Long-term independent projects like the multigenre research paper allow students room for such passionate learning. Teaching can support that. Teachers confer with students; they listen, respond, and teach. Students confer with each other. The prevailing attitude toward learning in the classroom should be one that expects students to be productive. If students do not produce a significant body of work, the process of reflecting, selecting, and perceiving becomes fraudulent. Self-assessment is short-circuited. Classroom activities that allow students time, choice, ownership, and response clear the way for portfolios to be used as a vital component in learning.

Students compile portfolios that contain a sampling of writing that represents their process of creation, their best work, *and* their near misses or unsatisfactory pieces. In portfolio cover letters, students explain the meaning of those artifacts. Final interviews with each student (not necessarily as long as my interview with Meg) cause students to reflect further. Teachers learn about students' learning. And, more importantly, students learn about their learning:

Here is what I did that is significant.

Here is why it is significant.

Here is the process I went through.

And here is what I've learned from that process.

When you get down to it, it's not the portfolio that matters most. The portfolio could become no more than a file, dog-eared, jammed in a desk or stored in a box high atop a cabinet. What does matter, however, is the portfolio *process*. That is the key to further learning and growth through writing and reading. After production of much work it is students' selection and reflection that solidifies learning, that explicitly reveals to them their perceptions.

12

AN ALTERNATIVE PORTFOLIO: GATHERING ONE CHILD'S LITERACIES

CINDY MATTHEWS

A seven-year-old redhead named Joey, who fit no school mold for success, taught me how portfolios can be used to record sophisticated forms of literacy. Unless we consider alternatives to the traditional forms of portfolios that are emerging, we lose children like Joey.

As a classroom researcher in an elementary school in New Hampshire, I observed Joey's emergent literacy for one year. I followed his journey, I shared and sometimes extended his vision, and I understood his feelings. What I learned of the complexity and idiosyncrasy of one child's literacies can be of use to all teachers.

Joey came to second grade in September nearly illiterate. He could not read and could barely write. As a result, Joey had very low self-esteem and acted out in a way that tended to anger teachers. He was tested for Learning Disability, Emotional Disability, and Attention Deficit Disorder.

But one thing Joey could do well was tell stories—stories that were interesting, funny, informative, and raucous. He once explained how to skin a catfish. At Halloween he recited from memory a recipe for dirt cake, which he said his mother had made for him.

Joey: Do you have a husband or a brother?

Cindy: Yes.

Joey: Okay, well, some day when you make it [dirt cake], put it out and see if he thinks it's real. Take a package of chocolate pudding and a package of banana pudding, then half a stick of cream cheese and a whole pack of oreos. And you gotta have a blender. You mix it all up in the blender, and it looks like dirt—soil. Oh yeah, you gotta remember the rubber worms—white—gummy worms.

"Language and literacy acquisition are forms of socialization," according to James Gee (1989a, 59). He contends that school demands a reacculturation from home literacy to school literacy. I began to see that Joey's disability, as it were, was school based.

Joey lives in an extended family situation, sharing his home with his grandfather, grandmother, father, stepmother, and older sister. Literacy in his home is social-interactional—orally based. Linguists contend that children who live in oral-style homes do not demonstrate the same school-based "essayist literacy" as children from mainstream homes. That does not mean that Joey is not in possession of a myriad of literacies. He is.

JOEY'S ORAL STORIES

Joey's socialization involves imitating a storytelling grandfather and emulating the adult talk he hears in his home in order to gain access to the adults' conversation. Joey tells many stories about his grandfather and tells adult jokes and stories, which he may be hearing from his granddad.

Joey: My grandfather . . . once my sister got a black fly bite on her eye and the kids called her "fly eye." My grandfather—well, I have fat cheeks and my grandfather calls me "horn pout lips."
Cindy: Nice guy!
Joey: He's bald. He just has little hairs and he said he wanted his hair cut. And I said, "Nan, how can you cut his hair?" and she said she cutted the little hairs with a scissors.

Joey responds to experience with oral stories. I transcribed Joey's responsive weaving of his own story in and out of a printed text about rivers, which a young friend, Timmy, read to Joey and me one day in early April. At one point Joey said, "This book really tells information. The Mississippi River is wicked deep." Timmy kept on reading as Joey created his own story. Joey said, "I go in rivers taller than this school. I've been rafting on a river with my cousins in Pittsburgh, up north. And I went with my cousin Peter, who is fourteen or fifteen. We were going down wicked fast. . . . We almost crashed and popped the raft. He had the big one tied to the little one." Timmy went on to read about fish jumping. Joey tuned back in to Timmy's story. Joey insisted, "But every fish hops out of the water—every fish is a hopping fish." Timmy disagreed. "Yes, they are. Trout is," Joey replied.

This episode illustrates the contrast between the oral versus the literate bent of these two children. For Timmy, the text is the authority. But Joey tends to move away from the text towards an oral account of personal experience, which for him wields more authority.

An earlier example of Joey's storying response, this one from the previous December, revealed much about Joey as a storyteller and language user. When classmate Alison asked what his favorite football team was, Joey did not respond with the standard "My favorite football team is . . . because . . . ." Rather, he responded by telling a story. In the following transcript, Joey's story is on the left, and thematic analysis is on the right.

1 My favorite team is the New York Jets.	ORIENTATION
2 I know one.	
3 Paul Fraze plays for the New York Jets.	
4 He's number 91.	
5 He grew up down by Witmer's candy.	
6 He lives in New York now.	COMPLICATING ACTION
7 I got his autograph. It says: "Dear Joey,	RESOLUTION
8 Paul Fraze, New York Jets,	
9 number 91."	
10 His father married my parents.	
11 (You know how they say, "Will you take this man to be your wedded, to love and to hold"?)	
12 Believe me, I've been in a wedding before.	EVALUATION

There are four standard components of a narrative in the literate style: orientation, complicating action, resolution, and evaluation. In lines 1–5, we learn who, what, when and where—the orientation. Line 6, "He lives in New York now," serves as the complicating action that separates Joey from his local hero. The resolution (lines 7–9) follows quickly, describing Joey's acquisition of Fraze's autograph. The autograph is the tangible connection between Joey and his favorite football star. Finally, although the last lines do not refer to Fraze explicitly, it can be inferred that Fraze's attendance at the wedding made the wedding superlative. "Believe me, I've been in a wedding before" functions as the evaluation. In other words, "What an experience it was to meet Paul Fraze at the wedding!"

According to Halliday (1985), repetition of nouns, pronouns, verbs, and ellipses create cohesion in a text. Hasan (1984) states that repetition of "functional information-via words having the same grammatic or syntactic function" lends more "cohesive harmony" to a text (Cox, Shanahan, & Sulzby, 1990). Although Joey does not repeat any of his verbs, he uses four verbs of existence: *'s, grew up,* and *lives;* six verbs of material action: *plays, got, married, will take, to love, to hold;* three verbs of mental action: *know* (twice) and *believe;* two verbs of oral action: *says* and *say;* and one stative verb: *is.* He makes consistent use of verbs and clusters of verb types that tighten the story text—for example, "I know one [of the New York Jets]," "take this man to be your wedded [husband]," and "Believe me [when I say] I've been in a wedding before." Joey thus makes his text connected and comprehensible.

The structure of Joey's oral story also involves tight parallelism. The text segments beginning "I know one" and "I got his autograph" are parallel, demonstrating the connection, the bond of familiarity between Joey and Paul Fraze. These two text segments act as stanzas. The stanzas match each other nearly identically, repeating a phrase of familiarity at the beginning of each stanza, repeating almost verbatim the phrase "Paul Fraze / New York Jets / number 91." Both stanzas conclude with a sentence in the past tense about Fraze. The sentences "He grew up down by Witmer's candy" and "His father married my parents" link Fraze, the subject, and Joey implicitly. (Witmer's is a candy store; Joey and his parents live in the same town as the store.)

Joey also uses sound play to hold his text together. "Favorite" and "Fraze," "Witmer's" (pronounced "Widmer's" by Joey) and "wedded" play on the ear with common sounds.

Joey also alternates tenses. Lines 1–4 are in the present tense. When he makes the connection between himself and Paul Fraze in line 5 he uses the past tense: "He grew up down by Witmer's candy." Then he jumps back to the present to reorient the listener in line 6—"He lives in New York now," anticipating the question "How he can play for a New York team and live in New Hampshire?" Joey maintains a present connection with a past action by stating, "I got his autograph," in line 7. The autograph, then, serves not only as the resolution to the complicating action, as the tangible connection to Paul Fraze, but becomes the link between past and present in Joey's text. Joey finishes the story with several present-tense appeals to the listener, lines 11 and 12.

Joey employs his keen sense of audience in this oral story. It is clear through all these parallels what it is that we as listeners are to infer: that sometime in the past, while Paul Fraze was growing up, his father and Joey's parents became acquainted. There is a unifying group concept, with a team at the beginning and a wedding party at the end. Joey the son meets Paul the son via an interaction between their fathers. Thus Joey has created a theme of bonds: local hero to hometown, local hero to hometown boy admirer, father to father, husband to wife, family to family, generation to generation. A chronology of human life is established in this story, childhood to maturation, with subplots of moving away, developing an identity, achieving success in one's vocation, returning home, and marrying.

Narratives of the mainstream literate tradition are considered "topic centered," while narratives of the oral tradition are "topic associating" (Michaels 1981). Joey's storytelling is in the oral style. His brief story is topic associative; it links anecdotes implicitly. He leaves it to his listener to infer that if Paul Fraze "grew up down by Witmer's," he is a local hero. He leaves it to us to infer that his parents are acquainted with Fraze's father and that he met Fraze at his parents' wedding and there received the autograph. Nowhere does Joey overtly state what sport Paul Fraze plays, or where Witmer's candy is located, assuming that his audience knows. He speaks to an intimate audience—people familiar with both the subject of the prompt for his story (Alison's query "What is your favorite football team?") and the local landmarks.

The ending of Joey's story is interesting for several reasons. The last two lines overtly invite the audience into the story. Though Joey has tacitly included the intimate listener up to this point through his "I" narration, with his last lines ("You know . . . " and "Believe me . . . ") he demands engagement. He does not explain who the generic "they" is who say "Will you take this man. . . . " He expects his audience to know that information. The line "Believe me, I've been in a wedding before" does not neatly wrap up his story by hearkening back to his beginning, but rather serves as a sort of punch line from which we can infer several things: Fraze's attendance at the wedding made the wedding superlative; Joey has still more stories to tell about that wedding; and we can only speculate as to what those other stories are, which is part of the fun of Joey's present story. This open ending is characteristic of the oral style.

A portfolio displaying a child like Joey as a literate person should include at least one taped oral story per month. That way the young, nonmainstream child's oral discourse can be examined for its inherent complexity, the child's oral and written language can be compared, and consistency among the discourse patterns can be seen. The "story" may be the child's share time talk, pre-writing storying, or any other extended talk in which the child fashions a text out of his or her own imagination and life experience.

The oral story is Joey's primary mode of discourse. Through his oral facility, his writing can increasingly assimilate his speech, and his speech can move beyond its present bounds. In early literacy language acts like a slinky continually climbing over and beyond itself. If the strength of Joey's oral literacy is highlighted in his classroom, not only would Joey's self-esteem rise, but he and his peers would come to value the ability to tell stories, which is at the root of all they write.

Ethnographic data and linguistic analysis of texts are necessary to preserve some of the fleeting growth that occurs every time a child uses language. A child's portfolio should include a list of narrative components and devices as the child introduces or acquires them. The child should be included in this process of identification of new abilities and their inclusion in the portfolio. This list would ideally be accompanied by transcribed examples of the child's oral language, analyzed in much the same way as I have done with Joey's oral stories.

JOEY'S WRITING: THE MAGIC CAVE STORY

What happened when Joey was asked to write in school? As shown below, Joey's written story makes clear several facts of his literacy:

1. Joey's writing looks very much like talk on paper.
2. Joey uses similar devices in his written and oral language, thus "represent[ing] a continuum rather than a dichotomy between oral and written language" (Cox, Shanahan, and Sulzby 1990).
3. Context is highly embedded in both Joey's oral and written stories. He speaks to a "society of intimates" (Givon 1979).

Joey's text is social-interactional in its prompting and its execution. Thus, both his written and his oral texts reflect a concept of storying as fostering connectedness—stories binding people.

Two months after Joey told his Paul Fraze story, on a day in early February, Joey was sitting at the round conference table at the head of the classroom for silent writing time (which in Mrs. Manning's classroom is never silent—fortunately for Joey). Jimmy and Peter, Joey's best buddies, were sitting with him. Joey had nothing in his writing folder. Jimmy opened a conversation with the title of a story he was about to write, "The Spooky Cave Story." As he wrote, he said, "One day me, Joey, Jimmy, Geoff and Jody went for a walk." Peter chimed in, "Look, The Waterfall Adventure!" and began to write. The atmosphere was ripe for Joey to begin a piece. He wrote: "Me and AnD Peter FanD a car in a cav." I asked Jimmy where he had gotten the idea for his story. He replied, "I had 'The Creepy Crawly Cave.' It came from a video called *Never Ending Stories* [sic] and Jody's book I had [read], 'The Spooky Old Cave.' "

By the time silent writing time had ended, Joey had completed one page of text with a picture. Below I submit Joey's entire Magic Cave story. The first segment (lines 1–5) indicates the text produced in that first writing session; the second segment (lines 6–13) was done nearly two months later, at the end of March; the last line was added on May 1.

1 Me and Peter found a car in a cave.	ORIENTATION
2 It was a magic car.	
3 We found it in a secret cave.	
4 It was a old, old car.	
5 It was our great-great-great-great-granddad's.	
6 We looked for the keys.	COMPLICATING ACTION
7 "Peter, over here."	
8 I pulled a rock out of the cave.	
9 Right there was the keys.	
10 Brm.	
11 It started right up.	RESOLUTION
12 We brought it home to show our mom.	
13 She said, (to be continued)	
14 "What in the walrus is that?"	EVALUATION

Nearly two months after starting this story, on March 29, Joey emptied out his writing folder before me, looking for something to write about. I asked if there was anything in his folder he wanted to "work on." He retrieved his Magic Cave story.

Joey: I gotta work on this one because it's old and I wanna fix it up. [*He reads the cave story aloud, adding an s to "wa" to clarify the word was. Then he begins a continuation of the story on a new sheet of paper. He writes, "We lookt."*] No, that's -ed, right?

Cindy: How did you know that?

Joey: 'Cause I'm smart. My grandfather had a blood clot in his brain. He knows more things now 'cause they fixed him. [*He goes back to his written text.*] Peter and me are brothers. [*Writes, "We looked for the keys."*] I can get more work done out here 'cause it's quiet. Over...how do you spell *over*? O-v-r? No. O-v-e-r-e?

Cindy: "Drop the last *e* and you'll have it.

Joey: Here. How do you spell *here*? H-e-r?

Cindy: One more letter.

Joey: A?

Cindy: How about silent *e*?

Joey: Our grandfather left it [the car] there for us—a mystery for us to do, me and Peter. It was a whole bunch of miles from my house. [*He then attempts to spell the word pulled.*] P-o-u-l-l-d—that's ed. [*He writes "poled."*]

At this point, several of Joey's buddies walked by as they returned from the library. "Boo!" one boy said. Joey was so intent on his writing that he didn't even look up.

Joey: "Show our mom." [*Writes, "Sh are mom."*] How do you spell *said?* S-i-d-a?
Cindy: Those are the letters, but in a different order.
Joey: [*immediately responding*]: S-a-i-d.
Cindy: Do you realize you are spelling differently?
Joey: Yeah, my brain is different, just like my grandfather's is.

Through my observations of Joey engaged in writing this year I can see that his Magic Cave story demonstrates significant growth. For one thing, this was the first piece of writing Joey had come back to all year. In addition, it was the first time all year he engaged totally in writing. Obviously, he gained much from the peer discussion that prompted this topic and wanted to join in the group activity. Also, this one piece of writing reflects some of the first self-corrections in spelling that Joey made this year.

Several features of Joey's written story situate it in the oral style. Joey speaks the words as he writes or attempts to write them; clearly, he sees writing as "speech written down," as Moffett (1968) and Britton (1975) describe early writing. Also, in contrast to the literate style of embedding additional information in relative clauses (Michaels and Collins 1984), in the first portion of his story Joey uses independent clauses to elaborate on the subject nouns *car* and *cave.* Linguist James Gee saw in the oral text of a young black child that "movement forward narratively is always done by holding a good bit of the structure and content constant" (Gee 1989a, 79). Joey builds the reader's knowledge of the subject while adhering to a tight parallel structure. The first portion of his text, written in February, is repetitive in something of an ababaa form. Lines 1, 2 and 4 elaborate on the car—found a car, it was a magic car, was a old, old car, was our great granddad's car. Lines 1 and 3 focus on the cave—in a cave, in a secret cave.

In the two different parts of his story—the February composition and the March—Joey has joined two linguistic styles, poetic and prosaic. (Gee 1989a). The February portion is poetic; it follows a parallel line and stanza structure. The March portion is not in parallel form. It bears some lexical links through the repetition of *keys* and *right*, but its form is more that of a paragraph than a stanza. Thus, it is more a school-based, essay style.

A second feature common to oral style is the preponderance of verbal complements (prepositional phrases) as opposed to nominal complements. (Michaels and Collins 1984). Joey's text is verb laden, and these verbs are often complemented with prepositional phrases: "found [a car] in a cave," "looked for the keys," "pulled a rock out of the cave," "brought it home to show our mom."

In terms of cohesive harmony there is striking parity in Joey's use of verb types and ellipsis in his written story and oral story about Fraze. The written text includes six verbs of material action with one repeated; four verbs of existence; and one verb of oral action. His oral text included five verbs of material action, three verbs of existence, two oral action verbs and two others.

In his story, Joey has chosen the past tense, with exception of one line of dialogue, which jars the reader into the present: "Peter, over here." Joey's tense choice is consistent with Langer's (1986) finding that eight-year-old writers tend to situate narratives in the past and exposition in the present tense. The past tense for his written story diverges from his mainly present tense oral text.

In the February segment, Joey has given the reader a spatial orientation and introduced the two main characters. As he remarked in his conversation with me, he and Peter are brothers in the story. Hence from the very beginning, Joey's story is fiction. Though Joey himself is a character in the story, it is a fictionalized version of himself, which serves to distance Joey from his audience. Yet his audience has not been fictionalized. He is assuming a "society of intimates" (Givon 1979) as his listening/reading audience in the opening "Me and Peter." The assumption is that the reader knows who "Me and Peter" are. Offering no temporal orientation in either his oral or written story, Joey has, however, chosen words that create a fantastical ambience with temporal cues in the Magic Cave story. The cave was "secret" and the car, "magic." The car was "old old," and belonged to a "great great great great granddad."

Joey wrote the February text during one writing session of approximately twenty minutes. The complicating action of his story was not written until late March, when Joey began his segment with "We looked for the keys." Joey re-entered his text by reading what he had written. As noted earlier, this second segment varies linguistically from the first. The difference may be attributed to a perceived difference in task. In his second writing session Joey had a text with which to interact. This interaction with an evolving text can be likened to a conversation with one's "other self" (Murray 1986) and could be seen as more akin to an oral telling than a writing session. The difference in text segments may derive from Joey's increasing awareness of the conventions of the essayist style or a broadening of his range of storying through increased awareness of TV and peer story strategies. The frequency of writing in

Joey's classroom clearly had the effect of enhancing and expanding Joey's storying.

That Joey could immediately re-enter his earlier text and link back episodically implies an understanding of his ability to do so. The "to be continued" at the end of his March text is a clear signal both that Joey can make that kind of link and that he knows he can.

The second portion of Joey's narrative has more of a sense of urgency and moves at a faster pace, like a TV serial episode. In it, he is directly communicating with the audience. He assumes that the reader carried all necessary information over from the previous segment—characters, setting, and plot. This segment differs lexically, syntactically, and structurally from the February one. Nearly every sentence begins with a different subject. Joey varies his sentence structure and alternates constructions. I recall in watching Joey that he worked less methodically on this second text segment than on the first. He was writing quickly, trying to capture the action as it unfolded in his head, anxiously demanding spell checks to avoid barriers to his storying. His preoccupation with standard orthography signifies the level of risk taking he was engaged in.

In this March segment, Joey used a device he had used in his earliest piece of writing in second grade: the sound effect. In September Joey had eked out a text about race cars, using few words other than sound effects. In March, Joey showed command of a wider repertoire of story devices: in addition to a sound effect, he used a line of dialogue.

After the March writing session Joey returned to his Magic Cave story twice, once to add the mother's reaction, "What in the walrus is that?" I inquired about the use of the word *walrus*. Joey explained, "I was looking for a word. I was looking for *world* in the dictionary, but I found *walrus*. I like walruses. I think they're awesome . . . but it was an accident." The fact that he chose to put *walrus* in place of *world* implies that he liked its effect in his text. He obviously felt it was consistent with the fantastical quality of the story. Weeks later Joey read the story to me and added "He laft a note." to the end of the February segment. He had realized the need for a connecting device to link the "great-great-great-great-granddad" and the boys' search.

The evolution of Joey's Magic Cave story showed me the dynamic nature of a child's writing process. This story was a task that Joey reopened several times, each time demonstrating tremendous growth. I saw him pushing the bounds of his storying abilities with each return. The fragments, slight changes, corrected spellings, inserted lines, and Joey's talk hold equal weight for me as an observer of his moment-to-moment development as storyteller, writer, thinker.

CONCLUSION

When Joey began second grade, his entering abilities in reading and writing tabbed him for school failure in a traditional classroom. Joey spent his mornings talking incessantly, orchestrating miniconferences, and looking at four-wheeler magazines. Fortunately Joey was in a process-oriented classroom, where he was free to write and read what he liked. His teacher had serious concerns about his reading deficiencies and was frustrated by his seeming lack of productivity during writing time. He was always talking, or working on some collaborative project in which he did little or no writing. Joey's talking usually got him in trouble. By March he had produced just ten pieces of writing. None was longer than a page. He had finished only two.

In April I spread all of Joey's writings before him—an impressive collection, to Joey. He smiled at the unfinished hieroglyphic scripts lifted from a disheveled writing folder. "Wow, I wrote all that!" he remarked. I asked Joey to pick out his best piece, his next best piece, and so on. His ranking system was interesting. Those pieces I considered Joey's best by standards based on his writing development—completeness, length, expression—Joey ranked lowest. For only one piece of writing he had selected as good was he able to explain why. A note he had taped to his pencil box was good, he said, because it was "funny."

note

That is a judgment of sorts. However, Joey is seven years old and is nearing the end of his second-grade year. What is more, Joey is a very verbal child. Yet Joey in traditional school settings would be labeled an emotionally disabled child. He has very poor self-esteem, despite his brassy, bold air. In examining a year's worth of observational notes I looked for signs of self-declarations of learning. I thought such verbalizations would demonstrate that Joey can evaluate his own learning. The only one I found was "Flunk and failure," a comment he made about himself when he was reprimanded for using foul language. I do believe, however, that Joey's behavior and his talk—what he does *and* does not say—tell much about how he values and devalues himself as a person, as a student, as a writer.

Though metacognitive information may not be on the tip of Joey's tongue when asked explicit questions regarding his thinking, writing, and the like, his behavior indicates that if unimpeded he knows what he needs as a writer and how to get it. The primary example is my observation of Joey asserting himself as a storyteller. I know that on some level he is aware of his prowess in this area.

How can we respect the integrity of the self-knowledge children demonstrate to us and somehow build into our educational system some receptivity to their literacies? Literacy is messy. It is individual and idiosyncratic. Portfolios allow us to be receptive to the children who come to us as they are. Our job is not to make them into people other than themselves. Our job is to take Joey as he is, show Joey who he is in his finest light, and then perhaps offer him the opportunity to expand who Joey may become.

A portfolio that portrays Joey's sophisticated literacy of necessity should include such complementary materials as I have shared here: ethnographic notes, anecdotal records, tapes and transcripts of conversations, share time talk, self-monitoring talk while writing, conferences and collaborations, and linguistic and thematic analyses of written and oral stories. Looking at both written and oral stories gives a rich picture of the child as a language user. With written texts, context is crucial: time of day, duration of work, how the work was initiated or prompted, who was writing what alongside this child, samples of the conversation that occurred during the writing, what support the child asked for and received during the writing, how fluently the child engaged in the writing of the particular piece.

A developmental approach to the portfolio has the potential of preserving the dynamic quality of learning. Anecdotal records readjust the teacher's vision of who and where the student is and sharpens teachers' insight into how each student travels along his or her own path to learning. Only when we look as if with a magnifying glass can we see and hear individual and idiosyncratic child-based standards of growth, accomplishment, and failure. If each child is seen as traveling a unique road, the perception of who the child is can be revealed to the teacher rather than imposed by the teacher.

I firmly believe that children are experts on their own learning. However, it is my experience that some children do not as readily articulate responses to explicit questioning of their writing process or thought patterns. Human beings, adults and children alike, can generally do a thing before they can talk about the doing. With young children, the bounds of their emergent language make it even harder for them to articulate what they can do. Children from nontraditional homes, who are not socialized into the school-based literacy patterns of book talk (which precede portfolio talk) also have difficulty responding to explicit questions about their learning.

None of these children are cognitively deficient; all can produce writing and grow as writers. And portfolios can be the best showcase of these students' learning and growth. But the questions we ask may be problematic. There is the risk of questions about the portfolio becoming formulaic and the responses contrived, and this may lead to more teacher expectations of better answers, better learning, more growth, and so on. "What is your best piece?" is a question most children can answer with reasonable facility. "Why?" is more difficult. "Which piece shows your learning?" Metacognitive questions are founded on school-based literacy. In evaluating the writing of young and nonmainstream children, we are assessing the rate of their reacculturation from home-based literacy to school literacy. Unfortunately, as James Gee writes, "schools as currently constituted tend to be good places to practice mainstream literacy once you have its foundations, but they are not good places to acquire those foundations" (Gee 1989a, 58).

If a portfolio is to serve both student and teacher, it can best be conceived as the ongoing creation of a conceptual framework for the learning and growth of each individual child. The contents of a portfolio, then, must encompass a larger vision. This means that all structures to portfolios must be designed to include such contents as: tape recordings, transcripts of oral narratives, artwork, and artifacts collected from both home and school.

13

ONE BILINGUAL CHILD TALKS ABOUT HIS PORTFOLIO

DAN-LING FU

I am an educator from the People's Republic of China studying for a PhD in Reading and Writing at the University of New Hampshire. I am interested in how people learn to read and write. I was surprised to find that a study of my son's use of portfolios was one of my best sources for learning about the power of literacy and how we might benefit from what children know in all schools, whether in China or the United States.

My son, Xiao-di, is almost eight years old. He joined me in the United States ten months ago and entered Oyster River Elementary School. He had had about one year of school in China and was a good reader and writer in Chinese for his age. He began his American school experience as a "speaker with limited English proficiency." Most of his English was learned the summer before he entered school. Now, seven months later, his teacher says, "he is a second-grade reader and writer like the others in the class."

When I first heard about portfolio assessment, I was fascinated by the idea and decided to do a study. The reason that I chose Xiao-di as the subject for the study was not just out of personal interest, but also out of my uncertainty about children's ability to assess their own work.

Before I interviewed Xiao-di, I was not sure what I could learn because I thought that children at his age knew nothing but Teenage Mutant Ninja Turtles or some other amusing things they may have picked up from cartoons on TV. I thought that an interview about them as learners might be too serious a topic for them. For this reason, I chose

Xiao-di to study, because I knew that at least he was a prolific writer; he constantly wrote and drew at home. There would also be the advantage of my being close to him and the fact that I could acquire my information more casually.

After I contacted Xiao-di's teachers, we started to collect all his work done at school and home. Seven months later, I took my collection of the work Xiao-di had done at home to Xiao-di's classroom and ESL (English as a second language) teachers, who had their school collection ready. I asked them to choose from the two folders the work that would best represent Xiao-di as a reader and a writer, and also to explain to me the reasons for their choices. Then I brought the two folders home and asked Xiao-di to do the same thing.

There was a big difference in what Xiao-di and his teachers selected. The pieces chosen by the teachers were invariably those done at school, and they were mainly connected with verbal skills. The work chosen by Xiao-di covers a much wider range. He selected thirteen pieces of work: bilingual writings, a letter to a friend, a birthday card to his mom, a picture, two published books, some reading-response writings, and several stories. It represented work done at school and at home, finished and unfinished, and teacher-assigned and self-assigned.

I didn't expect to make any discoveries when Xiao-di started to select his work, but he surprised me. At first Xiao-di misunderstood my request and thought that I had asked him to choose the best single piece of work that represented him as a learner. He spread everything on the couch and rummaged through all of it for quite a while. Finally he let out a sigh and said to me, "This is hard. I can't do it." Though mentally I was well prepared for the fact that I might not get much data, I didn't expect failure so soon. Disappointed, I said, half to myself and half to him, "I should have known this." He continued, "I can't find the one piece that can represent me." I realized his misunderstanding and explained again what I wanted him to do: "Not just one. You can choose as many as you want as long as you think that those pieces show your growth as a reader and a writer in English." "Oh, I can do that. That's easy," he said, relieved. I began to learn.

I almost aborted this experiment because of my preconditioned judgment of Xiao-di's ability. I was chilled by this near accident. I learned from Xiao-di's frustration that a learner knows that only one piece of work cannot represent him or her as anything. Every piece can only be part of a person; many pieces together can better portray him or her as a complete being. That is why Xiao-di was unable to choose one piece that can best represent his growth as a learner: there is no one piece that can do it, no matter how good it appears to be. This incident demonstrated to me the significance and the value of the child's participation in portfolio selection.

Besides the difference between Xiao-di's and the teachers' selections for the portfolio, the differences between Xiao-di's own and others' assessment of his work are striking. (By *others'* I mean mine and his two teachers'.) Sitting in Xiao-di's second-grade classroom, I opened the two folders full of Xiao-di's work that his teachers and I had collected during the last several months, and I said to the second-grade teacher, "First, I'd like you to choose some pieces that you think best represent Xiao-di's growth as a writer, and then talk about them." I was not sure whether I had made my point clear enough when she spread out *all* the pieces from the folder she had collected and started to talk about them:

> This is all the work Xiao-di has done since last September. From all this, we can see the emerging of Xiao-di's growth in writing. He came to us already with a good sense of story. At first, it was just the problem of the language, so we let him do picture-label activities, then from words to sentences, without much help for a couple of months. . . . [At] Christmastime, he began to put down ideas as stories.

While talking to me, she showed me Xiao-di's work piece by piece chronologically from the beginning of the year to the present. In the end, she concluded:

> All this shows the process of Xiao-di's growth as a writer. In his writings, we can also see the skills developing.

When I went to the resource room to see Xiao-di's ESL teacher, I tried to make my request clear. Among the work Xiao-di did at school, the ESL teacher selected five pieces: two responses to the readings, two published stories, and some writing about animals. She started to talk about them.

On the two responeses to the reading:

> Here the writing shows that not only the language, he also understood the ideas. He showed that he could understand the humor and pick up the subtleties in the stories. . . . He had the concept of characters.

On the published stories:

> He has the sense of plot—put the thoughts together and come to a conclusion. His ideas flowed and had a good command of English language. In this story he used "more scared," "far away," "very soon," and "very, very soon," and some transitional words.

On the writing about animals:

> This shows that he could pick up some sentence patterns on his own, without me modeling, such as S-V-O [subject–verb–object] pattern, and some grammar like, "It eats."

The two teachers' responses show that each had her own standards for judging Xiao-di's writing. The classroom teacher looked at Xiao-di's learning as a process of language learning: from words to sentences, from ideas to stories. Looking at Xiao-di's schoolwork shows us both Xiao-di's growth in learning and the classroom teacher's curriculum.

The ESL teacher mentioned more specifically what Xiao-di knew and could do: his sense of story; his concept of character and plot; his command of language structure; his understanding of ideas, humor, and subtlety. Like the classroom teacher's, the ESL teacher's response shows what she was trying to do. The classroom teacher was more concerned about Xiao-di's development on a normal track of skills learning, while the ESL teacher tended to see how she was helping Xiao-di adapt to a new language and new culture. Both were pleased with Xiao-di's development, as it fit right into their plans.

Xiao-di's own assessment of his work had many insights that would be hard for others (teachers or parents) to gain. The first pieces he picked up were ones he did during the end of September and the beginning of October. About them he said:

> They are my early writings—the first time I learned to sound out words. Though they were all wrong, they were still good. That was my first try. And I wrote the Chinese words and drew pictures there too. If people couldn't understand my spellings, they could read Chinese and look at pictures. [See Figure 13–1.]

Xiao-di had a different idea from his teachers on how he learned to write. He didn't think that he started "words" first. Rather, he started to put down ideas when he first began to write. He selected these early pieces for his portfolio because, as he mentioned, he was proud of what he learned to do so early in his use of English. He shifted from writing characters from memory to spelling out words by sounding them out, a big step in his learning. He knew that he had learned something entirely new. At that point he felt he was really writing, not just spelling out words, because he wanted people to understand him. He was conscious that his sounded-out words could hardly be understood, so he added Chinese characters and drew pictures to help his audience. He was proud of what he could do.

Looking at his bilingual piece, I was first impressed by his neat handwriting, both in Chinese and English. Having had only one year of formal education in Chinese and less than a month of learning in English, Xiao-di showed his excellent skills in both Chinese character and English letter writing. Like his Chinese, his English letters are well balanced, each word is separated, and the sentences are grammatically correct. But Xiao-di himself didn't mention any of these features when talking about his work.

FIGURE 13–1 Xiao-di's Selection From September–October

After I compared his Chinese with English, I figured out why. To be able to write neat English letters, to separate each word in a sentence, and to write those sentences in correct grammar was nothing new to him; he had already mastered those skills when he learned to write in Chinese. (The Chinese sentences in Figure 13–1 have the exact sentence structure as the English ones: Subject–Verb–Object.) To Xiao-di, learning meant to take a risk, to try something he never knew before. In that piece, for the first time, he learned to sound out words and tried to spell them. He felt excited about his new language skill. Certainly his evaluation of his learning was more truthful than mine.

After he talked about those bilingual writings, he put them aside and picked up some other pieces. One was a card he had made in December, shown in Figure 13–2:

> This is the first card I made. I wrote some English words, which I sounded out. I like the heart with a candle on it. That was what I imagined. It looks great.

Another was a picture book he had done in January:

> This is a picture book I made for small kids, with pictures and a few words on each page. This book can help them to learn language.

FIGURE 13-2 Xiao-di's Card from December

Then there was a picture of a teddy bear, which he had drawn in November (Figure 13–3):

This is a picture I drew out of my head. I didn't copy anything. I mean I drew it without looking at anything. It is just like my own teddy bear. Look at the lips. I like them. I also like the tie, that makes him look great. The other pictures that I did out of my head were not as good as this one. This one is

FIGURE 13–3   Xiao-di's Teddy Bear from November

really like a real one, as if it looks at me with feelings. I wrote a few words there too. I just like to draw animals.

He picked out another piece from November, this one a letter:

This is the longest letter I sent to Joshua, and . . . the best one too. I like the picture going along with the letter. That is my favorite pumpkin. And I like trick-or-treat. It is fun. Almost all the words in the letter are spelled right.

Xiao-di's remarks about each piece of work show us that not only was he a content writer at the very beginning of his new language acquisition, but he also had his own way of judging what a piece of good work was. I had thought that in his picture book he was just labeling pictures, as he had one or two words on each page with each picture in it—for example, "little dog" with the picture of a dog. But from what Xiao-di said about it, I understood that he was not just picture labeling but was actually writing, communicating. He was making a book "for small kids . . . to learn language." He had a clearly defined purpose and audience for his writing. To write a book, or to write one with a specific audience in mind, was a new concept to him. Chinese culture holds that only real writers can write books; learners only write to practice writing skills. It is premature for people who are still learners to have an audience in mind. But after just a few months of learning to write in English, Xiao-di had acquired the Western concept of being a writer.

Just as with his earlier, bilingual writings, Xiao-di's standard of judging good writing with these later pieces is what he had learned to do that he had never tried before and had been unable to do. He values first tries (sounding out words, the birthday card); originality (the picture he did out of his head, and the part he imagined); expressions of what he really likes (his favorite animal, activity, things); and length and correct spelling (his letter to Joshua). Xiao-di selected his portfolio based on his own standards.

Before he talked with me about it, I was puzzled by some of the work he selected for his portfolio. For instance, at first I could not understand why he chose the teddy bear picture. I thought there were many other drawings he'd done that looked far better than this one. After he talked about it, I not only understood the difference between the one he chose and his other work, but also realized that when we judge a piece of work only by the result, or by how it looks to us, we might miss the real quality of the work: what means the most to its producer.

When Xiao-di talked about the selections from his later writing, I understood even more. He was more serious about the later selections, which consist of a draft of a story he wrote on the computer at home, two published stories, a draft book of writing, a reading journal, and writings about animals. Following my request, before he talked about them, he put them in order from the one he liked best to the one he liked least:

1. The story "A dog and his frend."
2. Two published stories.
3. The draft book of writing.
4. The reading journal.
5. The writing about animals.

I was surprised both by his choice and by the order he arranged. I didn't expect that he would select the draft book for the portfolio. I never thought that he would select a draft of his writing as the best of the five rather than the two published stories. But after I heard Xiao-di talk about his selections, I was reassured about his sense of what good work was, and that this was consistent with what he had said about his other works.

This is why Xiao-di was most proud of the story "A dog and his frend":

It is long, longest story I ever wrote, and longer than some other kids' stories in the class. I like the title and words I used in the story. I also like the ending. It's a happy ending, and funny too. This is the first story I did on the computer. I was proud of myself. I really like it.

I asked him if he thought that this story was better even than the two published books, and he replied:

Yeah, because it is longer than them, the words are better. It has three characters. If you have more characters, your story can be long. And the title is better than those stories too.

I remember how excited he was after he wrote this story at home. He showed it to all his friends who happened to visit him that day and took it to the school the next day to show it to his teachers. But compared with the two bound and published stories, this one is still a draft, without any illustrations, printed on a piece of shabby computer paper. That is the reason I didn't expect he would choose this piece as the best. Clearly, Xiao-di, the producer, knows the real quality of his work; I am more attracted to his finished products.

What he had to say about his two published books is very interesting:

Other kids in the class published stories, and I can do the same. I am Chinese and can publish stories like them, I am very, very happy about it and very proud of myself. Some kids published one, some two, some five, six, and even ten, but I only got two. That is okay. My stories are long, longer than some of the kids', and my pictures are great. . . . Some kids asked me a question about the bear and shark story. They asked me how the bear could kill the shark when he was already in the shark's mouth. I want to revise that part, though it is already a published one.

This teddy bear story is my first published story. When I saw it on my desk that morning, I was so excited that I jumped and jumped as I could do just like the others!

With these two stories, Xiao-di stressed the publishing more than the quality of the writing. It shows that he can "do just like the others" and gives him a sense of belonging—membership in the American community. We all know that to be able to do things "just like the others" is a motivation, a common standard for learners of all ages. The most exciting thing I learned from Xiao-di's talk is that he did not take a published story as a finished product. He could consider his peers' advice about a published story and want to revise and make it better. This quality is more significant than the mechanical skills in learning to be a writer, I believe. It is a big step in his learning. In China, students, especially at Xiao-di's age, are never encouraged to share their writing with their peers. They take advice only from teachers, the authorities.

I would never have found this sophistication in him as a writer if I had judged his ability only by his products and had not listened to him talking about his work.

Xiao-di's insight about his own work came up again when he talked about his draft book. Both the teachers and I had excluded this from his portfolio, but he had chosen it to be included. The first draft that Xiao-di talked about from the book was a story called "The Monster in My Hous:"

> I like this dream story a lot, though I didn't choose it to publish. I want to work on this more and get it published too. The reason I wrote it as a dream was that I wanted to write a ghost story, but I wanted to make it true to life. So I wrote it in a dream. The reason I didn't choose this one but the teddy bear story to publish was because the teddy bear one was an adventure story. Actually when the teacher asked me to choose one of them, I had a tough time to make the choice, as I like both of them. It was just because the teddy bear one was an adventure, more exciting. I liked it better.

Obviously, this draft meant a lot to Xiao-di, but to both the teachers and me, it was just a draft that he failed to choose. Listening to his talk about this piece, I understood not only his standard for publication and his thinking strategies in making it a dream story, but also his affection for the work, his feeling guilty for his having to give it up at the time, and his plan to work on it more and "get it published too."

As the last part of the dream story happened to be on the same page as the first paragraph of the following story, called "My Friends," he went on to talk about it.

> I don't like this story at all and don't want to publish it. I can't write personal narrative. I don't know how to revise it. I just can't do it. I wish I would have written a fairy tale instead. I like to write fantasy better than personal experience. But I want to try this kind of writing later.

I am glad that, purely by chance, I could hear him talking about a truly abandoned piece. In writing a personal narrative, he was frustrated. But by trying it, he found out what he could do better and what he could not do well. I am glad to know that he did not give up the genre entirely, but just put it off for now.

Number four in his order was his reading journal. From this, he chose two of his responses to readings:

> I like my writing about reading the story "Pig and Blue Flag." It's long and good. I mentioned my favorite part. At first I thought I did a bad job. I tried to write long, but the teacher said I didn't have to and just wrote down the main points.

> I also like my writing about reading "Grownups Are Funny." At first I got the wrong main points. Then I thought that the main point should have something to do with the title, so I summarized the reading with "grownups are funny."

The ESL teacher had also selected his writing response to "Grownups Are Funny" in the portfolio and talked about it. She chose this piece as a reflection of growth in Xiao-di's concept of character, his ability to summarize main points, and his understanding of humor and subtlety. But to Xiao-di, this piece of writing reflects mainly a search for what his teacher wanted or what a reading response should be. Different from the other writings he talked about, this piece of writing seemed more for the teacher than for himself.

The writing he liked the least among his later portfolio selections was the writing about animals.

> They are my first writings, most are short, and some are long, like this chipmunk one. They are not stories but reports of animals. Stories should have characters. If you have more characters, you can write long stories. I like to write that kind of stories. I like to write stories with lots of characters in them. I don't like the writing here that much. I repeated a lot, as in this one: I mentioned "rabbit, rabbit" all the time. It is boring. The sentences are the same and the words are the same too.

By listening to his talk here, we can tell that Xiao-di has developed as a fiction writer. He cannot stand plain, reportlike writing any more. As his teacher said about him, he has a good sense of story, a concept of character and plot. He enjoys writing fiction more than nonfiction.

When I had looked at his writing about animals, I couldn't understand why he didn't like it. Afterall, he had been so excited about his bilingual writing (as was shown in Figure 13–1). He expressed his reasons: it was his early writing, it was short, it was report style, and it had a lot of repetition in sentence structure and words. But his bilingual writing shows the same features. That is also his early writing, it is also nonfiction, it is short, and it uses repetitive sentence structure and words. Why does the bilingual piece mean so much to him, while his animal writing strikes him as boring?

Later on I found out that the reading response and the animal writings he numbered as his least-liked writings were mainly assigned-topic work. I realized why he was bored by them. According to his standard of good writing, there was not much space for his imagination, creativity, or originality, which meant most to him. From his talk about those pieces we can see there was not much Xiao-di in them; in these pieces he was trying to make his writing fit what the teachers expected it to be. In contrast, he did the bilingual writing all by himself. When he saw that everybody in the class was writing, he started to try himself. He worked out his own strategies for being understood in writing: Chinese, English, and pictures. He wrote what he wanted to say and learned to spell out words he did not know how to write. Certainly he saw more evolutionary qualities in his bilingual writing and gave himself more credit there as a learner than the pieces he did for the teacher in the class.

Behind every piece of his writing, Xiao-di has a story that others can hardly tell just from looking at the products themselves. After talking with Xiao-di, I reread his work with a new perspective. Every piece to me became more meaningful and richer. Looking at his work with his words ringing in my ears, I thought about how much I had missed as a mother and a teacher. I had been a teacher for many years, but I had never thought of asking my students to select work for their own portfolios and evaluate that work. I always believed that I was the one who could or should evaluate their work. Now I realized that my selection and evaluation would only show my own standards and requirements, or it would show my work as a teacher. It would not show their work as learners.

Xiao-di's self-assessment shows that he knows when he has really learned and when he has not. He knows what he cannot do, what he has learned to do, and what he wants to improve. He has a sense of his past, his present, and his future. When others assess his work, no matter from what perspective, they would miss the perspective that Xiao-di sees himself as a learner. As Linda Rief discovered from her students' self-evaluation, "They [her students] thoughtfully and honestly evaluated their own learning with far more detail and introspection than I thought possible" (1990, 26). Learners know best their own zone of proximal development (Vygotsky 1982).

In my ninety-minute interview with Xiao-di about his writing portfolio, I learned more about children, about learners, and about the significance of portfolio assessment than I did by being both a mother and a teacher for many years and a graduate student for four years. It is Xiao-di and his writing portfolio that made me realize that one single piece of work, no matter how good it appears to be, cannot represent a learner. Every piece is only part of a person; many pieces put together can portray the complete person.

By comparing and contrasting what Xiao-di and his teachers said, I have found that self-assessment reveals different standards learners may have from their teachers for evaluating themselves as learners and for setting goals for their own improvement in study. Xiao-di's talk about his own work not only convinced me that learners can have more control of their own learning if they can be included in the evaluation of their learning, but also taught me that we, teachers and parents, will understand our children better if we are willing to listen to what they say about themselves instead of judging them by our own standards of what we want them to be. For years we have evaluated students passively and never allowed them to be part of the assessment themselves. They accept and believe what they are told. They do what they are told to do in their learning. But when they don't control their learning, they don't understand themselves as learners. We, teachers and parents, tend to believe, too, that we know them better than they do. Xiao-di's talk about his writing told me that this is just not true. Learners know themselves better than anybody else knows them. They know what they are doing, what they want to do next, and what means most to them in their learning.

Xiao-di's self-selection of his portfolio represents the best of who he is and what he can do. He is a writer, a reader, an artist, and a loving son. He loves animals and small children and has many friends. He can use a computer and "do just like the others." He enjoys learning. His self-selected portfolio represents him as a whole person.

Clearly, learners know themselves better than anybody else. If we teachers include them as participants in the evaluation of their own learning, not only will they gain more control of their own study and development, but also we will have a better understanding of them as learners and as people. Learner-centered assessment should be considered a necessary part of student-centered instruction. Based on what our students say about their own learning and what they want to achieve, we ought to work out a curriculum that best meets their needs and connects their learning with their lives.

NOTES ON CONTRIBUTORS

ELIZABETH CHISERI-STRATER is assistant professor of English at the University of Illinois, Chicago, Illinois. She is a graduate of the Ph.D. program in Reading and Writing Instruction at the University of New Hampshire. She is author of *Academic Literacies: The Public and Private Discourse of University Students* (Boynton-Cook, 1991) as well as chapters and articles in books and journals about composition and education.

DAN-LING FU is assistant professor of English at Nanjing University in the People's Republic of China and a doctoral candidate at the University of New Hampshire, Durham, New Hampshire. She has written in English for *Language Arts,* as well as for various publications in China.

DONALD H. GRAVES is professor of Education at the University of New Hampshire, Durham, New Hampshire. He has received numerous awards for his research in composition. He speaks internationally and is the author of an array of books and articles about teaching and writing, the latest of which is *Explore Poetry,* the fifth in the *Reading/Writing Teacher's Companion* series (Heinemann, 1992).

JANE HANSEN is professor of Education at the University of New Hampshire, Durham, New Hampshire, and director of the Writing Lab. She has worked with language arts teachers around the world, authored *When Writers Read* (Heinemann, 1987), co-edited *Breaking Ground* (Heinemann, 1985), and published articles and chapters in many books and professional journals.

CINDY MATTHEWS is a researcher, instructor, and doctoral candidate at the University of New Hampshire, Durham, New Hampshire. Her background includes both teaching and research with young children in traditional urban classrooms and Montessori schools.

MARK MILLIKEN teaches fifth grade in Stratham, New Hampshire, and is an instructor in the New Hampshire Summer Writing Program. His chapter in this book is reprinted from *Workshop 3* edited by Nancie Atwell. (Heinemann, 1991).

LINDA RIEF teaches seventh- and eighth-grade Language Arts in Durham, New Hampshire, and is an instructor in the New Hampshire Summer Writing Program. Her new book, *Seeking Diversity: Language Arts with Adolescents* (Heinemann, 1992), from which her chapter is taken, offers more details about her own classroom.

TOM ROMANO is assistant professor of English at Utah State University in Logan, Utah, and a graduate of the Ph.D. program in Reading and Writing Instruction at the University of New Hampshire, Durham, New Hampshire, and teaches in the New Hampshire Summer Writing Program. His book, *Clearing the Way,* (Heinemann, 1987) describes writing in the Ohio high school in which he taught for many years.

F. DAN SEGER teaches middle school in Boulder Valley, Colorado, where he consults widely in language arts instruction and teaches in the Colorado Writing Project. He is also a doctoral candidate at the University of New Hampshire, Durham, New Hampshire.

JAY SIMMONS has consulted in portfolio assessment across the country, and has published several related articles. He is a graduate of the Ph.D. program in Reading and Writing Instruction at the University of New Hampshire, Durham, New Hampshire. He has taught at all levels, elementary through college, and currently teaches third grade in Madbury, New Hampshire.

BONNIE S. SUNSTEIN is assistant professor of English Education at the University of Iowa, in Iowa City, and a graduate of the Ph.D. program in Reading and Writing Instruction at the University of New Hampshire, Durham, New Hampshire. She has taught in secondary schools and colleges throughout New England, including the New Hampshire Summer Writing Program. She consults widely and has published many journal articles and book chapters.

MARGARET M. VOSS is an instructor and doctoral candidate at the University of New Hampshire, Durham, New Hampshire. A classroom teacher and writing specialist, she has published articles in various regional journals as well as *Language Arts.* She currently works as an educational consultant.

REFERENCES AND
SELECTED BIBLIOGRAPHY

Airasian, P. 1988. Measurement driven instruction: A closer look. *Educational Measurement: Issues and Practice* 7(4):6–11.

Allis, S. 1991. Testing, testing, testing. *Time Magazine*, July 15, 2–63.

Anson, C. M., R. L. Brown, Jr., and L. Bridwell-Bowles. 1989. "Portfolio assessment across the curriculum: Early conflicts." In K. Greenburg and G. Slaughter, eds., *Notes from the National Testing Network in Writing*. Vol. 3 of a University of Minnesota document. Bloomington, IN: ERIC Clearinghouse on Reading and Communication Skills (ED 301 888).

Applebee, A., J. Langer, and I. Mullis. 1989. *Understanding direct writing assessments.* Princeton, NJ: Educational Testing Service.

Aristotle. 1984. *The rhetoric and poetics of Aristotle.* New York: Modern Library.

Arizona looks at a new assessment. 1989. *Centerspace* 4(2):1.

Atwell, N. 1987. *In the middle: Writing, reading, and learning with adolescents.* Portsmouth, NH: Boynton/Cook.

Au, K., J. Scheu, A. Kawakami, and P. Herman. 1990. Assessment and accountability in a whole literacy curriculum. *The Reading Teacher* 43(8):574–78.

Bannister, S. 1988. Preparing and assessing portfolios in east central colleges: The professor's perspective. Heidelberg College, Tiffin, Ohio. Typescript.

Beers, S. 1985. Use of a portfolio writing assignment in a course on developmental psychology. *Teaching of Psychology* 12(2):94–96.

Belanoff, P., and M. Dickson, eds. 1991. *Portfolios: Process and product.* Portsmouth, NH: Boynton/Cook.

Benedict, S. 1989. Looking at their own words: Students' assessment of their own writing. Typescript.

Berger, S., M. L. Dertouzos, R. K. Lester, R. M. Solow, and L. C. Thurow. 1989. Toward a new industrial America. *Scientific American* 260(6):39–47.

Bourque, J., et al. 1983. Portfolio and presentation of self. In *Curriculum development in craft sewing as a vocation: Final report.* Kirkland, WA: Lake Washington Vocational Technical Institute.

Boy, A. V. 1990. "The reflective process." In A. V. Boy and G. J. Pine, *A person-centered foundation for counseling and psychotherapy,* 23–54. Springfield, IL: Charles C. Thomas.

Brandt, R., ed. 1990. *Educational Leadership* 47(8) (entire issue).

———. 1988. On assessment in the arts: A conversation with Howard Gardner. *Educational Leadership* 45(4):30–34.

Britton J., T. Burgess, N. Martin, A. McLeod, and H. Rosen. 1975. *The development of writing abilities, 11–18.* London: Macmillan.

Broadfoot, P. 1988. Profiles and records of achievement: A real alternative. *Educational Psychology* 8(4):291–97.

Brown, R. 1991. *Schools of thought: How the politics of literacy shape thinking in the classroom.* San Francisco: Jossey-Bass.

———. 1989. Testing and thoughtfulness. *Educational Leadership* 46(9):31–33.

———. 1987a. Literacy and accountability. *The Journal of State Government* 60(2):68–72.

———. 1987b. Who is accountable for "thoughtfulness"? *Phi Delta Kappan,* September, 49–52.

Budnick, D., and S. Beaver. 1984. A student perspective on the portfolio. *Nursing Outlook* 34(5):268–69.

Burnham, C. 1986. "Portfolio evaluation: Room to breathe and grow." In C. W. Bridges, ed., *Training the new teacher of college composition.* Bloomington, IN: ERIC Clearinghouse on Reading and Communication Skills (ED 264 589).

Business Council for Effective Literacy. 1990. Standardized tests: Their use and misuse. *BCEL Newsletter for the Business Community* 22(1):2–3.

Calkins, L. 1986. *The art of teaching writing.* Portsmouth, NH: Heinemann.

Camp, R. 1983. The ETS writing portfolio: A new kind of assessment. Typescript.

Carter, F. 1976. *The education of Little Tree.* Albuquerque: University of New Mexico Press.

Carter, M., and R. Tierney. 1988. Reading and writing growth: Using portfolios in assessment. Paper presented at the National Reading Conference, Tucson, Arizona.

Clay, M. 1985. *The early detection of reading difficulties.* 3rd ed. Portsmouth, NH: Heinemann.

Cohen, M. 1990. Test questions: A subject for the nineties. *The Boston Sunday Globe,* December 2, A33, A42.

Collins, J. and S. Michaels. 1986. "Speaking and Writing: Discourse Strategies and the Aquisition of Literacy." In J. Cook-Gumperz, ed., *The social construction of literacy.* New York: Cambridge University Press.

Connors, R., and A. Lunsford. 1988. Frequency of formal errors in current college writing or: Ma and Pa Kettle do research. *College English* 39(4):395–409.

Cooper, W., and J. Davies, eds. 1990. *Portfolio news.* Encinitas, CA: Portfolio Assessment Clearing House.

Corey, M. S., and G. Corey. 1987. Groups: Process and practice. 3rd ed. Pacific Grove, CA: Brooks/Cole.

Cormier, R. 1974. *The chocolate war.* New York: Dell.

———. 1985. *Beyond the chocolate war.* New York: Dell.

Costa, A. L. 1989. "Re-assessing assessment." *Educational Leadership* 46(9): 35–37.

Cox, B., T. Shanahan, and E. Sulzby. 1990. Good and poor elementary readers' use of cohesion in writing. *Reading Research Quarterly* 25(1):47–65.

Crowhurst, M., and G. L. Piche. 1979. Audience and mode of discourse effects on syntactic complexity in writing at two grade levels. *Research in the Teaching of English* 13:101–9.

Csikszentmihalyi, M. 1990. *Flow: The psychology of optimal experience.* New York: Harper and Row.

Cuban, L. 1988. Constancy and change in schools (1880s to the present). In P. Jackson, ed., *Contributing to educational change: Perspectives on research and practice.* Berkeley, CA: McCutchan.

Degavarian, D. A. 1989. *Portfolio assessment.* Bloomington, IN: ERIC Clearinghouse on Reading and Communication Skills (ED 306 894).

Dewey, J. 1938. *Experience and education.* New York: Collier, Macmillan.

———. 1934. *Art as experience.* New York: Perigree, G. Putnam's Sons.

———. 1916. *Democracy and education.* New York: Collier, Macmillan.

Diedrich, P. 1974. *Measuring growth in English.* Urbana, IL: National Council of Teachers of English.

Dillon, D., ed. 1990. "Evaluation of language and learning." *Language Arts* 67(3) (entire issue).

Eisner, E. 1990a. Synopsis of "Winning race not a valid goal, ASCD Told." *ASCD update* 32(4):1–3.

———. 1990b. Keynote speech presented at the Alternate Assessment Conference (Concord, NH, schools and the NH Department of Education), Merrimack, New Hampshire.

———. 1982. *Cognition and curriculum: A basis for deciding what to teach.* New York: Longman.

Elbow, P., and P. Belanoff. 1986. Portfolios as a substitute for proficiency examinations. *College Composition and Communication* 37(3):336–39.

Emig, J. 1983. *The web of meaning.* Portsmouth, NH: Boynton/Cook.

Faigley, L. 1989. Judging writing, judging selves. *College Composition and Communication* 40(12):395–412.

Feinstein, H. 1989. The art response guide: How to read art for meaning, a primer for art criticism. *Art Education* 42(5):43–53.

Flagg, F. 1987. *Fried green tomatoes at the whistle stop cafe.* New York: Random House.

Flood, J., and D. Lapp. 1989. Reporting reading progress: A comparison portfolio for parents. *The Reading Teacher* 42(7): 508–14.

Flower, L. 1981. "Writer-based prose: A cognitive basis for problems in writing." In G. Tate and E. P. Corbett, eds., *The writing teacher's sourcebook,* 268–93. New York: Oxford University Press.

Ford, J. E., and G. Larkin. 1978. The portfolio system: An end to backsliding writing standards. *College English* 39(8):950–55.

Freedman, S. W. 1983. Student characteristics and essay test writing performance. *Research in the Teaching of English* 17:313–25.

Gannett, C. 1992. *Gender and the journal: Diaries and academic discourse.* Ithaca, NY: SUNY Press.

Gardner, H. 1983. *Frames of mind: The theory of multiple intelligences.* New York: Basic Books.

Gardner, H., and J. Greenbaum. 1986. *The assessment of artistic thinking: Comments on the national assessment of educational progress in the arts.* Bloomington, IN: ERIC Clearinghouse on Reading and Communication Skills (ED 279 677).

Gardner, H., and T. Hatch. 1989. Multiple intelligences go to school. *Educational Researcher* 18:4–10.

Gee, J. 1989a. Literacy, discourse, and linguistics: Collected essays. *Journal of Education* 171(1) (entire issue).

———. 1989b. *What is literacy?* Technical Report no. 2. Newton, MA: Literacies Institute, Educational Development Center.

Geertz, C. 1973. "Thick description: Toward an interpretation of culture." In *The interpretation of cultures.* New York: Basic Books.

Gentile, J. R., and N. C. Murnyack. 1989. How shall students be graded in discipline-based art education? *Art Education* 46(11):33–41.

Givon, T. 1979. *On understanding grammar.* New York: Academic Press.

Glickman, C. C. 1990. Open accountability for the '90's: Between the pillars. *Educational Leadership* 47(7):38–42.

Goldman, W. 1973. *The princess bride.* New York: Ballantine.

Goodman, K. S., Y. M. Goodman, and W. J. Hood, eds. 1989. *The whole language evaluation book.* Portsmouth, NH: Heinemann.

Graves, D. H. 1984. *A researcher learns to write.* Portsmouth, NH: Heinemann.

———. 1983. *Writing: Teachers and children at work.* Portsmouth, NH: Heinemann.

Griffith, D., R. Stout, and P. Forsyth, eds. 1988. *Leaders for America's schools.* Berkeley, CA: McCutchan.

Hall, N. 1987. *The emergence of literacy.* Portsmouth, NH: Heinemann.

Halliday, M. A. K. 1985. *An introduction to functional grammar.* Kent, England: Edward Arnold.

Hansen, J. 1987. *When writers read.* Portsmouth, NH: Heinemann.

Harp, B, ed. 1991. *Assessment and evaluation in whole language programs.* Norwood, MA: Christopher-Gordon.

Hasan, R. 1984. "Coherence and cohesive harmony." In J. Flood, ed., *Understanding reading comprehension,* 181–219. Newark, DE: International Reading Association.

Hayden, T. 1980. *One child.* New York: Avon.

Hiebert, E., and R. Calfee. 1989. Advancing academic literacy through teacher's assessment. *Educational Leadership* 46(9):50–54.

Hoffa, H. 1987. Preparing high school students for admission to college art departments. *Art Education* 40(1):16–22.

Howard, K. 1990. Making the writing portfolio real. *The Quarterly of the National Writing Project and the Center for the Study of Writing* 12(2):4–7, 27.

Innocenti, R. 1985. *Rose Blanche.* Mankato, MN: Creative Education.

Jervis, K. 1989. Daryl takes a test. *Educational Leadership* 46(9):11–15.

John-Steiner, V. 1985. *Notebooks of the mind: Explorations of thinking.* Albuquerque: University of New Mexico Press.

Jones, N. L. 1982. Case study, course study: A context investigation of a writing course. Typescript.

Jongsma, K. S. 1989. Questions & answers: Portfolio assessment. *The Reading Teacher* 43(4):264–65.

Joyce, R. 1988. Preparing and assessing portfolios in east central colleges: The administrator's perspective. Heidelberg College, Tiffin, Ohio. Typescript.

Kirby, D. 1990. Panelist for "When bad things happen to good ideas." NCTE convention, Atlanta, Georgia, November 18.

Krass, P. 1988. *Sojourner Truth.* New York: Chelsea House.

Krest, M. 1990. Adapting the portfolio to meet student needs. *English Journal* 79(2):29–34.

Lammon, K. 1985. Job search techniques for fine artists: An adviser's handbook. Paper presented at the American College Personnel Association, Boston, Massachusetts, March.

Langer, J. 1986. *Children reading and writing.* Norwood, NJ: Ablex.

Levi, R. 1990. Assessment and educational vision: Engaging learners and parents. *Language Arts* 67(3):269–73.

Los Alimitos Unified School District, CA. 1990. Samples of language arts portfolio, grades K-12. Typescript.

Lunsford, A. L. 1981. Cognitive development and the basic writer. In G. Tate and E. P. Corbett, eds., *The writing teacher's sourcebook*, 257–67. New York: Oxford University Press.

Malamud, B. 1983. An interview by Daniel Stern conducted in 1975. In J. C. Oates, ed., *First person singular: Writers on their craft*, 41–56. Princeton, NJ: Ontario Review Press.

Marzano, R. J., and A. L. Costa. 1988. Question: Do standardized tests measure general cognitive skills? Answer: No. *Educational Leadership* 45(8): 66–71.

Mathews, J. 1990. From computer management to portfolio assessment. *The Reading Teacher* 43(6):420–21.

McLean, L. 1987. Emerging with honor from a dilemma inherent in the validation of educational achievement measures. Paper presented at the American Educational Research Association, April.

Michaels, S. 1984. Oral discourse styles: Classroom interaction and the acquisition of literacy. In D. Tannen, ed., *Coherence in spoken and written discourse*, 219–44. Norwood, NJ: Ablex.

———. 1981. Sharing time: Children's narrative styles and differential access to literacy. *Language in Society* 10: 423–42.

Mills, R., and W. R. Brewer. 1990. Working together to show results. *Vermont Education* 14(3):5–8.

Moffett, J. 1981. *Active voice*. Portsmouth, NH: Heinemann.

———. 1968. *Teaching the universe of discourse*. Boston, MA: Houghton Mifflin.

Morrison, T. 1987. *Beloved*. New York: Signet Books.

Murphy, J. 1990. "Preparing school administrators for the twenty-first century: The reform agenda." In B. Mitchell and L. L. Cunningham, eds., *Educational leadership and changing contexts of families, communities, and schools*. 89th Yearbook of the National Society for the Study of Education, part II. Chicago, IL: University of Chicago Press.

Murphy, S., and M. A. Smith. 1990. Talking about portfolios. *The Quarterly of the National Writing Project and the Center for the Study of Writing* 12(2):1–3.

Murray, D. 1990. *Shoptalk*. Portsmouth, NH: Heinemann.

———. 1989. *Expecting the unexpected*. Portsmouth, NH: Boynton/Cook.

————. 1986. "Teaching the other self: The writer's first reader." In T. Newkirk, ed., *To compose: Teaching editing in high school and college,* 113–23. Portsmouth, NH: Heinemann.

New Hampshire Association of Teachers of English. 1990. State board plans to kick the CAT. *NHATE Newsletter* 10(2):1.

New York State Literacy Program. 1987. My child as a writer: An observation guide for parents. The child as an emergent writer: An observation guide for teachers. Me as writer: An observation guide for young writers. A series adapted from a letter developed by Dawn Jamieson, Armstrong, British Columbia. Photocopy.

Newkirk, T. 1984. How students read student papers. *Written Communication* 1(3):283–305.

Ondaatje, M. 1984. *The collected works of Billy the Kid.* New York: Penguin.

Paulsen, G. 1987. *Hatchet.* New York: Viking Penguin.

Paulson, F. L., P. R. Paulson, and C. A. Meyer. 1991. What makes a portfolio a portfolio? *Educational Leadership* 48(7): 60–63.

Poplin, M. S. 1987. Self-imposed blindness: The scientific method of education. *Remedial and Special Education* 8(6):31–37.

Prokesch, S. 1990. Three U.S. economists win Nobel. *The New York Times* (National edition), October 17, D1.

Rief, L. 1992. *Seeking diversity: Language arts with adolescents.* Portsmouth, NH: Heinemann.

————. 1990. Finding the value in evaluation: Self-assessment in a middle school classroom. *Educational Leadership* 47(8):24–29.

Rolls, D. M. 1987. *Documenting experiential learning: Preparation of a portfolio for college credit.* Bloomington, IN: ERIC Clearinghouse on Reading and Communication Skills (ED 281 043).

Romano, T. 1990. "The multigenre research paper: Melding fact, interpretation, and imagination." In D. Daiker and M. Morenberg, eds., *The writing teacher as researcher.* Portsmouth, NH: Boynton/Cook.

Rosenblatt, L. 1978. *The reader, the text, the poem.* Carbondale, IL: Southern Illinois University Press.

Rothman, R. 1990. Large 'faculty meeting' ushers in the pioneering assessments in Vermont. *Education Week* 10(6):1.

Saint-Exupery, A. de. 1971. *The little prince.* Orlando, FL: Harcourt Brace Jovanovich.

Sansregret, M. 1987. *A rationale for assessing adults' prior learning.* Bloomington, IN: ERIC Clearinghouse on Reading and Communication Skills (ED 284 988).

Scheffler, I. 1984. On the education of policymakers. *Harvard Educational Review* 54(2):152–65.

Schon, D. 1987. *Educating the reflective practitioner.* San Francisco: Jossey-Bass.

———. 1983. *The reflective practitioner: How professionals think in action.* New York: Basic Books.

Seigel, S. 1989. Even before portfolios: The activities and atmosphere of a portfolio classroom. *Portfolio* 1(5):6–9.

Shepard, L. 1989. Why we need better assessment. *Educational Leadership* 46(9):4–9.

Shulman, L. 1988. A union of insufficiencies: Strategies for teacher assessment in a period of educational reform. *Educational Leadership* 46(4):36–46.

Simmons, J. 1991. Large-scale portfolio evaluation of writing. PhD diss. University of New Hampshire, Durham.

———. 1990a. Adapting portfolios for large-scale use. *Educational Leadership* 47(6):28.

———. 1990b. Portfolios as large-scale assessment. *Language Arts* 67:262–68.

Smith, E. 1984. *Who shall teach English?* Bloomington, IN: ERIC Clearinghouse on Reading and Communication Skills (ED 249 498).

Steinbergh, J. 1988. *A living anytime.* Boston, MA: Troubadour Press.

Strasser, T. 1981. *The wave.* New York: Dell.

Suhor, C. 1985. Objective tests and writing samples: How do they affect instruction in composition? *Phi Delta Kappan,* May, 635–39.

Sunstein, E. 1989. *Mary Shelley: Romance and reality.* Boston, MA: Little, Brown.

Taylor, D. 1990a. *Learning denied.* Portsmouth, NH: Heinemann.

———. 1990b. Teaching without testing. *English Education* 22(1): 4–74.

———, 1983. *Family literacy.* Portsmouth, NH: Heinemann.

Teale, W. 1988. Developmentally appropriate assessment of reading and writing in the early childhood classroom. *The Elementary School Journal* 89(2): 173–83.

ten Boom, C. 1971. *The hiding place.* New York: Bantam.

Thomson, P. 1988. *The school of hard knocks: A study on assessment of experiential learning.* TAFE National Centre for Research and Development, Payneham Australia. Bloomington, IN: ERIC Clearinghouse on Reading and Communication Skills (ED 295 034).

Tierney, R., M. A. Carter, and E. Desai. 1991. *Portfolio assessment in reading-writing classrooms.* Norwood, MA: Christopher-Gordon.

Torbert, W. 1990. "Reform from the center." In B. Mitchell and L. L. Cunningham, eds., *Educational leadership and changing contexts of families, communities, and schools.* 89th Yearbook of the National Society for the Study of Education, part II. Chicago, IL: University of Chicago Press.

Tsuchiya, Y. 1988. *Faithful elephants.* Boston, MA: Houghton Mifflin.

Vaughn, D., and P. Vaughn. 1985. *Handbook for rural students: Finding employment and adjusting to urban areas.* Las Cruces, NM: New Mexico State University.

Vermont Department of Education. 1989. *Vermont writing assessment: The portfolio.* Montpelier, VT: Vermont Department of Education.

Voigt, C. 1987. *Sons from afar.* New York: Fawcett-Juniper.

———. 1985. *The runner.* New York: Fawcett-Juniper.

———. 1981. *Homecoming.* New York: Fawcett-Juniper.

Vygotsky, L. 1978. *Mind in society: The development of higher psychological processes.* Cambridge, MA: Harvard University Press.

Walker, A. 1982. *The color purple.* New York: Washington Square Press.

Weathers, W. 1980. *An alternate style: Options in composition.* Portsmouth, NH: Boynton/Cook.

Wiesel, E. 1960. *Night.* New York: Bantam.

Williams, V. 1982. *A chair for my mother.* New York: Mulberry Books.

Wixson, K., C. Peters, E. Weber, and E. Roeber. 1987. New directions in statewide reading assessment. *The Journal of State Government* 60(2):73–75.

Wolf, D. P. 1989. Portfolio assessment: Sampling students work. *Educational Leadership* 46(9):35–39.

———. 1988. Opening up assessment. *Educational Leadership* 45(4): 24–29.

Wolf, D. P., et. al. 1987. *Designing portfolios for the assessment of elementary literacy teaching.* Bloomington, IN: ERIC Clearinghouse on Reading and Communication Skills (ED 302 842).

INDEX